Occupation in International Law

ELEMENTS OF INTERNATIONAL LAW

Series Editors

Mark Janis is William F. Starr Professor of Law at the University of Connecticut.

Douglas Guilfoyle is Associate Professor of International and Security Law at UNSW Canberra.

Stephan Schill is Professor of International and Economic Law and Governance at the University of Amsterdam.

Bruno Simma is Professor of Law at the University of Michigan and a Judge at the Iran–US Claims Tribunal in The Hague.

Kimberley Trapp is Professor of Public International Law at University College London.

Elements of International Law represents a fresh approach in the literature of international law. It is a long series of short books. *Elements* adopts an objective approach to its subject matter, focusing on narrowly defined core topics in international law. Eventually, the series will offer a comprehensive treatment of the whole of the field. In this volume, Eliav Lieblich and Eyal Benvenisti explore the framework and dilemmas of the international law on occupation.

Previously published titles in this series

Arms Control and Disarmament Law
Stuart Casey-Maslen

International Law of Taxation
Peter Hongler

Jus Cogens
Dinah Shelton

The International Tribunal for the Law of the Sea
Kriangsak Kittichaisaree

International Law in the Russian Legal System
William E. Butler

Occupation in International Law

Eliav Lieblich
and
Eyal Benvenisti

OXFORD
UNIVERSITY PRESS

OXFORD
UNIVERSITY PRESS

Great Clarendon Street, Oxford, OX2 6DP,
United Kingdom

Oxford University Press is a department of the University of Oxford.
It furthers the University's objective of excellence in research, scholarship,
and education by publishing worldwide. Oxford is a registered trade mark of
Oxford University Press in the UK and in certain other countries

First Edition published in 2022

Impression: 1

Published in the United States of America by Oxford University Press
198 Madison Avenue, New York, NY 10016, United States of America

British Library Cataloguing in Publication Data

Data available

Library of Congress Control Number: 2022945707

ISBN 978–0–19–886103–4 (hbk.)
ISBN 978–0–19–886104–1 (pbk.)

DOI: 10.1093/law/9780198861034.001.0001

Printed and bound in the UK by
TJ Books Limited

Series Editors' Preface

Elements of International Law represents a fresh approach to the literature of international law. It is a long series of short books. Following the traditional path of an international law textbook, *Elements*, rather than treating the whole of the field in one heavy volume, focuses on more narrowly defined subject matters.

There is nothing like *Elements*. It treats particular topics of international law much more extensively and in significantly more depth than traditional international law texts or encyclopedias. As each book in the *Elements* series has a relatively narrow focus, it provides a comprehensive treatment of a specialized subject matter, in comparison to the more limited treatment of the same subject matter in other general works.

Like a classic textbook, *Elements* aims to provide objective statements of the law. The series does not concern itself with the academic niches filled ably by doctoral theses, nor include works which take an strictly argumentative point of view, already well done by the OUP *Monograph* series. Except in length and integration, *Elements* is for substantive topics comparable to OUP's *Commentary* series on individual treaties. Each book is exhaustively footnoted in respect of international legal practice and scholarship, including treaties, diplomatic practice, decisions by international and municipal courts and arbitral tribunals, resolutions and acts of international organizations, and commentary by the most authoritative jurists.

Elements adopts an objective approach to its many subject matters and constitutes a reliable go-to source for practicing international lawyers, judges and arbitrators, government and military lawyers, and scholars, teachers, and students engaged in the discipline of international law.

Mark Janis
Douglas Guilfoyle
Stephan Schill
Bruno Simma
Kimberley Trapp

Contents

List of Abbreviations

API	Additional Protocol I
APII	Additional Protocol II
BIT	bilateral investment treaty
CEDAW	Convention on the Elimination of All Forms of Discrimination against Women
CJEU	Court of Justice of the European Union
CPA	Coalition Provisional Authority [U.S./Iraq]
DoD	Department of Defense [U.S.]
DPH	directly participate in hostilities
ECHR	European Convention on Human Rights
ECtHR	European Court of Human Rights
EEZ	exclusive economic zone
EU	European Union
FSA	Free Syrian Army
GCIV	Geneva Convention Relative to the Protection of Civilian Persons in Time of War of 12 August 1949 [Fourth Geneva Convention]
HCJ	High Court of Justice [Israel]
IAC	international armed conflict
ICC	International Criminal Court
ICCPR	International Covenant on Civil and Political Rights
ICESCR	International Covenant on Economic, Social and Cultural Rights
ICJ	International Court of Justice
ICTY	International Criminal Tribunal for the Former Yugoslavia
IDF	Israel Defense Forces
IHL	international humanitarian law
IHRL	international human rights law
ISDS	investor-state dispute settlement
ISIL	Islamic State of Iraq and the Levant
KFOR	Kosovo Force [NATO]
MAG	Military Advocate General [Israel]
NATO	North Atlantic Treaty Organization
NGO	nongovernmental organization
NIAC	non-international armed conflict

NSA	non-state actor
POW	prisoner of war
SOFA	status of forces agreement
UNGA	United Nations General Assembly
UNSC	United Nations Security Council
WWI	World War I
WWII	World War II

Table of Authorities

TREATIES AND OTHER AGREEMENTS

INTERNATIONAL TRIBUNALS

European Court of Human Rights (ECtHR)

European Court of Justice (ECJ)

International Arbitration

International Court of Justice (ICJ)

International Criminal Court (ICC) (Cases and Other Official Documents)

International Criminal Tribunal for the Former Yugoslavia (ICTY)

International Military Tribunals, World War II

Israel and the Territories Occupied by Israel

OTHER DOCUMENTS

Expert Opinions

National and Supranational Documents, Including by Occupation Authorities

UN Resolutions and Documents

Introduction*

I General

The international law of occupation is a branch of international humanitarian law (IHL), which regulates actions of states—and possibly other actors such as international organizations—that gain effective control over hostile territory during armed conflict. As part of the *Elements of International Law* series, this book provides an entry point for those seeking to familiarize themselves with the topic. Accordingly, Part 1 of this book discusses the law of occupation's principles, concepts, and frameworks, while Part 2 addresses the scope of the occupant's powers and obligations, both generally and in relation to specific issues.

The law of occupation attempts to balance several competing interests. Its most fundamental principle is that occupation does not confer sovereignty, and that the occupant's powers are limited accordingly. The law of occupation envisions the occupant as a temporary trustee, empowered only to maintain public order and safety in the territory, including the security of its own forces. Inherent in this "trusteeship" are fundamental conflicts of interest, which the law of occupation aims to mitigate. As a consequence of the occupant's limited powers, and as a response to these conflicts of interests, the law of occupation requires that the occupant respect the status quo ante in the territory. It furthermore requires that the occupant respect and ensure the individual rights of the local population, and would not violate their right to self-determination—or the rights of the absent sovereign—by introducing massive changes or by treating the territory as its own.

Since the law of occupation is a framework for territorial administration, it potentially relates to every aspect of life in occupied territories. This

* During our work on this book, we benefited from the work of excellent, and extremely dedicated, research assistants. We wish to thank Ott Arava, May Dar, Widad Elias, Tamir Gur, Eden Swisa, Ori Yaniv, Tamar Yehezkely, and Yuval Yekutiel. The extensive research required for this book was supported by the Israel Science Foundation (Grant no. 2150/19).

book, of course, cannot touch upon all of these aspects. Rather, it elaborates on general principles and key rules, which should serve to guide relevant actors—whether states, academics, NGOs, or individuals under occupation—when assessing or challenging the conduct of occupants.

A significant challenge in writing a book on the law of occupation concerns the fact that this law is rarely applied. Usually, states go out of their ways to argue that, for this or that reason, *their* control is not an *occupation*. Moreover, even when the law of occupation *is* applied, states often advance exceedingly permissive interpretations of their powers. This is facilitated by the law of occupation's frequent reference to vague terms such as military necessity or security considerations, as preconditions for an action's lawfulness. As this book shows, reading security considerations too broadly positions the law of occupation as a legitimating, rather than constraining, body of law. Therefore, our underlying approach is to highlight legal interpretations which have constraining potential and to provide meaningful vocabulary for assessing occupants' actions. In other words, while this book is generally doctrinal, our analysis gives precedence to interpretations of the law "in its best light," in accordance with its object and purpose.[1]

The vast majority of practice and jurisprudence on occupation in recent decades stems from Israel's post-1967 occupation of Gaza and the West Bank, and in particular from the rulings of the Supreme Court of Israel, sitting as the High Court of Justice (HCJ). The reason that this is so is definitely *not* because Israel has been the only occupant in this period. As we shall see throughout this book, there were indeed other instances of occupation in the early 21st century: for example, the U.S.-led coalition's occupation of Iraq in 2003; Turkey's occupation in north Syria since 2016; and Russia in Ukraine—first in Crimea and parts of Donbas since 2014, and then in territories it occupied during its invasion of March 2022. The majority of practice comes from Israel, however, because it has been one of the few states to admit, even if imperfectly, that the law of occupation applies in territories it controls; and additionally, the HCJ has extended its judicial review to acts in the occupied territories, and has rendered hundreds of decisions applying the law of occupation.

While it is tempting to do so—and many cases and examples referred to in this book relate to this occupation—we have consciously refrained from making this a book *about* the Israeli occupation. First, although instructive

[1] *Compare* Ronald Dworkin, Law's Empire 90 (1986).

at times, much of the HCJ's reasoning on occupation is marked by its attempt to reconcile law with Israel's understanding of its security concerns, as well as its settlements in the occupied territories (while refraining from ruling on their legality in general).[2] This makes it difficult to extrapolate from the HCJ's jurisprudence to other contexts. Second, owing to its duration and specific policies, critical interventions have cast doubts on the accuracy of analyzing Israel's control strictly from the point of view of the law of occupation, arguing that the latter is mainly used to legitimate de facto annexation and colonization.[3] Naturally, since this book aims to provide an account of the law of occupation applicable beyond the Israeli–Palestinian context, we cannot focus on, nor do justice to, this specific debate.

II Neighboring Frameworks and Concepts: Occupation and Fragmentation

The law of occupation interacts nowadays with many "neighboring" international legal frameworks and institutions. When the law of occupation emerged in the 19th century, it was virtually the only body of law that regulated military control over hostile territory. Today, as part of the (in)famous fragmentation of international law[4] it is impossible to delineate the legal frameworks potentially applicable to every aspect of occupation. If, for example, one wishes to analyze the occupant's obligations in relation to pandemics, an analysis of article 59 of the Fourth Geneva Convention (GCIV), which addresses this issue directly, is not enough. It would also be necessary to discuss the right to health under the various instruments of international human rights law (IHRL). Furthermore, it would be impossible to neglect

[2] *See* David Kretzmer & Yaël Ronen, The Occupation of Justice: The Supreme Court of Israel and the Occupied Territories (2d ed. 2021).

[3] This point of view has been frequently made by Palestinian scholars. *See, e.g.*, Noura Erakat, Justice for Some: Law and the Question of Palestine (2019); Raja Shehadeh, From Occupation to Interim Accords: Israel and the Palestinian Territories (1997); Raja Shehadeh, Occupier's Law: Israel and the West Bank (1988); Nimer Sultany, *Activism and Legitimation in Israel's Jurisprudence of Occupation*, 23 Soc. & Leg. Studies 315 (2014); Ardi Imseis, *On the Fourth Geneva Convention and the Occupied Palestinian Territory*, 44 Harv. Int'l L.J. 65 (2003); George Emile Bisharat, Palestinian Lawyers and Israeli Rule: Law and Disorder in the West Bank (1989); Omar M. Dajani, *Israel's Creeping Annexation*, 111 Am. J. Int'l L. Unbound 51 (2017); Mona Rishmawi, *The Administration of the West Bank Under Israeli Rule*, *in* International Law and the Administration of Occupied Territories 271 (Emma Playfair ed., 1992).

[4] *See generally* Anne Peters, *The Refinement of International Law: From Fragmentation to Regime Interaction and Politicization*, 15 Int'l J. Const. L. 671 (2017).

bodies and norms of global health governance, such as the World Health Organization and its recommendations and regulations. As if this were not enough, many other bodies, from the International Monetary Fund to the International Maritime Organization, might issue formal and informal regulations that could be applicable or relevant to the actions of occupants in this field.[5]

Legal frameworks neighboring to the law of occupation include, for example, the law on the use of force (*jus ad bellum*), the law on the conduct of hostilities under IHL, IHRL, international criminal law, the law on state responsibility, the law of international organizations, and international economic law. This book cannot exhaust the potential interactions between the law of occupation and all of its neighboring legal fields and relevant institutions. Rather, it focuses on the law of occupation from within, while occasionally highlighting instances in which neighboring frameworks might be especially consequential. Unsurprisingly, this is most commonly the case concerning IHRL.

Beyond the fragmentation of legal frameworks, the current international system is characterized by a plurality of actors. Not only states and international organizations are relevant in situations of occupation, but also private actors, such as private security contractors, importers and exporters, energy companies, and mining firms. Due to the increasing prevalence of private actors, the field of business and human rights has become a bourgeoning area of scholarship and practice—both in general and in relation to occupation. This field seeks to hold corporations accountable for their involvement in human rights violations, and to strengthen states' obligations to ensure that corporations respect human rights, domestically and transnationally.[6] In occupation, considerations of business and human rights would be relevant to corporations that conduct business with occupants; to occupants, in relation to corporations which operate in the occupied territory; and to third-party states, regarding the transnational activities of their corporations in occupied territories.[7] Notwithstanding

[5] Sivan Shlomo Agon, *Farewell to the F-Word? Fragmentation of International Law in Times of the Covid-19 Pandemic*, TORONTO L.J. (2022); *see generally* EYAL BENVENISTI, THE LAW OF GLOBAL GOVERNANCE (2014).

[6] *See generally* NADIA BERNAZ, BUSINESS AND HUMAN RIGHTS: HISTORY, LAW AND POLICY—BRIDGING THE ACCOUNTABILITY GAP (2016); Steven R. Ratner, *Corporations and Human Rights: A Theory of Legal Responsibility*, 111 YALE L.J. 443 (2001).

[7] *See, e.g.*, MARYA FARAH, AL-HAQ & GLAN, BUSINESS AND HUMAN RIGHTS IN OCCUPIED TERRITORY: GUIDANCE FOR UPHOLDING HUMAN RIGHTS (2020); Daria Davitti, *Business Actors in Western Sahara: Heightened Obligations and Responsibilities Under the UNGP?*, *in*

the importance of these issues, we do not address them here, since the key legal problems that arise in this context do not stem from the law of occupation *as such*, but from the more general problem of corporate accountability under international law.

Similarly, as in any field of international law, a question of much importance concerns the consequences of breaches. Consequences of breaches of the law of occupation can extend to personal liability of individuals under international criminal law;[8] to the state responsibility of the occupant;[9] as well as to obligations of third-party states. That is, third-party states might be bound by the triple obligation not to recognize the illegal situation created by the breach; to refrain from aiding or assisting in its maintenance; and to cooperate in bringing it to an end.[10] The exact content of the duty of nonrecognition varies across contexts, and its modalities remain unclear.[11] Much of the contemporary discussion of nonrecognition relates to states' attempts to extend trade treaties to annexed territories, or in relation to imports from settlements in occupied territories.[12] Ultimately, the scope of third-party obligations in relation to breaches is a matter of general international law, and as such it remains a distinct question which we do not discuss at length here.

The Legality of Economic Activities in Occupied Territories 199 (Antoine Duval & Eva Kassoti eds., 2020)

[8] *See, e.g.*, ICC, Office of the Prosecutor, Situation in Palestine: Summary of Preliminary Examination Findings ¶ 4.

[9] Legal Consequences of the Construction of a Wall in the Occupied Palestinian Territory, Advisory Opinion, 2004 I.C.J. Rep. 136 ¶¶ 149–153 (July 9) [hereinafter Wall Opinion].

[10] *Id.* ¶¶ 154–159. A similar conclusion possibly arises from the status of the basic rules of IHL as peremptory norms of international law (*jus cogens*). *See* Int'l Law Comm'n, Peremptory Norms of General International Law, Draft Conclusion 19, U.N. Doc. A/CN.4/L.936 (May 29, 2019).

[11] *See, e.g.*, Stefan Talmon & Hannah Janknecht, *Legal Consequences of Germany's Non-Recognition of the Russian Annexation of Crimea*, GPIL—German Practice in International Law (Aug. 27, 2021), https://gpil.jura.uni-bonn.de/2021/08/legal-consequences-of-germanys-non-recognition-of-the-russian-annexation-of-crimea/.

[12] *See, e.g.*, Eva Kassoti & Antoine Duval, *Setting the Scene: The Legality of Economic Activities in Occupied Territories*, *in* Duval & Kassoti, *supra* note 7; Case C-104/16 P, Council of the E.U. v. Front Polisario, ECLI:EU:C:2016:973, ¶¶ 86–99 (Dec. 21, 2016), https://curia.europa.eu/juris/liste.jsf?language=en&num=C-104/16; James Crawford, Third Party Obligations with Respect to Israeli Settlements in the Occupied Palestinian Territories ¶ 51 (Jan. 24, 2012); *see also* Commission Interpretative Notice 2015/C 375/05 on indication of origin of goods from the territories occupied by Israel since June 1967, 2015 O.J. (C 375) 4; Cedric Ryngaert, *Indications of Settlement Provenance and the Duty of Non-Recognition Under International Law*, 4 European Papers 791 (2019); *compare* Eugene Kontorovich, *Some State Practice Regarding Trade with Occupied Territories: From the GATT to Today*, *in* Duval & Kassoti, *supra* note 7, at 65.

PART 1

CONCEPTS AND GENERAL FRAMEWORKS

1
Occupation
History, Normative Framework, Concepts

1.1 Occupation: General Concept

Occupation, most commonly understood, occurs when armed forces—usually of a state—gain effective control over foreign territory, without the consent of the territorial state. The basic point of departure of international law is that occupation does not confer sovereignty over the territory. Accordingly, the law of occupation—a branch of international humanitarian law (IHL)—defines situations in which occupation exists, and circumscribes the powers that an occupant may lawfully exercise. Three interrelating limitations undergird the entire law of occupation: (a) that occupation is presumed temporary; (b) that the occupant possesses fewer powers than the sovereign; and (c) that occupation does not grant title over the territory.

In light of these limitations, the law of occupation attempts to balance between three poles: the rights and interests of the local population (including self-determination); the interests of the absent sovereign; and the security interests of the occupying forces.[1] For these purposes, the law of occupation envisions the occupant as a "trustee," in the sense that its powers are limited to promote these interests only.[2] The fundamental obligation resulting from this trusteeship is that once an occupation exists, the occupant incurs positive duties to restore and ensure public order and safety in the territory. Yet, as a trustee only, it must do so while respecting the physical

[1] Note that while the interests of the sovereign were in the past equated with the interests of the ousted government, the emergence of the principle of self-determination and of IHRL shifted the focus to the interests of the local population as such, rather than that to those of the government strictly speaking. EYAL BENVENISTI, THE INTERNATIONAL LAW OF OCCUPATION 6–7 (2d ed. 2012).

[2] GERHARD VON GLAHN, THE OCCUPATION OF ENEMY TERRITORY: A COMMENTARY ON THE LAW AND PRACTICE OF BELLIGERENT OCCUPATION 31 (1957).

and legal status quo. Furthermore, it cannot act in its own interests beyond what is needed to provide either for the occupied population or for the security of its forces.[3] Taking this into account, it is clear that a rampant potential for conflicts of interest exists at the basis of the law of occupation. International law seeks to manage these conflicts, for fear that occupation would become a form of conquest, colonialism, or apartheid.[4]

Both the existence of a separate legal status of occupation and the idea that there are limits to powers that can be exercised in territory captured in war are relatively modern developments. It was only in the mid-19th century that a clear distinction emerged between *conquest*—a situation in which a state acquired sovereign title over captured territory—and occupation, in which title remained in the hands of the territorial sovereign.[5] Furthermore, the notion that the occupied population enjoys certain protections, and is not subject to the occupant's unlimited discretion, is also a product of that era.[6]

Importantly, the legal distinction between occupation and conquest which emerged in the 19th century did not imply that conquest was *always* ruled out. At the time, it was generally accepted that the victor could eventually annex territory captured in war: either through a peace treaty (and regardless of the origins of the war); or unilaterally, when the enemy state was completely subjugated (*debellatio*); or, according to some, when hostilities ceased, and the occupant remained in control of territory which the sovereign has in fact given up.[7] The law of occupation was the default law applicable in the interim phase *before* possible conquest.

[3] *See* Convention (IV) respecting the Laws and Customs of War on Land and Its Annex: Regulations Concerning the Laws and Customs of War on Land, art. 43, Oct. 18, 1907, 187 C.T.S. 227 [hereinafter Hague IV].

[4] Benvenisti, *supra* note 1, at 4; Aeyal Gross, The Writing on the Wall: Rethinking the Law of Occupation 20 (2017); Miles Jackson, *Expert Opinion on the Interplay Between the Legal Regime Applicable to Belligerent Occupation and the Prohibition of Apartheid Under International Law* (2021), https://apidiakoniase.cdn.triggerfish.cloud/uploads/sites/2/2021/05/expert-opinion-apartheid-and-occupation.pdf/; *compare* John Dugard & John Reynolds, *Apartheid, International Law, and the Occupied Palestinian Territory*, 24 Eur. J. Int'l L. 867 (2013) *with* Yaffa Zilbershats, *Apartheid, International Law, and the Occupied Palestinian Territory: A Reply to John Dugard and John Reynolds*, 24 Eur. J. Int'l L. 915 (2013). For a critical debate, see Rania Muhareb, *Apartheid, the Green Line, and the Need to Overcome Palestinian Fragmentation*, EJIL: Talk! (July 7, 2021), https://www.ejiltalk.org/apartheid-the-green-line-and-the-need-to-overcome-palestinian-fragmentation/.

[5] *See* 2 Lassa Oppenheim, International Law: A Treatise § 166 (2d ed. 1912); Von Glahn, *supra* note 2, at 7; *see also* Nehal Bhuta, *The Antinomies of Transformative Occupation*, 16 Eur. J. Int'l L. 721, 724–25 (2005).

[6] 2 Oppenheim, *supra* note 5, § 166; Benvenisti, *supra* note 1, at 21.

[7] 1 Oppenheim, International Law § 239 (2d ed. 1912); 2 Oppenheim, *supra* note 5, §§ 263, 273.

It was only after World War I (WWI), when European public opinion shifted against expansionism—and with the advent of the idea of self-determination—that the international norm of non-acquisition of territory by force gradually solidified.[8] Since 1928's Kellogg–Briand Pact, and certainly after the UN Charter's embrace of territorial integrity as a basic principle, the idea of lawful conquest virtually disappeared from international law.[9] In this era, the law of occupation emerged as the law that regulates the *outer limits* of a state's power over territories captured in war.

To sum up, the law of occupation aims to safeguard the principles of self-determination and territorial integrity against annexations, while protecting the basic rights of individuals.[10] By distinguishing the powers of the occupant from those of the sovereign, the distinction between occupation and conquest, between administration and annexation, are meant to be preserved.

1.2 The Law of Occupation: A (Very) Brief History and Enduring Challenges

In terms of the history of ideas, the development of the concept of occupation as distinct from conquest must be read in conjunction with the development of the idea of national sovereignty. The idea that occupation does not confer sovereignty, and that the occupant must respect the sovereignty of the ousted government, is intertwined with the 19th-century European view that sovereignty over a particular territory is vested in a certain nation.[11] In fact, it is the principle of national self-determination—as it developed from the French Revolution onward—that provided the groundwork for the two basic notions of the law of occupation: that occupation alone cannot result in title over the territory;[12] and that the occupant must respect

[8] Sharon Korman, The Right of Conquest: The Acquisition of Territory by Force in International Law and Practice 135–39 (1996).

[9] Oona A. Hathaway & Scott J. Shapiro, The Internationalists: And Their Plan to Outlaw War 309–36 (2017); Andrew Clapham, War 112–18 (2021); *but see* Victor Kattan, *U.S. Recognition of Golan Heights Annexation: Testament to Our Times*, 48 J. Palestine Stud. 79 (2019); Yoram Dinstein, The international Law of Belligerent Occupation 58–60 (2d ed. 2019).

[10] Eyal Benvenisti, *The Origins of the Concept of Belligerent Occupation*, 26 Law. Hist. Rev. 621 (2008).

[11] *Id.* at 622–23.

[12] This notion can be traced to August Wilhelm Heffter, Das Europäische Völkerrecht der Gegenwart 220–21 (1844).

the status quo ante in the territory ("the conservationist principle").[13] During that time, occupation began to be distinguished from both conquest and *debellatio* (subjugation). The latter referred to situations in which the sovereign was completely defeated, its international legal personality effectively extinguished. In such cases, the temporary status of occupation was deemed irrelevant, and the occupant would acquire full sovereignty.[14]

Unsurprisingly, this idea of occupation was markedly European. It served, to a large extent, to distinguish between European territories and those inhabited by "uncivilized peoples" incapable, in European eyes, of sovereignty—concerning which occupation and conquest were one and the same.[15] In this sense, like most laws of war of the time, the law of occupation served some humanitarian purposes, but was also a colonial marker of distinction between subjects and nonsubjects of international law.[16] Only in the 20th century, with the advent of the principles of sovereign equality and self-determination, did international law cease to make that distinction formally. These principles now require that the law of occupation apply to the territories of *all* states or peoples.

Beyond this well-recognized "dark side" of the laws of war, there were other, realpolitik considerations that contributed to the formation of the ideas undergirding the law of occupation. For example, European nation-states sought to guarantee the protection of their own citizens should they fall under enemy control; but they were also interested in safeguarding the eventual return of their territories, and sought to prevent the possibility that their citizens would secede and unite with the enemy.[17]

The immediate impetus for the codification of the law of occupation was the Franco-Prussian War (1870–71). In the ensuing debates on the conduct of belligerents during that war, a key point of contention concerned

[13] This idea can be traced to PASQUALE FIORE, NUOVO DRITTO INTERNAZIONALE PUBBLICO 177 (1865); *see* Benvenisti, *supra* note 10, at 628, 632–33; Gregory H. Fox, *The Occupation of Iraq*, 36 GEO. J. INT'L L. 195, 199 (2005).

[14] *See* Melissa Patterson, *Who's Got the Title? Or, the Remnants of Debellatio in Post-Invasion Iraq*, 47 HARV. INT'L L. J. 467, 475–77 (2006).

[15] *See* ANTONY ANGHIE, IMPERIALISM, SOVEREIGNTY AND THE MAKING OF INTERNATIONAL LAW 83–84 (2004); for clarity it should be noted that in the 19th century the term "occupation" referred to the unilateral acquisition of colonial territory, alongside with "occupation of enemy territory" (or "belligerent occupation") to connote temporary control of territory during war between states. *Compare* 1 OPPENHEIM, *supra* note 7, §§ 220–28 *with* 2 OPPENHEIM, *supra* note 5, § 166.

[16] *Compare* Frédéric Mégret, *From "Savages" to "Unlawful Combatants": a Postcolonial Look at International Humanitarian Law's "Other"*, *in* INTERNATIONAL LAW AND ITS OTHERS 265, 305 (Anne Orford ed., 2006).

[17] Benvenisti, *supra* note 10, at 634–35.

the declarations made by some Prussian officials that territories taken from France were under German sovereignty, and Prussia's wish to annex Alsace and Lorraine. This sparked a debate—chiefly between German scholars and others—both on the authority of occupants, and the existence of a right of conquest, and galvanized the effort to clarify the rules governing occupation.[18]

The 1874 Brussels Declaration was the first instance in which the basic principles of the modern law of occupation were included in an international document (albeit a nonbinding one).[19] While not explicitly endorsing the principle of non-annexation—indeed, this idea would take its final shape only with the advent of the UN Charter—the Brussels Declaration solidified the concept of occupation as distinct from sovereignty.[20] The Institut de Droit International's Oxford Manual of 1880—aimed to complement the Brussels Declaration[21]—further established these principles, and stated, perhaps more clearly than before, that occupation does not confer sovereignty, and that as long as the territory is contested, transfer of title does not occur.[22]

To be sure, these ideas were under severe pressure from their inception. Already in the Russo-Turkish War (1877–78), Russia found reasons to disapply elements of the law of occupation. During its occupation of Bulgaria, for example, it overhauled the local administrative system, arguing that it did not benefit the local population, and that reforming it conformed with the Brussels Declaration, which required that the occupant further local interests.[23] This was a harbinger of a key predicament that has haunted the law of occupation ever since: that states seek exceptions either to the application of the law of occupation, or to the conservationist principle at its core.[24]

[18] *Id.* at 642–43. *See, e.g.*, Gustave Rolin-Jaequemyns, *Essai complémentaire sur la guerre franco-allemande dans ses rapports avec le droit international*, 3 Revue de Droit International et de Legislation Comparée 335 (1871). For a critical take on the development of the law of war at the time, *see* Eyal Benvenisti & Doreen Lustig, *Monopolizing War: Codifying the Laws of War to Reassert Governmental Authority, 1856–1874*, 31 Eur. J. Int'l L. 127 (2020); Samuel Moyn, Humane: How the United States Abandoned Peace and Reinvented War 81–86 (2021).

[19] Project of an International Declaration concerning the Laws and Customs of War, Aug. 27, 1874, 69 B.F.S.P. 1059 [hereinafter Brussels Declaration].

[20] Article 1 of the Brussels Declaration establishes the idea of occupation as de facto authority.

[21] The Laws of War on Land, Preface, Sep. 9, 1880, 5 Institut de Droit International, Annuaire 156 (1881–82).

[22] *Id.* art. C(a).

[23] Benvenisti, *supra* note 10, at 645–46.

[24] We shall see this, for example, when we discuss transformative occupation in Chapter 4.

When European states assembled again at the 1899 Hague Peace Conference, they were already aware of this problem. Two camps emerged during the negotiations on The Hague Conventions of 1899–1907: the stronger, potentially occupying states on the one hand, and the weaker—potentially occupied—states on the other. The key achievement of the latter was the strengthening of the conservationist principle in the Fourth Hague Convention of 1907, which stated that the status quo ante in occupied territories must be preserved "unless absolutely prevented."[25]

Notwithstanding the early misgivings, the basic principles of the law of occupation have remained quite stable until today: indeed, nobody argues seriously that they no longer apply as the *lex lata*.[26] This is quite remarkable considering that the political and legal upheavals of the 20th century intensified the pressure on these ideas.[27] During WWI, the German occupying authorities deployed the necessity doctrine (*Notstand*) in justification of far-reaching security powers, effectively rendering the limitations of the law of occupation meaningless.[28] The atrocities of World War II (WWII), many of them committed in occupied territories, do not necessitate repeating.[29]

These developments led to an increased focus on the rights of individuals under occupation, as manifested, chiefly, in the Fourth Geneva Convention of 1949 (GCIV).[30] GCIV widened the protection of individuals significantly, since until then, the law of occupation focused mainly on the protection of property, rather than of persons as such.[31] This broadening, however, brought about new tensions within the law: once individual rights became the focal point, the justification for maintaining the status quo ante—to the extent that it did not conform to these rights—became difficult to defend.[32] The advent of international human rights law (IHRL) also added to this

[25] Benvenisti, *supra* note 10, at 646–47. This formulation is found in Hague IV, art. 43, *supra* note 3. Previous formulations required maintaining the legal status quo "unless necessary."

[26] *Compare* Martti Koskenniemi, *Occupation and Sovereignty—Still a Useful Distinction?*, *in* Law at War—The Law as it Was and The Law as It Should Be 163, 164 (Ola Engdahl & Pål Wrange eds., 2008).

[27] Some argued that the law of occupation was defunct already by 1914. Ernst H. Feilchenfeld, The International Economic Law of Belligerent Occupation 23 (1942).

[28] *See* Isabel V. Hull, A Scrap of Paper: Breaking and Making International Law During the Great War 133 (2014).

[29] *See* Raphael Lemkin, Axis Rule in Occupied Europe: Laws of Occupation, Analysis of Government, Proposals for Redress (1st ed. 1944).

[30] Convention (IV) relative to the Protection of Civilian Persons in Time of War, Aug. 12, 1949, 6 U.S.T. 3516, 75 U.N.T.S. 287 [hereinafter GCIV].

[31] *See* Benvenisti, *supra* note 1, at 22–24.

[32] *Compare* Koskenniemi, *supra* note 26, at 165–66.

pressure: if occupants are bound by human rights law, how can this be reconciled with the conservationist principle?[33]

Furthermore, the conservationist principle was challenged by the total war of WWII, in which the subordination of Germany and the defeat of Japan was viewed as requiring—and legally justifying—a complete constitutional reconstruction of these states.[34] Nor could this principle be easily reconciled with the dynamics of the cold war, in which many military interventions by the great powers aimed *precisely* to impose a certain political and ideological system.[35] This motivation led states to rely on the real or manufactured consent of local authorities in order to disapply the law of occupation—a tendency that we also see today.[36]

Several other developments contribute to the limited contemporary application of the law of occupation. One stems from the changes in the normative environment of the law of occupation itself. In the 19th century, the law granted many powers to occupants while entailing only thin obligations—in light of the then-prevalent laissez-faire approach of government. The occupied population possessed minimal individual rights and had no legally recognized right to resist. As noted, occupation was a prelude to conquest. Under these assumptions, states had interests in becoming occupants and pushed for low thresholds for the existence of occupation.[37] However, in the latter half of the 20th century, the realignment of the law of occupation toward the protection of individuals was also buttressed by a more robust conception of government in political theory. Along with the advent of IHRL, this led to increasingly burdensome positive obligations on occupants. Unsurprisingly, the status of "occupying power" became much less attractive.[38]

For these and other reasons explored later, states nowadays go a long way to deny that occupation exists. In fact, there are only two cases in recent decades in which states consistently admitted that the law of occupation applied to their actions, and these, too, are far from textbook examples.[39] The

[33] *Compare* Aeyal M. Gross, *Human Proportions: Are Human Rights the Emperor's New Clothes of the International Law of Occupation?*, 18 Eur. J. Int'l L. 1 (2007); Smadar Ben-Natan, *Self-Proclaimed Human Rights Heroes: The Professional Project of Israeli Military Judges*, 46 Law & Soc. Inq. 755 (2021).

[34] *See* Section 4.2.4.

[35] *See* Koskenniemi, *supra* note 26, at 167.

[36] Bhuta, *supra* note 5, at 734–35.

[37] Benvenisti, *supra* note 1, at 7–8.

[38] *Id.* at 9–10.

[39] Koskenniemi, *supra* note 26, at 164.

first is the Israeli control of the West Bank and Gaza—which is fraught with difficulties, not least because of the prolonged—"indefinite," really—nature of this occupation.[40] The second is the early stages of the U.S. control over Iraq in 2003–04.[41]

Importantly, contemporary challenges to the law of occupation do not only arise from unilateral state interests. The multilateralism of the 20th century, and the turn to global governance, also challenges the basic ideas of the law of occupation, including the conservationist principle. From the League of Nations' mandate system—which transformed the allied states from occupants to mandate holders[42]—to the extensive powers granted to the U.S.-led coalition in post-2003 Iraq,[43] multilateral forms of territorial administration are also in tension with the idea that foreign forces should not alter the status quo in territories they control.[44]

Last, it should also be considered whether in times of rising nationalism, the trusteeship idea that undergirds the law of occupation can hold. The assumptions that form the basis of this idea are cosmopolitan, as they require that enemy territory be administrated while excluding the wider national interest. These requirements are in direct tension with nationalist and authoritarian tendencies that might inform the development of international law in the near future.[45]

1.3 General Normative Framework

As mentioned above, the point of departure for the modern law of occupation is the Fourth Hague Convention of 1907, and its annexed Regulations (in short—Hague IV).[46] The basic rules on occupation are set out in Section III of the Regulations, in articles 42–56. These articles define occupation, and outline the general powers and duties of the occupant, including the

[40] *See, e.g.*, Adam Roberts, *Prolonged Military Occupation: The Israeli-Occupied Territories Since 1967*, 84 Am. J. Int'l L. 44 (1990). We discuss the problems of prolonged occupation in Chapter 4.

[41] Koskenniemi, *supra* note 26, at 164.

[42] League of Nations Covenant, art. 22.

[43] *See, e.g.*, S.C. Res. 1483 (May 22, 2003); S.C. Res. 1511 (Oct. 16, 2003); S.C. Res. 1546 (June 8, 2004).

[44] *Compare* Ralph Wilde, International Territorial Administration: How Trusteeship and the Civilizing Mission Never Went Away (2008).

[45] Tom Ginsburg, *Authoritarian International Law?*, 114 Am. J. Int'l L. 221 (2020).

[46] Hague IV, *supra* note 3.

conservationist principle.[47] They include some provisions on respecting individual rights, in particular—but not limited to—the protection of private property.[48] They also set out provisions on taxation,[49] requisitions,[50] and the administration of public property (including natural resources).[51] The Hague Regulations, although over a century old, are still in force and were widely recognized as reflecting customary international law as early as in 1947.[52]

After WWII, Hague IV was supplemented by the GCIV.[53] As its title suggests, GCIV focuses almost exclusively on the protection of civilians. It regulates many aspects of war; for our purposes, it suffices to recall its most relevant parts. Part I, which establishes general provisions, outlines the scope of the Convention's application, and defines the key term "protected persons," which refers, inter alia, to individuals belonging to the "enemy" in occupied territories.[54] Importantly, GCIV does not offer its own definition of occupation, but piggybacks for this purpose on Hague IV. Part III deals with the status and treatment of protected persons, whether in occupied territories or otherwise. This part, in Section I, entrenches the protection of basic rights of protected persons everywhere, including, for instance, the prohibition on torture, collective punishment, and reprisals.[55] Section III includes GCIV's specific provisions on occupation. Some of this section's most notable provisions establish the inviolability of rights under the Convention;[56] the prohibition on forcible transfers and deportations, including the transfer of the occupant's civilian population to the occupied territory;[57] positive duties concerning food and medical supplies;[58] and duties concerning humanitarian access.[59] Furthermore, this section includes key provisions on legislation in occupied territories, courts, due process, and criminal punishment.[60] It provides for security measures against

[47] *Id.* arts. 42–43.
[48] *Id.* arts. 46–47, 50.
[49] *Id.* arts. 48–49.
[50] *Id.* art. 52.
[51] *Id.* arts. 48–49, 52, 55.
[52] *Trial of the Major War Criminals Before the International Military Tribunal, Nuremberg, Judgment*, 41 AM. J. INT'L L. 172, 248–49 (1947).
[53] GCIV, *supra* note 30, art. 154.
[54] *Id.* arts. 2, 4, 6.
[55] *Id.* arts. 27, 32–33.
[56] Whether by changes to the local law, agreement with the local authorities, or by annexation. *Id.* art. 47.
[57] *Id.* art. 49.
[58] *Id.* art. 55.
[59] *Id.* art. 59.
[60] *Id.* arts. 64–76.

protected persons, including security internment.[61] The Convention also includes detailed rules concerning the treatment of detainees and internees.[62]

The question whether GCIV has attained customary status is of limited importance from an international perspective, owing to the Convention's universal membership.[63] Yet, since in some states, in the absence of adopting legislation, only customary norms of international law can be invoked in domestic courts, this question can have much practical importance.[64] This has been pertinent regarding the Israeli occupation, since Israel argued for decades that the Convention has not attained such status, and therefore could not be invoked in domestic courts.[65] The universal membership of GCIV results in a paradox: on the one hand, it reflects a wide consensus on its norms; on the other, it makes it difficult to identify practice relevant to the development of customary norms, since such practice must be primarily external to the Convention qua treaty.[66] Nonetheless, the International Court of Justice (ICJ) has recognized that "a very widespread and representative participation" in a treaty might suffice to elevate its norms to customary status,[67] and, according to Meron, it is generally accepted today that GCIV reflects customary international law.[68]

Some additional norms pertaining to occupation are scattered in other IHL treaties, including in the First Additional Protocol to the Geneva Conventions (in short—API),[69] and importantly, in treaties relating to the protection of cultural property.[70]

[61] *Id.* art. 78.

[62] *Id.* art. 76, Section IV.

[63] *See* Theodor Meron, *The Geneva Conventions as Customary Law*, 81 Am. J. Int'l L. 348, 348 (1987).

[64] *Id.* 348–49.

[65] In practice many HCJ decisions rely on GCIV, mostly because the State declared that its actions were compatible with GCIV, and was willing to adjudicate on that basis. *See* David Kretzmer, *The Law of Belligerent Occupation in the Supreme Court of Israel*, 94 Int'l Rev. Red Cross 207, 211–13 (2012).

[66] Meron, *supra* note 63, at 365.

[67] *Id.* at 366–67; North Sea Continental Shelf, Judgment (Ger. v. Neth.), 1969 I.C.J. Rep. 4, ¶ 73 (Feb. 20).

[68] Theodor Meron, *The West Bank and International Humanitarian Law on the Eve of the Fiftieth Anniversary of the Six-Day War*, 111 Am. J. Int'l L. 357, 361 (2017).

[69] Protocol Additional to the Geneva Conventions of 12 August 1949, and relating to the Protection of Victims of International Armed Conflicts (Protocol I), June 8, 1977, 1125 U.N.T.S. 3 [hereinafter API].

[70] Convention for the Protection of Cultural Property in the Event of Armed Conflict, art. 5, May 14, 1954, 249 U.N.T.S. 215; (First) Protocol to the Hague Convention for the Protection of Cultural Property ¶ 1, May 14, 1954, 249 U.N.T.S. 358; Convention on the Means of Prohibiting and Preventing the Illicit Import, Export and Transfer of Ownership of Cultural Property, art. 2(2), Nov. 14, 1970, 823 U.N.T.S. 231.

Last, an increasingly important normative framework regulating occupation is IHRL. The application of IHRL during occupation raises two key questions concerning the limits of human rights law: whether, and the extent to which, IHRL applies beyond a state's territory (extraterritorial application); and whether, and in what manner, IHRL applies in parallel with IHL.[71] These questions have been addressed extensively in the literature.[72] For now, it suffices to say that of all cases of potential extraterritorial application of IHRL, situations of occupation are the least controversial, since in these a state clearly exercises effective control over foreign territory. While some states still argue otherwise, this is clearly the minority view.[73] As held by the European Court of Human Rights (ECtHR), when there is occupation under IHL, it can also be inferred that there is effective control for the purpose of IHRL.[74]

Similarly, while some states contest the parallel application of IHRL and IHL—and the law of occupation, as a branch of the latter[75]—it is widely accepted nowadays that these bodies of law apply concurrently.[76] Determining the exact model of their interaction—whether based on any form of *lex generalis/lex specialis* relations, or on mutual complementarity between these regimes—is beyond our scope.[77] A helpful point of reference

[71] *See generally* Yutaka Arai-Takahashi, The Law of Occupation: Continuity and Change of International Humanitarian Law, and Its Interaction with International Human Rights Law (2009). For a historical account, see Boyd van Dijk, *Human Rights in War: On the Entangled Foundations of the 1949 Geneva Conventions*, 112 Am. J. Int'l L. 553 (2018).

[72] For a list of sources, see Gross, *supra* note 4, at 339 n.8.

[73] Legal Consequences of the Construction of a Wall in the Occupied Palestinian Territory, Advisory Opinion, 2004 I.C.J. Rep. 136, ¶¶ 107–12 (July 9) [hereinafter Wall Opinion]; Armed Activities on the Territory of the Congo (Dem. Rep. Congo v. Uganda), Judgment, 2005 I.C.J. Rep. 168, ¶¶ 178–80 (Dec. 19); Al-Skeini v. United Kingdom, 2011-IV Eur. Ct. H.R. 99, ¶¶ 138–40; Georgia v. Russia (II), App. No. 38263/08 (Jan. 21, 2021), (holding that while extraterritorial jurisdiction for the purpose of the ECHR's application does not materialize during active hostilities, it does materialize when occupation commences).

[74] Georgia v. Russia (II) ¶ 196.

[75] These states view IHL as a whole as the *lex specialis* during armed conflict and occupation. *See* Wall Opinion ¶ 102.

[76] *Id.* ¶ 106; Legality of the Threat or Use of Nuclear Weapons, Advisory Opinion, 1996 I.C.J. Rep. 226, ¶¶ 24–25 (July 8); *Dem. Rep. Congo v. Uganda* ¶ 178; Human Rights Committee, General Comment No. 36 on article 6 of the International Covenant on Civil and Political Rights, on the Right to Life, U.N. Doc. CCPR/C/GC/36, ¶ 64 (Oct. 30, 2018); Benvenisti, *supra* note 1, at 12–15. Additionally, in the specific context of occupation, the occupant might be subject to IHRL as part of the treaty obligations in force in the occupied territory. *see* Section 6.1.5.

[77] *See* Oona A. Hathaway, Rebecca Crootof, Philip Levitz, and Haley Nix, *Which Law Governs During Armed Conflict? The Relationship Between International Humanitarian Law and Human Rights Law*, 96 Minn. L. Rev. 1883 (2012).

is the method applied by the ECtHR in cases where it acknowledged that the law of occupation applied (and no derogation was filed by the occupant). In general, where it concluded that no conflict existed between the relevant rights and the law of occupation, it proceeded to examine the facts in light of these rights, unaltered, under the European Convention on Human Rights (ECHR).[78] Where it found that such a conflict might exist—namely, concerning administrative detention—it interpreted the rights under the ECHR in light of the relevant rule of the law of occupation, while supplementing that rule with procedural safeguards.[79]

1.4 Key Theoretical Aspects

1.4.1 The Authority or Power of the Occupant

The law of occupation is triggered once a territory "is actually placed under the authority of the hostile army."[80] As such, an occupation administration is based on de facto power, rather than on widely accepted sources of legitimate political authority—such as the social contract, the consent of the governed, or self-determination.[81] This raises complex questions concerning the nature of occupation. Does the occupant exercise "naked power" lacking any form of legitimacy?[82] If so, it can be said that law under occupation resembles an Austinian legal system, where the source of obligation is only the threat of sanction. On this view, from the perspective of the occupied, the occupant is no more than a "gunman writ large."[83] Another view, however, would be that the power of occupants derives from

[78] Without much debate, it held that there was no such conflict with regard to the right to life (art. 2 of the Convention), the prohibition on torture (art. 3), the right to private and family life (art. 8), the right to property (art. 1 of Protocol No. 1); freedom of movement (art. 2 of Protocol No. 4); and the right to education (art. 2 of Protocol No, 1); *Georgia v. Russia (II)*, ¶ 199, ¶¶ 290–291, ¶¶ 310–311.

[79] Hassan v. UK, 2014-VI Eur. Ct. H.R. 1 ¶¶ 102–07; *Georgia v. Russia (II)*, ¶ 236. We elaborate on this issue in Chapter 5.

[80] Hague IV, *supra* note 3, art. 42.

[81] On legitimate authority, see Max Weber, *The Three Types of Legitimate Rule*, 4 Berkeley Publications in Society and Institutions 1 (1958).

[82] Bhuta, *supra* note 5, at 727; Lassa Oppenheim, *Legal Relations Between an Occupying Power and the Inhabitants*, 33 Law Q. Rev. 363, 364 (1917).

[83] H.L.A. Hart, The Concept of Law 7 (3d ed. 2012). But see the Razian conception mentioned infra note 94.

international law, and, as such, they *do* enjoy some form of legitimate authority, beyond possessing arbitrary power.

A key theoretical question is thus whether an occupation administration enjoys any form of legitimate authority.[84] In fact, the implications of this question were central during the drafting of the early law of occupation. The question came up, indirectly, in the disagreement on the status of individuals that resisted occupation. Were they entitled to immunity from prosecution, like combatants, or, rather, could the occupant punish them as common criminals? During the negotiations on the Brussels Declaration, weaker states argued that citizens possessed a "sacred duty" to resist occupation, and the law must reflect this duty, in a disconnect from the occupants' duties toward the occupied population.[85] Conversely, stronger states—which viewed themselves as potential occupants—sought to condition the rights of the local inhabitants on a duty to obey.[86] This caused a stalemate at Brussels, and also haunted the negotiations at the 1899 Hague Peace Conference. Eventually, the parties dodged the problem through the Martens clause, which provides that issues unaddressed explicitly in the Hague Conventions remain regulated by the "the usages established among civilized peoples, from the laws of humanity, and the dictates of the public conscience."[87] In practice, this indecision resulted in the peculiar arrangement that on the one hand, international law did not explicitly prohibit resistance to occupation, but on the other, recognized the occupant's power to treat resistant fighters as criminals, subject to the protection of their basic rights—as enshrined, nowadays, in GCIV.[88]

Early scholarship sought to find grounds for the occupant's legitimate authority, inter alia as a source for a duty to obey and the power to punish. One argument was that occupation spawned authority simply because the occupant was in fact responsible for the well-being of the occupied population.[89] Some 19th-century writers even conceived occupation as a tacit "quasi-contract" between the occupant and the occupied, where protection is guaranteed in return for obedience.[90] On this view, the legitimacy

[84] We do not address here the broader question of the *morality* of occupation. *See, e.g.*, Jeff McMahan, *The Morality of Military Occupation*, 31 Loy. L.A. Int'l & Compar. L. Rev. 101 (2009).

[85] Benvenisti, *supra* note 1, at 16.

[86] *Id.*

[87] Hague IV, *supra* note 3, preamble.

[88] Benvenisti, *supra* note 1, at 16.

[89] *See* Oppenheim, *supra* note 82, at 368; *see* Adil Ahmad Haque, Law and Morality at War 31 n.43 (2017).

[90] *See* Oppenheim, *supra* note 82, at 368; Von Glahn, *supra* note 2, at 45.

of an occupying authority stems from a Hobbesian notion of protection.[91] But this position was never unchallenged. The concept of quasi-contract has been thoroughly discredited, not least because there is no free consent under occupation.[92] Furthermore, even if it were true that authority could stem from de facto protection[93]—consider, for instance, a situation where an occupant provides relative order where anarchy prevailed before[94]—it would only provide for a thin form of legitimacy, not only paternalistic, but also easily eroded once we consider real-world occupants. For this reason, even traditional writers like Oppenheim denied that occupation can enjoy legitimacy that spawns a "true" duty to obey.[95]

When analyzing the contemporary law of occupation as a whole, the question whether positive law recognizes any form of legitimate authority under occupation is difficult to answer.[96] On the one hand, article 43 Hague IV juxtaposes the "authority of the legitimate power" with the power "in fact passed into the hands of the occupant." The latter's obligations are phrased as duties stemming from factual control only.[97] Furthermore, the prohibitions on compelling protected persons to furnish information to the occupant;[98] to swear allegiance to the occupant;[99] or to serve in the occupant's

[91] *See* Henry W. Halleck, International Law: or, Rules Regulating the Intercourse of States in Peace and War § 14, at 791 (1861); *compare* Anne Orford, International Authority and the Responsibility to Protect 36 (2011); Bhuta, *supra* note 5, at 727. This conception of authority explains the 19th-century (controversial) view that resistance in occupied territories was "war rebellion" or "war treason." *See* Richard Baxter, *The Duty of Obedience to the Belligerent Occupant*, 27 Brit. Y.B. Int'l L. 235, 253 (1950); Lassa Oppenheim, *On War Treason*, 33 L. Q. Rev. 266 (1917).

[92] *Compare* Oppenheim, *supra* note 82, at 369.

[93] Bhuta, *supra* note 5, at 727, *citing* Carl Schmitt, The Nomos of the Earth in the International Law of Jus Publicum Europeaн 206 (G.L. Ulmen trans., 2003).

[94] *Compare* Koskenniemi, *supra* note 26, at 171; arguably, in such a hypothetical situation the occupant can be said to enjoy some form of Razian authority, meaning, that it would be better for the occupied to obey the law of the occupant for reasons that apply to them, than to decide what to do on their own. *See* Joseph Raz, The Morality of Freedom Pt. I (1986).

[95] Oppenheim, *supra* note 82, at 369. Interestingly, after WWII, a question has arisen in domestic courts whether individuals were under a duty to obey *at least* the lawful orders of the German occupation, or, rather, they could be trialed as collaborators. Dutch courts held that occupation does not "create rights against the population of an occupied territory; they [provisions of the law of occupation] merely limit the *de facto* authority of the occupant," and that accordingly, the duty to obey does not stand as a defense. *See* Baxter, *supra* note 91, at 257. Yet, the same courts conceded that "measures designed exclusively for the benefit of the occupied country might create legal obligations for individuals." *Id.* at 257 n.1.

[96] This relates to the larger debate regarding IHL as a permissive or prohibitive normative framework. *See generally* Anne Quintin, The Nature of International Humanitarian Law: A Permissive or Restrictive Regime? (2020).

[97] Hague IV, *supra* note 3, art. 43.

[98] *Id.* art. 44.

[99] *Id.* art. 45.

military[100] suggest that occupation does not create relations of legitimate authority. Additionally, while the occupant may subject protected persons to penal provisions,[101] GCIV qualifies that "[t]he courts or authorities shall in passing sentence take ... into account the fact that the defendant is not a national of the Detaining Power,"[102] and stress that the accused is not bound to the occupant "by any duty of allegiance."[103] Last, in contemporary law, at least in certain situations, those resisting occupation might enjoy combatant immunity, meaning entitlement to prisoner-of-war (POW) status.[104] This, too, challenges the view of occupation as legitimate authority.

Conversely, if it were true that occupation provides no authority, it would be difficult to explain normatively—beyond by reference to the pragmatic compromises of the Hague Peace Conference—why the accordance of POW status to participants in *levée en masse* is explicitly preconditioned on the territory not yet being occupied—while during occupation similar actions could lead to criminal punishment.[105]

Last, an additional challenge to the legitimate authority of the occupant stems from the equal application of the laws of war, and its intersection with questions of just war. Like all other aspects of IHL, the law of occupation is subject to the principle of *belligerent equality*: the law of occupation applies equally to—and recognizes the powers of—aggressors as well as defenders.[106] That is, an occupation does not only impose itself on individuals, but may also do so in the context of an unjust or unlawful war. It is clear therefore that occupation may suffer a normative deficit even if conducted in accordance with the law.

These questions cannot be fully resolved here. Nonetheless the following propositions seem reasonable. First, if there can be any legitimate authority under occupation, it is thin and heavily contingent. Second, since in any case, occupied peoples are unlikely to accept the legitimacy of their occupation and any duty to obey it, a realistic conception of the law cannot assume that occupation entails any meaningful authority.[107]

[100] GCIV, *supra* note 30, art. 51.
[101] *Id.* art. 64.
[102] *Id.* art. 118.
[103] *Id.* art. 68(4).
[104] GCIV, *supra* note 30, art. 4(A)(2); API, *supra* note 69, arts. 1(4), 43, 44(3).
[105] *See* Hague IV, *supra* note 3, art. 2; GCIV, *supra* note 30, art. 4(A)(6); Francis Lieber, Instructions for the Government of Armies of the United States in the Field ¶52 (1863).
[106] Dinstein, *supra* note 9, at 2–3; *see generally* Adam Roberts, *The Equal Application of the Laws of War: A Principle Under Pressure*, 90 Int'l Rev. Red Cross 931 (2008).
[107] *See* Baxter, *supra* note 91, at 259.

Nonetheless, regardless of the theoretical nature of the power of the occupant, the legitimating potential of the law of occupation should not be disregarded. Drawing from the tradition of legal realism, Gross points out that unlike conquest, colonialism, or apartheid—which are per se illegal—occupation is considered an "accepted legal phenomenon" that might provide a "stamp of international legality" on practices that would be otherwise condemned.[108] It follows that in order to fully grasp the character of the occupant's power, this body of law should be approached from both a conceptual *and* realist point of view, paying attention to law in books as well as law in action.[109]

1.4.2 Occupation and Sovereignty

In previous sections, we introduced the basic principle that occupation does not confer sovereignty. In a sense, this basic principle underlines the law of occupation in its entirety, and much of this book addresses the specific manifestations of this notion. In this section, therefore, we discuss this distinction more generally.

In order to establish the relationship between sovereignty and occupation, we need first a conception of "sovereignty." In general, almost all conceptions of sovereignty share two interrelated meanings: one is *spatial*, and concerns title in territory; and the other is *substantive*, and relates to the sovereign's scope of authority.[110] Beyond this general observation, sovereignty—and its scope—is one of the most contested concepts in political theory and jurisprudence.[111] Since the most basic attribute of occupation is its distinction from sovereignty, our understanding of the former is inevitably bound with that of the latter.[112]

In any case, since occupation does not amount to sovereignty, it must mean that the powers it accords fall short of whatever is considered sovereignty, both spatially and substantively. Concerning the *spatial* aspect, the situation is relatively simple. A fundamental principle of modern

[108] Gross, *supra* note 4, at 20–21. *See generally*, in this context, David Kretzmer & Yaël Ronen, The Occupation of Justice: The Supreme Court of Israel and the Occupied Territories (2d ed. 2021).

[109] *See* Roscoe Pound, *Law in Books and Law in Action*, 44 Am. L. Rev. 12 (1910).

[110] 1 Oppenheim, *supra* note 7, § 168.

[111] *See, e.g.*, Lars Vinx, The Guardian of the Constitution: Hans Kelsen and Carl Schmitt on the Limits of Constitutional Law (2015).

[112] *See* Koskenniemi, *supra* note 26, at 165–70.

international law is that the territorial integrity of states is inviolable.[113] The resulting rule is that occupation, in itself, cannot confer title over territory. This, in turn, also affects the scope of the occupant's powers. Obviously, the occupant cannot transfer the territory to others. Moreover, since it does not own the natural resources in the territory, the occupant can only administer them under a trusteeship regime known as *usufruct*.[114]

Substantively, the limits on the occupant's powers—as a non-sovereign—stem from the principle of self-determination, meaning, at its most basic, that political status cannot be imposed on peoples by a foreign power.[115] Accordingly, the occupant cannot act as a supreme authority in the territory; rather, its powers are delineated by the international law of occupation itself.[116] The law of occupation imposes the obligation to respect the status quo ante in the territory precisely in anticipation of the return of the sovereign in line with the principle of self-determination.[117]

Importantly, occupation differs from sovereignty not only when the occupant seeks to promote its *own* interests in the territory. Perhaps counterintuitively, the occupant is restricted also when it claims to change the status quo ante to promote human rights.[118] In this sense, grounding the limitations on the occupant's powers in the principle of self-determination requires understanding the latter as not necessarily including individual rights, or a certain conception of them, at its core.[119]

Ultimately, it is difficult to pinpoint exactly how occupation differs from sovereignty in the substantive sense, precisely because the meaning of sovereignty is itself indeterminate. Indeed, commentators have for decades held both the convictions that on the one hand, "[t]here is not an atom of sovereignty in the authority of the occupying power,"[120] and, on the other,

[113] *See* Montevideo Convention on the Rights and Duties of States, art. 11, Dec. 26, 1933, 165 L.N.T.S. 19; UN Charter, art. 2(4); G.A. Res. 2625 (XXV), annex, Declaration on Principles of International Law concerning Friendly Relations and Cooperation among States in accordance with the Charter of the United Nations, principle (d) (Oct. 24, 1970) [hereinafter Declaration on Friendly Relations].

[114] Hague IV, *supra* note 3, art. 55. We discuss usufruct in Section 6.3.1.

[115] *See, e.g.*, Declaration on Friendly Relations, *supra* note 113, Principle (e).

[116] Koskenniemi, *supra* note 26, at 164; HCJ 393/82 Jam'iat Iscan Al-Ma'almoun v. IDF Commander of Judea and Samaria, 37(4) PD 785, ¶ 23 (1983) (Isr.).

[117] Koskenniemi, *supra* note 26, at 164.

[118] *See* TRISTAN FERRARO, ICRC, EXPERT MEETING, OCCUPATION AND OTHER FORMS OF ADMINISTRATION OF FOREIGN TERRITORY 61–72 (2012) [hereinafter ICRC EXPERT MEETING].

[119] *Compare* Koskenniemi, *supra* note 26, at 167–68; BENVENISTI, *supra* note 1, at 17–18. Alternatively, even if self-determination *is* understood as including individual rights, arguably occupants should not be the ones assessing them in occupied territories.

[120] Oppenheim, *supra* note 82, at 364.

that "how far short of sovereignty the authority of a belligerent occupant falls" is a contested issue.[121]

The Israeli High Court of Justice (HCJ) attempted, in the *Jam'iat Iscan* case, to conceptualize the distinction between occupation and sovereignty in the substantive sense.[122] There, the question was whether Israel, as the occupant in the West Bank, could expropriate land for the purpose of constructing a highway.[123] The landowners argued that as a temporary administrator, the occupant could not enact far-reaching, permanent infrastructural changes. Rather, it could only administer and maintain the existing infrastructure.[124] The Court noted that the occupant "is not sovereign" and therefore possesses temporary authority only.[125] Yet, it conceded that this notion is in tension with its duty, under the law of occupation itself, to ensure public order and to act as a "proper government."[126] The Court addressed this problem by reformulating it as a balancing exercise.[127] Within this balance, as occupation is prolonged, "proper government" requires wider powers to act in favor of the local population.[128] If this view is adopted, the gap between occupation and sovereignty narrows as time passes, and becomes harder to grasp. To the Court, it seems, the minimum gap that must be always maintained is that the occupant "must not bring about a substantive change in the fundamental institutions of the [occupied] Area."[129] Yet, this formulation fails to provide a clear distinction between occupation and sovereignty, because even a domestic, civilian executive usually cannot enact such changes within its own state. Under this view, it remains unclear how, *at least* in prolonged occupation, an occupation administration differs from a sovereign acting in its own territory.

Owing to these and other difficulties, Koskenniemi suggested that "it seems both impossible and somehow pointless or counter-productive to insist on a formal distinction between occupation and sovereignty."[130] Nonetheless, he still argued against completely erasing this formal distinction in favor of a functional, "purpose"-based analysis of the occupant's

[121] Feilchenfeld, *supra* note 27, at 87.
[122] *Jam'iat Iscan*, 37(4) PD 785.
[123] *Id.* ¶ 1.
[124] *Id.* ¶ 3.
[125] *Id.* ¶ 12.
[126] Hague IV, *supra* note 3, art. 43; *Jam'iat Iscan*, 37(4) PD 785, ¶¶ 18–19.
[127] *Jam'iat Iscan*, 37(4) PD 785, ¶ 20.
[128] *See id.* ¶ 22.
[129] *Id.* ¶ 28.
[130] Koskenniemi, *supra* note 26, at 170.

actions. This is because such a view fails to take seriously the inherent value of political participation, which is reflected—ideally—in sovereignty, but denied under occupation.[131]

In sum, the relationsship between sovereignty and occupation are in flux precisely because the understanding of sovereignty is unstable.[132] This tension reappears in many forms in our discussions of particular issues throughout this book.

1.4.3 Occupation and Temporariness

The idea that occupation is *temporary* underlines the law of occupation in its entirety.[133] Since occupation is a state of exception, it *must* be temporary—otherwise the distinction between the exception and the norm collapses.[134] Of course, the idea of temporariness is intrinsically tied with the discussion above on occupation and sovereignty. While sovereignty is presumed to be eternal, occupation "anticipates the restoration of sovereignty."[135] If occupation is indefinite, a fair question is what remains of the distinction between occupation and sovereignty, between trusteeship and military dictatorship or colonialism.[136] This tension undergirds the problematics of "prolonged occupation," as mentioned briefly above. We discuss prolonged occupation specifically in Chapter 4. Here, we only point out some general considerations.

Only under the presumption that occupation is temporary, can we rationalize both the wide security powers possessed by the occupant, and its obligation to respect the status quo ante. The Fourth Geneva Convention , to an extent, reflects this assumption, by stipulating in article 6(3) that the application of the Convention in occupied territories shall cease a year after "the general close of military operations."[137] This provision anticipates that when significant time passes after active hostilities end, most governmental functions would be handed back to the local authorities, and that "stringent

[131] *Id.* at 173–74.
[132] *Compare* Benvenisti, *supra* note 1, at 21.
[133] *See* Gross, *supra* note 4, at 29–35.
[134] *See* Benvenisti, *supra* note 1, ch. vii, 93; Bhuta, *supra* note 5, at 723.
[135] Koskenniemi, *supra* note 26, at 164.
[136] *See* Orna Ben-Naftali, Michael Sfard & Hedi Viterbo, The ABC of the OPT: A Legal Lexicon of the Israeli Control over the Occupied Palestinian Territory 400 (2018).
[137] GCIV, *supra* note 30, art. 6(3).

measures against the civilian population will no longer be justified."[138] Nonetheless, the article stipulates that to the extent that the occupant continues to exercise governmental functions, it remains bound by certain provisions; but provisions allowing security internment, for instance, no longer apply.[139] Yet, these limitations notwithstanding, article 6(3) does not circumscribe a time limit for occupation as a whole.

Be that as it may, even GCIV's limited allusion to temporariness has been effectively quashed, "[o]nce it became clear that the drafters' [of GCIV] assumption regarding the short duration of occupations was not supported by reality."[140] Article 6(3) arguably fell into desuetude, and was reversed in API, which provides that the entire scope of the law of occupation remains applicable until the occupation is terminated.[141]

This legal situation leads to the odd conclusion that occupation could be at once temporary *and* potentially indefinite.[142] For example, the HCJ held that although occupation is "temporary by nature,"[143] international law "does not set a time limit thereto."[144] This idea of an indefinite occupation is subject to much criticism. Gross argues, in this context, that indefinite occupation contradicts the law of occupation's basic principles, and if it were recognized as a lawful possibility, occupation's "distance from the illegal regimes of conquest, colonialism, and apartheid may become thin or blurred."[145]

138 ICRC, Commentary on IV Geneva Convention 63 (Jean S. Pictet ed., 1958) [hereinafter ICRC, Commentary 1958]; *see also* Gross, *supra* note 4, at 31–34.

139 GCIV, *supra* note 30, art. 6(3); ICRC, Commentary 1958, *supra* note 138, at 63. There are many inconsistencies in this article. *See* Gross, *supra* note 4, at 32–33; Roberts, *supra* note 40, at 57.

140 Gross, *supra* note 4, at 33.

141 API, *supra* note 69, art. 3(b). *See also* Benvenisti, *supra* note 1, at 80; Arai-Takahashi, *supra* note 71, at 18; Gross, *supra* note 4, at 32–33; curiously, the ICJ applied article 6(3) of GCIV in the Wall Opinion. However, this is an obiter dictum at most since the articles relevant to the Wall Opinion would apply in any case. *See* Ardi Imseis, *Critical Reflections on the International Humanitarian Law Aspects of the ICJ Wall Advisory Opinion*, 99 Am. J. Int'l L. 102, 106 (2005); Orna Ben-Naftali, *"A la Recherche du Temps Perdu": Rethinking Article 6 of the Fourth Geneva Convention in the Light of the Legal Consequences of the Construction of a Wall in the Occupied Palestinian Territory Advisory Opinion*, 38 Isr. L. Rev. 211 (2004); ICRC Expert Meeting, *supra* note 118, at 77–78.

142 Ben-Naftali et al., *supra* note 136, at 401.

143 HCJ 393/82 Jam'iat Iscan Al-Ma'almoun v. IDF Commander of Judea and Samaria, 37(4) PD 785 ¶ 12 (1983) (Isr.).

144 *Id. See also* Meir Shamgar, *Legal Concepts and Problems of the Israeli Military Government: The Initial Stage*, *in* Military Government in the Territories Administered by Israel, 1967–1980, 13, 43 (Meir Shamgar ed., 1982).

145 Gross, *supra* note 4, at 35. *See also* David Hughes, *Of Tactics, Illegal Occupation and the Boundaries of Legal Capability: A Reply to Ardi Imseis*, 31 Eur. J. Int'l L. 1087 (2020).

To sum up, the law of occupation presupposes temporariness; yet, the black-letter law does not circumscribe a period of time after which occupation must end. This led some to argue that indefinite occupations are unlawful. We return to this question in Section 1.4.5.

1.4.4 De Jure and De Facto Annexation

That occupation does not grant title in the territory is a widely accepted bright-line rule.[146] In the past, however, an occupation could transform into title in two main situations. First, when the territorial state was subjugated and ceased to exist (*debellatio*). Second, when the defeated state still existed but agreed, in a final peace treaty, to cede the territory.[147] Another possibility, according to Oppenheim, was when formal cession of territory has not taken place, yet the vanquished state ceases fighting and "submits silently to the annexation."[148]

In contemporary law, the territorial integrity of states is permanent and inviolable; the principle of non-acquisition of territory by force is widely recognized; and peoples enjoy the right to self-determination.[149] This limits significantly the situations in which an occupation can be converted to title. The annexation of occupied territory following a negotiated peace treaty—while entailing some complications[150]—could be lawful, *at least* when it transfers title from the aggressor to the victim.[151] Conversely, the idea of unilateral annexation through *debellatio* quite clearly contravenes the principles of territorial integrity and self-determination.[152] It seems that the Geneva Conventions, by providing that they apply to "all cases of partial or total occupation," clarify that *debellatio* is no longer possible, and even situations in which states are completely subjugated remain instances of occupation.[153]

[146] *See* GCIV, *supra* note 30, art. 47; API, *supra* note 69, art. 4; *see also* Council of the European Union Press Release, Declaration by the High Representative on behalf of the EU on the Golan Heights (Mar. 27, 2019).
[147] 1 Oppenheim, *supra* note 7, § 236.
[148] *Id.* § 239.
[149] *See supra.*
[150] In particular, emanating from GCIV, art. 47 regarding the inviolability of rights.
[151] Dinstein, *supra* note 9, at 291.
[152] Notably, Dinstein still views *debellatio* as a possible outcome. *Id.* at 2; yet he concedes that in post-2003 Iraq, no one doubted that Iraq continued to be a state. *Id.* at 16. He also concedes that even in situations that could amount to *debellatio*, "the right to self-determination of the local people has to be taken into account." *Id.* at 59.
[153] GCIV, *supra* note 30, Common Article 2.

Traditionally, annexation was effected through a formal act.[154] Nowadays, due to the absolute prohibition on unilateral annexation, states might avoid formal declarations, in favor of incremental changes that would eventually amount to de facto annexation—without admitting that one took place. Avoiding formal annexation also facilitates refraining from extending full citizenship to the occupied population.[155] There is a wide array of measures which might amount to de facto annexation.[156] For example, Russia's policies in South Ossetia and Abkhazia, which involve economic and legal integration, passportization and the appointment of Russian officials to key posts, were described as "creeping annexation."[157] De facto annexation can also be effected through infrastructural and demographic changes. The ICJ, for instance, opined that Israel's construction of settlements in the West Bank, along with a wall to reinforce them, amounted to a permanent "fait accompli" regardless of the temporary characterization of the wall by Israel.[158] Legal changes, too, can raise such a suspicion. This can be the case when the occupation administration enacts far-reaching changes to the local law, which mirror the law in the occupying state itself.[159] Another technique for de facto annexation could be the extraterritorial application of the occupant's domestic laws. For instance, Israel's controversial Settlements Regularization Law—eventually annulled by the HCJ—sought to regulate the use of private property in the West Bank extraterritorially.[160]

[154] A recent case is the Russian annexation of Crimea, enacted through a domestic law. Note, however, that Russia did not see this as annexation of occupied territory, but rather the joining together of two sovereign states. *See* Thomas D. Grant, *Annexation of Crimea*, 109 Am. J. Int'l L. 68, 68 (2015).

[155] *See* Omar M. Dajani, *Israel's Creeping Annexation*, 111 Am. J. Int'l L. Unbound 51, 52, 54 (2017).

[156] An especially interesting case of a mixed de jure and de facto annexation concerns Israel's approach to the Golan Heights, Syrian territory occupied in 1967. In 1981, Israel extended its "law, jurisdiction and administration" to the Golan, justifying it as a functional measure and actively refraining from using the term "annexation." Yet, the UNSC treated this as a clear case of annexation. S.C. Res. 497 (Dec. 17, 1981); *compare* Leon Sheleff, *Application of Israeli Law to the Golan Heights Is Not Annexation*, 20 Brook. J. Int'l L. 333 (1994), *with* Asher Maoz, *Application of Israeli Law to the Golan Heights Is Annexation*, 20 Brook. J. Int'l L. 355 (1994).

[157] 2 Independent International Fact-Finding Mission on the Conflict in Georgia, Report, at 18–19 (Sept. 2009).

[158] Wall Opinion ¶¶ 115, 117, 119, 121.

[159] *See* Von Glahn, *supra* note 2, at 94–95; Yesh Din, Annexation Legislation Database, https://www.yesh-din.org/en/legislation/ (last visited July 30, 2020).

[160] HCJ 1308/17 Silwad Municipality v. The Knesset, Nevo Legal Database (June 9, 2020) (Isr.).

An interesting question, in this context, is whether the occupation administration must be strictly *military*. The concern is that subjecting the territory to the direct civilian rule of the occupying state would again amount to de facto annexation. This concern has both expressive and substantive aspects. Expressively, insisting on a military administration highlights the exceptional and provisional nature of the control.[161] Substantively, the military chain of command is formally and functionally distinct from most states' civilian government. Since the administration in occupied territories is ideally envisioned as a trusteeship that may not take into account the political interests of the occupying state, it should enjoy some independent discretion—at least concerning the day-to-day administration of the territory.[162] Presumably, keeping the territory under military administration prevents its integration with the state apparatus and helps to maintain such independence.

This "independence" of the military administration—to the extent possible—is frustrated when the civilian government micro-manages it to a point in which it does not enjoy administrative discretion.[163] When the civilian government does so we might have, again, an instance of de facto annexation. The difficult question, of course, is the extent of independent discretion that must be granted to the military administration. While it is expected that the administration will execute the *general* policy of the state, it must enjoy some functional independence in its micro decision-making.[164]

The idea that an occupation administration must be military is implied in article 42 of Hague IV, which defines occupied territory as placed under the authority of the "hostile *army*."[165] Dinstein, accordingly, argues that the "government of an occupied territory is military *par definitionem*."[166] That is not to say that the occupant cannot establish an administration with civilian components, such as the Israeli "civil administration" (1981)[167] or the Coalition Provisional Authority (CPA) in Iraq (2003).[168] Still, the law of occupation presumes that the military command is the top authority in the territory, and all civilian components are ultimately subject to it.[169]

161 Schmitt, *supra* note 93, at 207–09.
162 Benvenisti, *supra* note 1, at 4.
163 *See, e.g.*, HCJ 390/79 Duweikat v. Government of Israel, 34(1) PD 1, 20 (1979) (Isr.).
164 *Compare* Dinstein, *supra* note 9, at 56.
165 Hague IV, *supra* note 3, art. 42.
166 Dinstein, *supra* note 9, at 56.
167 *Id.*
168 Benvenisti, *supra* note 1, at 5.
169 Dinstein, *supra* note 9, at 131.

In sum, holding the territory under a military administration is presumed, ideally, to better ensure the insulation of the occupied territory from the politics of the occupying state, and to signify its provisional nature. This presents the occupation administration as a peculiar hybrid construct. From the perspective of domestic law, it derives its power from internal legislation, and is of course subject to the civilian government; from the point of view of international law, however, it derives its powers from the law of occupation and therefore, to an extent, is an organ of international law.[170]

1.4.5 Occupation and Illegality

To some, the question whether occupation can be illegal is a category mistake.[171] Occupation, on this view, is simply a factual condition regulated under *jus in bello*, just like any other military operation.[172] Since *jus in bello* applies equally to all parties to the conflict, regardless of the legality of their war or other considerations, the only relevant question would be whether the occupant complied with the law of occupation in specific instances.[173] Complementing this view is the general approach which views occupation as a neutral concept:[174] it is a "legitimate aim of warfare,"[175] and perhaps even "a natural phenomenon in war."[176]

This view, however, focuses on the law of occupation in isolation. When broadening the picture, other arguments can be made. First, potential illegalities arise when considering the law of occupation in relation to *jus ad bellum*. Consider a situation in which an occupation is a product of a war of aggression. Since a war of aggression is a violation of a peremptory norm (*jus cogens*),[177] it could be said that states are under a duty not to recognize such occupations as lawful on the whole (nonrecognition).[178] This remains

[170] *Jam'iat Iscan*, 37(4) PD 785, ¶ 10.
[171] *See* Dinstein, *supra* note 9, at 2–3.
[172] *Id.*; Shamgar, *supra* note 144, at 43.
[173] Dinstein, *supra* note 9, at 3.
[174] Gross, *supra* note 4, at 19; *compare* Benvenisti, *supra* note 1, at 15–16.
[175] Shamgar, *supra* note 144, at 28.
[176] Dinstein, *supra* note 9, at 1.
[177] *See, e.g.*, Int'l Law Comm'n, Dire Tladi (Special Rapporteur), *Fourth Rep. on Peremptory Norms of General International Law (Jus Cogens)*, U.N. Doc. A/CN.4/727, ¶¶ 62–68 (Jan. 31, 2019).
[178] Int'l Law Comm'n, Draft Articles on Responsibility of States for Internationally Wrongful Acts, *extract from* the *Rep. of the International Law Commission on the Work of Its Fifty-third Session*, U.N. Doc. A/56/10, art. 41 (2010); *see also* Valentina Azarova, *An Illegal Territorial Regime? On the Occupation and Annexation of Crimea as a Matter of International Law*, *in*

true although an exception to this duty might exist for administrative acts which, if deemed invalid by third-party states, would only harm the local population (the *Namibia exception*).[179] Importantly, nonrecognition would not necessarily mean that the occupant has violated the law of occupation; rather, in line with the general separation between *jus ad bellum* and *jus in bello*, the fact that its actions might be lawful under the latter do not render them lawful under the former, and therefore it could be said that they are still a part of the illegal whole.[180]

In this sense, some argue that an occupation can be illegal overall even if it results from initially lawful self-defense.[181] If territory is held well after the threat from the attacking state has subsided, then maintaining the occupation of that state's territory could be an unnecessary and disproportionate use of force.[182]

Of course, such constructions suffer from the constant predicament of *jus ad bellum*, that in most cases third parties would not be able to identify the aggressor. Practically, it follows that in most cases occupations would not be treated as illegal per se by third parties.[183] Yet, this might not be the case where the United Nations Security Council (UNSC) identifies the aggressor;[184] where a binding UNSC resolution designates an occupation as

The Use of Force against Ukraine and International Law 41 (Sergey Sayapin & Evhen Tsybulenko eds., 2018); Yaël Ronen, *Illegal Occupation and Its Consequences*, 41 Isr. L. Rev. 41 (2008).

[179] Legal Consequences for States of the Continued Presence of South Africa in Namibia (South West Africa) notwithstanding Security Council Resolution 276 (1970), Advisory Opinion, 1971 I.C.J. Rep. 16, ¶ 125 (June 21) [hereinafter Namibia Opinion]; *compare*Demopoulos v. Turkey, 2010-I Eur. Ct. H.R. 365, ¶ 94 (ruling that "an illegal occupation does not deprive all administrative or putative legal or judicial act therein of any relevance").

[180] *See, e.g.*, API, *supra* note 69, preamble ("nothing in this Protocol or in the Geneva Conventions of 12 August 1949 can be construed as legitimizing or authorizing any act of aggression or any other use of force inconsistent with the Charter of the United Nations"); Benvenisti, *supra* note 1, at 17; *compare* Rotem Giladi, *The Jus ad Bellum/Jus in Bello Distinction and the Law of Occupation*, 41 Isr. L. Rev. 246, 301 (2008); Alejandro Chehtman, *Occupation Courts, Jus Ad Bellum Considerations, and Non-State Actors: Revisiting the Ethics of Military Occupation*, 21 Legal Theory 18, 37–43 (2015); *see also* Ralph Wilde, *Using the Master's Tools to Dismantle the Master's House: International Law and Palestinian Liberation*, 22 Pal. Y.B. Int'l L. 3, 21–35 (2019–20).

[181] *See* Ariel Zemach, *Can Occupation Resulting from a War of Self-Defense Become Illegal?*, 24 Minn. J. Int'l L. 313 (2015).

[182] On necessity and proportionality, see Military Aid and Paramilitary Activities in and Against Nicaragua (Nicar. v. U.S.), Judgment, 1986 I.C.J. Rep. 14, ¶ 176 (June 27).

[183] For a classic statement, see 3 Emer De Vattel, The Law of Nations ch. XII (1758).

[184] *See, e.g.*, S.C. Res. 660 (Aug. 2, 1990).

illegal, or otherwise demands ending the occupation;[185] or, perhaps, where there is wide consensus that aggression has occurred, such as in the case of Russia's invasion of Ukraine in 2022.[186]

The same logic applies when a state that was mandated to administer a territory remains there after its mandate is revoked. In such cases, an occupation can become per se illegal. The paradigmatic example for such cases is South Africa's continuing control of Namibia long after its mandate was terminated.[187] Additionally, when a state withdraws its consent to the presence of foreign forces on its territory, and the latter refuse to leave, then it might become an illegal occupant, to the extent that the other conditions for occupation exist.[188]

Others suggest that illegality, and a duty to end the occupation, can spawn from violations of principles *internal* to the concept of occupation. In this context, one of us has suggested that an occupation regime that refuses to earnestly promote a peaceful settlement of the dispute would be per se illegal. This is because such a behavior reveals that the occupant acts in bad faith: it does not hold the territory for legitimate security reasons, but seeks to retain it for other purposes, such as de facto annexation.[189] On this view, if the occupant's conditions for peaceful settlement are not motivated by "reasonable security interests," its continued occupation would be internationally wrongful.[190]

The notion of per se illegality of occupation is most frequently invoked regarding the Israeli occupation. Drawing from the practices of this occupation, some conclude that an occupation can indeed become illegal on the whole.[191] They criticize the "factual" approach which views occupation as a neutral construct of *jus in bello*, and urge viewing occupation as a *normative* phenomenon—meaning, one generated by the operation of law itself—which can therefore be subjected to judgments of legality and illegality.[192] On this view, violation of one of the three basic tenets of the

[185] Such was the case concerning South Africa in Namibia and Iraq in Kuwait; S.C. Res. 276 (Jan. 30, 1970), S.C. Res. 661 (Aug. 6, 1990). Concerning Israel and the Palestinian Territories, see S.C. Res. 242 (Nov. 22, 1967); Benvenisti, *supra* note 1, at 245.

[186] G.A. Res A/ES-11/L.1 (Mar. 1, 2022).

[187] S.C. Res. 276 (Jan. 30, 1970); Namibia Opinion.

[188] *See* Eliav Lieblich, International Law and Civil Wars: Intervention and Consent 19–20 (2013).

[189] Benvenisti, *supra* note 1, at 17, 245.

[190] *Id.* at 246.

[191] Orna Ben-Naftali, Aeyal M. Gross & Keren Michaeli, *Illegal Occupation: Framing the Occupied Palestinian Territory*, 23 Berkeley J. Int'l L. 551 (2005).

[192] *Id.* at 552–54.

law of occupation—(a) non-acquisition of sovereignty; (b) occupation as trusteeship; and (c) temporariness—renders an occupation illegal per se.[193] Gross suggested, in this context, a distinction between *jus ad occupation* and *jus in occupation*. The former consists of these three basic principles, while the latter of the specific norms of the law of occupation. Violations of *jus ad occupation*, to Gross, render an occupation illegal.[194]

Common to the views that condition the legality of occupation on its adherence to internal basic principles of the law of occupation is that they seek to identify situations in which an occupation becomes an instrument to suppress the right to self-determination. In such cases, it might become indistinguishable from unlawful regimes such as colonial domination and apartheid.[195] Imseis has suggested that in such situations a state must end its occupation as an international wrongful act—and a violation of a peremptory norm (*jus cogens*)—and that this obligation cannot be preconditioned on negotiations.[196]

Undoubtedly, even if an occupation is illegal, the occupant is still bound by the laws of occupation, just as it is bound by IHL as a whole, regardless of the justness of its cause. In the rest of the book, therefore, we set the question of per se illegality aside.

[193] *Id.* at 555.

[194] Gross, *supra* note 4, at 3–4, 23–35.

[195] *Compare* John Dugard, *Preface*, *in* The Legality of Economic Activities in Occupied Territories (Antoine Duval & Eva Kassoti eds., 2020).

[196] Ardi Imseis, *Negotiating the Illegal: On the United Nations and the Illegal Occupation of Palestine, 1967–2020*, 31 Eur. J. Int'l L. 1055 (2020).

2
Definition, Beginning, and End of Occupation

In this chapter, we address the threshold questions of the law of occupation: how occupation is defined, what territory can be occupied, who can occupy it, and, relatedly, when does occupation begin and end. When answering these questions, the main challenge stems from the centrality of the indeterminate concept of "effective control" within the law of occupation. This indeterminacy leaves ample space for manipulation by potential occupants wishing to evade the burdens imposed by the law of occupation.

Several general observations are helpful. From the standpoint of the protection of individuals, defining occupation is essentially about identifying the point at which belligerents acquire enhanced *positive* obligations toward the civilian population. Negative obligations concerning civilians—for instance, not to attack them, or not to interfere with humanitarian aid—are *always* applicable.[1] Yet, at least traditionally, certain positive duties kick in only once occupation is established.[2] For example, it is only in occupation that belligerents must *actively* protect persons against third parties.

Two issues complicate this observation. First, underlying the entire debate is the question whether occupation is a formal concept, which applies in a binary fashion once a certain threshold of control is reached; or, rather, that occupation-like duties arise *functionally* whenever—and to the extent to which—individuals are under the power of a belligerent. This question is increasingly important, considering the modern capacity of states to exert significant control from afar, and over disaggregated elements of

[1] Convention (IV) relative to the Protection of Civilian Persons in Time of War arts. 23, 70, Aug. 12, 1949, 6 U.S.T. 3516, 75 U.N.T.S. 287 [hereinafter GCIV].

[2] *See id.* arts. 43, 55, and Protocol Additional to the Geneva Conventions of 12 August 1949, and relating to the Protection of Victims of International Armed Conflicts (Protocol I) art. 69, June 8, 1977, 1125 U.N.T.S. 3 [hereinafter API].

government.[3] If occupation is not a binary concept, the distinction between the stage of hostilities and of occupation becomes harder to grasp.

Second, identifying the point at which occupation exists has been especially important in times when there were no *other* possible sources of positive obligations. When GCIV was drafted, there were no parallel IHRL treaties, nor were belligerents subject to the obligations to take precautionary measures, as was enshrined in API of 1977. However, nowadays, competing sources for positive obligations might be found in both IHRL and in the law on the conduct of hostilities. The law of occupation, like all international law, is affected by the process of fragmentation, in which multiple normative frameworks and institutions govern any given instance.[4] The law of occupation is but one framework within what may be termed the "international law of control": the corpus of norms that apply once states exercise control or power over territory or individuals.

Accordingly, to fully grasp the implications of the threshold for the law of occupation, the relations between the law of occupation and parallel sources should be clarified. For example, if one adopts a high threshold for occupation, the question arises whether in liminal situations—in which the belligerent exercises powers over individuals but not effective control over territory—positive duties can derive from IHRL. Some point out that IHRL, due to its greater flexibility, might be the "superior avenue" to fill gaps in such cases.[5] Conversely, if one adopts a functional approach to occupation—and accordingly sets a low threshold for occupation-like duties—then the potential parallel application between the law of occupation and IHRL expands. Whether, in such cases, occupation law adds or detracts from IHRL—or is roughly equivalent—is a complex question which cannot be resolved here.[6]

When considering the normative framework better suited to apply in liminal cases, the politics of the term "occupation" cannot be overlooked.

[3] We discuss the functional approach to occupation in more detail in Section 2.6.

[4] Int'l Law Comm'n, Rep. on the Fragmentation of International Law: Difficulties Arising from the Diversification and Expansion of International Law, U.N. Doc. A/CB.4/L.682 (Apr. 13, 2006). The notion of "control" itself has been given different meanings in different contexts. *See* Natia Kalandarishvili-Mueller, Occupation and Control in International Humanitarian Law 3–11 (2021).

[5] Yuval Shany, *Binary Law Meets Complex Reality: The Occupation of Gaza Debate*, 41 Isr. L. Rev. 68, 86 (2008).

[6] Some argue that in occupation, IHRL might actually *lessen* the protection of individuals in relation to IHRL. *See* Aeyal M. Gross, *Human Proportions: Are Human Rights the Emperor's New Clothes of the International Law of Occupation?*, 18 Eur. J. Int'l L. 1 (2007).

Because of its negative connotations, states might be more willing, in gray situations, to recognize duties under competing frameworks rather than under the law of occupation.[7]

Furthermore, as mentioned above, some pre-occupation positive duties can be read into the law on the conduct of hostilities, most notably the duties to take precautionary measures. A wide reading of the latter can also result in the duty, for instance, to provide for the civilian population in order to minimize the adverse effects of an attack.[8] In sum, to the extent that parallel positive duties can be derived from other sources of law, the practical importance of the threshold for occupation lessens.

2.1 Point of Departure: Article 42 Hague 1907

The widely accepted definition of occupation is found in article 42 of Hague IV:

> Territory is considered occupied when it is actually placed under the authority of the hostile army.
>
> The occupation extends only to the territory where such authority has been established and can be exercised.

Article 42 is usually understood as establishing three cumulative conditions for occupation: (a) the presence of foreign forces in the territory; (b) the exercise of control ("authority") over the territory, in a manner that excludes control by others; and (c) the nonconsensual nature of the presence ("hostile army").[9]

Yet, as this chapter shows, none of these elements are self-explanatory.[10]

[7] Tristan Ferraro, ICRC, Expert Meeting, Occupation and Other Forms of Administration of Foreign Territory 28 (2012) [hereinafter ICRC, Expert Meeting].

[8] Eyal Benvenisti, *The Law on Asymmetric Warfare*, *in* Looking to the Future: Essays on International Law in Honor of W. Michael Reisman 931, 946–47 (Mahnoush H. Arsanjani, Jacob Cogan, Robert Sloane & Siegfried Wiessner eds., 2010).

[9] *See, e.g.*, ICRC, Expert Meeting, *supra* note 7, at 10; ICRC, Commentary on I Geneva Convention for the Amelioration of the Condition of the Wounded and Sick in Armed Forces in the Field ¶ 304 (2016) [hereinafter ICRC, Commentary 2016].

[10] *See* Kalandarishvili-Mueller, *supra* note 4, at 20–21.

2.2 Occupation of Whose Territory?

2.2.1 Territories of Other States

Before analyzing the constitutive elements of occupation, a preliminary question needs addressing: Which territory could be subject to occupation to begin with? Section III of Hague IV refers to military authority over the territory of the "Hostile State." Similarly, GCIV provides that the Convention applies "to all cases of partial or total occupation of the territory of a *High Contracting Party*, even if the said occupation meets with no armed resistance."[11] It is clear, on its face, that occupation is a phenomenon of an *international* armed conflict and not of internal conflicts.[12]

Accordingly, when a state regains control over its own territory during civil war, that territory is not subject to the law of occupation but to the state's own domestic law, and internationally, to IHRL—under which, perhaps, some form of martial law can be declared as a derogation from IHRL.[13] This remains true although in the quintessential historical example of a highly legalized civil war—the American Civil War—the Union Government drew extensively from the notion of occupation in its actions in the retaken Confederate states.[14]

Furthermore, an increasingly important question concerns situations where organized armed groups gain control over territory in a non-international armed conflict (NIAC). Are such groups bound by occupation-like rules, over and above those that explicitly govern conduct in NIAC?[15] We address this issue in Section 2.4.4.

[11] GCIV, *supra* note 1, art. 2 (emphasis added).

[12] *See* Danish Ministry of Def., Military Manual on International Law Relevant to Danish Armed Forces in International Operations 431 (2016) [hereinafter Danish Manual].

[13] International Covenant on Civil and Political Rights, art. 4, Dec. 16, 1966, 999 U.N.T.S. 171 [hereinafter ICCPR]; Convention for the Protection of Human Rights and Fundamental Freedoms, art. 15, Nov. 4, 1950, 213 U.N.T.S. 222.

[14] *See* Stephen C. Neff, Justice in Blue and Gray: A Legal History of the Civil War 110 (2010).

[15] Those being the provisions of Common Article 3 to the Geneva Conventions, and those of Protocol Additional to the Geneva Conventions of 12 August 1949, and relating to the Protection of Victims of Non-International Armed Conflicts (Protocol II), June 8, 1977, 1125 U.N.T.S. 609 [hereinafter APII].

2.2.2 "Non-Sovereign" and Disputed Territories

Occupation in general applies to *external* territories. This, in turn, raises the question whether the said territory must belong to another sovereign *state*. In the past, and in line with the colonial underpinnings of international law, "uncivilized" peoples were not deemed entitled to sovereignty over territory. Their territories were accordingly not subject to the law of occupation, and could be simply absorbed.[16] Traces of this logic have endured in contemporary times, albeit in modified forms. In several instances, states argued that external territories under their control are not de jure occupied, mainly because of their previous, allegedly non-sovereign status.

Four main cases come to mind, all relating to territories that fell under the control of semi-peripheral states after the collapse of empires. Common to these cases, is that despite the objection of these states, the alleged gap created by the absence of a previous sovereign was filled by the principle of self-determination, or in some cases, by the purposive reading of the provisions controlling the applicability of the law of occupation.

After WWI, South Africa was granted a mandate over Namibia (Southwest Africa) by the League of Nations. However, following the demise of the League, South Africa argued that it was no longer bound by the mandate. Rather, it claimed that it gained title in the territory inter alia because no "State or organization can have a better title to it."[17] The ICJ rejected this claim, holding that the mandate system endured within the UN system.[18] In 1966, the UNGA terminated South Africa's mandate, owing to its failure to abide by its terms. Yet, the result was not, as South Africa hoped, that it would now gain the territory. Rather, the UNGA declared that absent the mandate South Africa had no right to administer the territory.[19] UNSC Resolution 276 of 1970 added that the continued presence of South Africa in Namibia was "illegal," and that the "occupation" of the territory had grave consequences.[20] Importantly, South Africa's absence of rights did not derive from Resolution 276.[21] Rather, the normative source of its duty to withdraw was the principle of self-determination, which

[16] *See* Section 1.2.

[17] Legal Consequences for States of the Continued Presence of South Africa in Namibia (South West Africa) notwithstanding Security Council Resolution 276 (1970), Advisory Opinion, 1971 I.C.J. Rep. 16, ¶ 82 (June 21) [hereinafter Namibia Opinion].

[18] *Id.* ¶ 78.

[19] G.A. Res. 2145 (XXI), ¶¶ 3–4 (Oct. 27, 1966).

[20] S.C. Res. 276, ¶¶ 3–4 (Jan. 30, 1970).

[21] Namibia Opinion, ¶ 106.

articulated the rights of colonial peoples to freely determine their political status.[22] In the Namibia case, therefore, the principle of self-determination replaced, so to speak, the absent sovereign state, and the territory was considered occupied.

A comparable argument was advanced by Israel concerning its occupation of the West Bank and Gaza since June 1967. Immediately after establishing control, the Israeli MAG stated that the territories would be subject to Hague IV and GCIV, and this was also reflected in Israel's early military orders.[23] This soon changed, however, in favor of the view that the law of occupation did not apply de jure in the territories, but was only applied by Israel de facto for pragmatic reasons.[24] The argument was that neither Jordan—which held the West Bank before Israel—nor Egypt—which occupied Gaza—were lawful sovereigns, since they unilaterally occupied the territories in 1948, when the mandatory power (Great Britain) withdrew from Palestine. Accordingly, the argument went, since the territories did not belong to any state before 1967, they could not be de jure occupied.[25] This argument was refocused later mainly against the application of GCIV in the occupied territories. According to this version of the claim, GCIV did not apply since the territories were not taken from a "High Contracting Party," as Common Article 2 required.[26] Rather, as Israel claimed, it voluntarily applied the "humanitarian provisions" of GCIV to avoid a legal vacuum in a *sui generis* situation.[27] In truth, the reason for the focus on GCIV is that while Hague IV is relatively convenient for occupants, GCIV is more constraining: significantly, it prohibits the transfer of civilians to occupied territories, which contradicts Israel's settlement policy.[28]

Yet, Israel's argument has been almost universally rejected.[29] A string of UNSC resolutions called upon Israel, as the occupying power, to abide by

[22] G.A. Res. 1514 (XV), ¶¶ 1–2 (Dec. 14, 1960); *see* also Namibia Opinion, ¶¶ 108–110.

[23] Eyal Benvenisti, *The Missing Argument: The Article that Changed the Course of History?*, 111 Am. J. Int'l L. Unbound 31, 31 (2017).

[24] Meir Shamgar, *The Observance of International Law in the Administered Territories*, 1 Isr. Y.B. Hum. Rts. 262, 265–66 (1971). The HCJ, however, arguably held that at least parts of the law of occupation apply de jure to the territories. *See* HCJ 393/82 Jam'iat Iscan Al-Ma'almoun v. IDF Commander of Judea and Samaria, 37(4) PD 785, ¶¶ 10–11 (1983) (Isr.).

[25] Yehuda Z. Blum, *The Missing Reversioner: Reflections on the Status of Judea and Samaria*, 3 Isr. L. Rev. 279, 293 (1968).

[26] Meir Shamgar, *Legal Concepts and Problems of the Israeli Military Government: The Initial Stage*, *in* Military Government in the Territories Administered by Israel, 1967–1980: The Legal Aspects 1, 34 (Meir Shamgar ed., 1982).

[27] Shamgar, *supra* note 24, at 266.

[28] Benvenisti, *supra* note 23, at 33.

[29] *But see* Abraham Bell & Eugene Kontorovich, *Palestine,* Uti Possidetis Juris *and the Borders of Israel*, 58 Ariz. L. Rev. 633 (2019).

GCIV.[30] In its 2004 Wall Advisory Opinion, the ICJ rejected the argument on GCIV's inapplicability on the basis of the principles of treaty interpretation.[31] First, it held that according to Common Article 2, GCIV applies *whenever* a territory is occupied in a conflict between two High Contracting Parties, regardless of the previous status of the territory. Since the West Bank was taken during an armed conflict between Israel and Jordan—both parties to GCIV—this was sufficient to trigger GCIV.[32] Admittedly, this reasoning is imprecise. Taken literally, it could mean that when a state recovers its *own* territory during an international armed conflict, it becomes an occupant. It seems, therefore, that what is meant here is only territory taken during international armed conflict, concerning which the occupant did not possess clear title previously.

The second, more principled reason, was purposive: since the object and purpose of GCIV was "to protect civilians who find themselves, in whatever way, in the hands of the occupying power," Common Article 2 should not be read restrictively.[33] The Court also applied the framework of self-determination to analyze the lawfulness of the Wall and its associated regime.[34]

Also pertinent, in this context, is the case of Western Sahara, which had been a Spanish colony since the 19th century. It was considered a non-self-governing territory with the advent of the UN,[35] and the people of Western Sahara were internationally recognized as entitled to self-determination.[36] In 1975, Morocco took over part of the territory—through a massive march of civilians—citing precolonial rights.[37] Spain, in turn, withdrew from the territory.[38] Yet, that the territory did not belong previously to another state did not yield sovereign rights for Morocco, nor did it—in and of itself—exclude the territory from occupation. In Resolution 34/37, the UNGA asserted that the territory was occupied by Morocco.[39] In 2016, the CJEU

[30] *See, e.g.*, S.C. Res. 2334 (Dec. 23, 2016); S.C. Res. 478 (Aug. 20, 1980); S.C. Res. 446 (Mar. 22, 1979).

[31] Vienna Convention on the Law of Treaties, May 23, 1969, arts. 31–32, 1155 U.N.T.S. 331.

[32] Legal Consequences of the Construction of a Wall in the Occupied Palestinian Territory, Advisory Opinion, 2004 I.C.J. Rep. 136 ¶ 95 (July 9) [hereinafter Wall Opinion].

[33] *Id.*

[34] *Id.* ¶¶ 118, 122, 149.

[35] Subjectto the UN Charter, art. 73.

[36] G.A. Res. 2229 (XXI) (Dec. 20, 1966).

[37] *See* Western Sahara, Advisory Opinion, 1975 I.C.J. Rep. 12, ¶ 162 (Oct. 16); Case C-104/16 P, Council of the E.U. v. Front Polisario, ECLI:EU:C:2016:973, ¶¶ 28–30 (Dec. 21, 2016).

[38] *Front Polisario*, ECLI:EU:C:2016;973, ¶ 32.

[39] G.A. Res. 34/37 (Nov. 21, 1979), ¶ 5.

held that trade agreements between the EC and Morocco did not apply to Western Sahara, inter alia because they affected the rights and interest of a third party—here, the Sahrawi people qua bearers of the right to self-determination—without its consent.[40]

The last case is that of East Timor, which had been a Portuguese colony since the 16th century. In 1974 a process of decolonization began, but was interrupted in 1976 with the invasion and annexation of the territory by neighboring Indonesia.[41] The international reaction was initially vehement, emphasizing the East Timorese right to self-determination.[42] Thereafter, the international community gradually lost interest, but at no point was there significant recognition of Indonesia's annexation.[43] Eventually, in 1999, a UN-sponsored referendum established that an overwhelming majority of East Timorese preferred independence.[44] This result sparked massive violence, and eventually, the UNSC adopted a Chapter VII resolution, authorizing—with Indonesian consent—a multinational force to restore "peace and security" in East Timor.[45] Following the intervention, a transitional UN administration was established,[46] and in 2002, East Timor became independent.[47] In sum, the four cases discussed above illustrate that the previous, non-sovereign status of territories, does not in itself exclude occupation, or grant occupants title.[48]

Importantly, title over territory can be contested also between fully independent states. Even in the contemporary international system, border disputes abound.[49] The question arises whether an occupant can claim that owing to the disputed legal title over a certain territory, it would not be considered occupied if taken in war. This possibility has been rightfully rejected. As held by the Eritrea–Ethiopia Claims Commission, nothing in the law of occupation suggests "that only territory the title to which is clear and uncontested can be occupied territory."[50] This makes sense, since the cause

[40] *Front Polisario*, ECLI:EU:C:2016:973, ¶¶ 81–108.

[41] Eyal Benvenisti, The International Law of Occupation 172–73 (2d ed. 2012).

[42] *See* G.A. Res. 3485 (XXX) (Dec. 12, 1975).

[43] Benvenisti, *supra* note 41, at 175–76.

[44] Mark Rothert, *U.N. Intervention in East Timor*, 39 Colum. J. Transnat'l L. 257, 26[illegible] (2000).

[45] S.C. Res. 1264 (Sept. 15, 1999).

[46] S.C. Res. 1272 (Oct. 25, 1999).

[47] *See* S.C. Res 1392 (Jan. 31, 2002).

[48] *See* Christine Gray, International Law and the Use of Force 74–75 (4th ed. 2018).

[49] *See generally* Border Disputes: A Global Encyclopedia (Emmanuel Brunet-Jailly ed., 2015).

[50] Eritrea–Ethiopia Claims Commission—Partial Award, Central Front—Ethiopia's Claim 2, XXVI (Part V) UN Reports of International Arbitral Awards 155, ¶ 29 (2004); *see*

of many territorial conflicts is precisely disputes over title. If disputed title would alone exclude occupation, a major loophole would exist. Yet, this conclusion should not be taken to absurdity. For example, it is obvious that if State A occupies State B's previously undisputed territory and annexes it, the territory would not be considered occupied if B succeeds in recovering it—only because A's claim to the territory made it "disputed." A state must have *at least* a minimally plausible legal claim to a territory in order to argue that it is occupied by another.

2.3 Occupation of What Territory?

2.3.1 Land, Air, Waters, and Maritime Zones

Article 42 Hague is clear that occupation extends only to parts of the territory controlled by the hostile army, but no further.[51] Now, in international law, sovereignty over land entails also full sovereignty over the territorial waters;[52] and, under the modern law of the sea, some exclusive rights over the exclusive economic zone (EEZ)[53] and continental shelf.[54] Likewise, sovereignty over land includes sovereignty over the airspace above the land and territorial sea.[55] The question is whether the powers and duties arising from occupation of land extend automatically also to airspace and waters, and, if so, to which "types" of waters.[56] If they do, the occupant would be required to administer these spaces in accordance with the duties of trusteeship imposed by the law of occupation, and would be empowered to manage the natural resources and to impose security measures that limit activities there.[57]

also Aeyal Gross, The Writing on the Wall: Rethinking the Law of Occupation 76 (2017); Hanne Cuyckens, Revisiting the Law of Occupation 48 (2017).

[51] *See* Cuyckens, *supra* note 50, at 40.

[52] United Nations Convention on the Law of the Sea, art. 2, Dec. 10, 1982, 1833 U.N.T.S. 3 [hereinafter UNCLOS]; Andrew Clapham, Briely's Law of Nations ch. V (7th ed. 2012).

[53] UNCLOS, *supra* note 52, art. 55.

[54] *Id.* art. 77.

[55] Convention on International Civil Aviation, arts. 1–2, Dec. 7, 1944, 15 U.N.T.S. 295.

[56] *See generally*, Marco Longobardo, *The Occupation of Maritime Territory Under International Humanitarian Law*, 95 Int'l L. Stud. 322 (2019).

[57] These duties are discussed in subsequent chapters.

Regarding airspace, the question is rather easy, since control over territory would almost *ipso facto* entail control over the adjacent airspace.[58] Concerning territorial waters, occupation of coastal land is traditionally viewed as a prerequisite for the occupation of the adjacent territorial waters.[59] Furthermore, the presumption would be that occupation of the former also entails the occupation of the latter.[60] In any case, regarding occupied territorial waters, the actions of the occupant at sea would be subject to the same principles applying on land.[61]

It is easy, however, to imagine complicated scenarios in this context. For example, a belligerent could gain effective control over the coastal land, but the adversary's navy would still control the territorial waters.[62] In such cases, it is difficult to argue that these waters are occupied, just because the land is.[63] The opposite may also happen. Consider a situation where a state, through its navy, gains control only over the territorial waters of another state. A functional approach might entail, for example, that in such cases the controlling state would have to administer fisheries (and other resources) in the area in accordance with the law of occupation.[64] This, of course, strains the traditional view that occupation of land is a prerequisite for the occupation of waters.[65]

The question is far more complicated regarding maritime zones *beyond* the territorial waters, namely EEZs and continental shelves. As a preliminary issue, these areas—as distinct legal zones—were not yet developed when the law of occupation was formed. This has raised the question whether the modern law of the sea, which establishes these zones, continues to apply concurrently with the law of occupation. On most contemporary views, these two frameworks apply in parallel, and the mere fact that

[58] Yoram Dinstein, The international Law of Belligerent Occupation 56 (2d ed. 2019).

[59] *See* Manual on the Laws of Naval War, art. 88, Aug. 9, 1913, *reprinted in* Dietrich Schindler and Jiri Toman, The Laws of Armed Conflicts 1123 (4th ed. 2004) [hereinafter Manual on the Laws of Naval War]. A different question is whether withdrawal of land forces also entails the end of the occupation of territorial waters. On the end of occupation, see Section 2.6.2.

[60] Dinstein, *supra* note 58, at 56.

[61] Manual on the Laws of Naval War, *supra* note 59, art. 88.

[62] An opposite situation might be the case of the Gaza strip. *See* Section 2.6.2.

[63] *See* Longobardo, *supra* note 56, at 343–45.

[64] *Compare* Trung Nguyen Quoc Tan, *"Occupant" Status for China in South China Sea Islands?* Opinio Juris (Apr. 17, 2021), http://opiniojuris.org/2021/04/17/occupant-status-for-china-in-south-china-sea-islands/. On the functional approach, see Section 2.6.

[65] *See* Longobardo, *supra* note 56, at 341–43.

a territory is occupied does not exclude the application of the law of the sea to questions that might arise concerning adjacent marine areas.[66]

However, the application of the law of the sea during occupation does not mean that EEZs and continental shelves can be "occupied." First, the coastal state itself does not possess full sovereignty over these zones.[67] Rather, it only possesses some sovereign-like rights over natural resources, some limited enforcement powers relating to these rights, and some duties to coordinate activities in these areas.[68] Beyond these rights, and since the coastal state *itself* cannot gain effective control over marine areas beyond its territorial waters—generally, except for the coastal state's enumerated rights, the freedom of the sea applies there[69]—it follows that these zones cannot be occupied by another.[70]

Still, some argue that the principles of the law of occupation should be extended to EEZs and continental shelves.[71] A functional approach supports this conclusion, *at least* in cases where the occupied state conducted activities in these zones prior to the occupation. Arguably, to the extent that there were activities in these areas before the occupation—and after the occupation, the ousted government cannot regulate this activity—it makes sense that the occupant should incur the powers and obligations to administer *these specific activities* in accordance with the law of occupation.[72] Otherwise, a gap in responsibility might occur.[73] Of course, this is not a license to exploit marine resources. To the extent that such activities take place in these areas, the occupant would be limited by the law of occupation's specific rules on natural resources.[74] Beyond the administration of *existing* activities, it would be difficult to justify granting

[66] *See* Shani Friedman, *The Application of the Law of Occupation in Maritime Zones and Rights to "Occupied" Marine Resources*, 36 Int'l J. Marine & Coastal L. 1, 2–3, 6–7 (2021).

[67] *See id.* at 5; Surabhi Ranganathan, *The Law of the Sea and Natural Resource*, *in* Community Interests Across International Law 121 (Eyal Benvenisti & Georg Nolte eds., 2018).

[68] *See* UNCLOS, *supra* note 52, arts. 56–73, 77–81.

[69] *Id.* art. 58.

[70] *See, e.g.*, Longobardo, *supra* note 56, at 347–48; Friedman, *supra* note 66, at 5–6.

[71] *See* Dinstein, *supra* note 58, at 56.

[72] *See* Tassilo Singer, *Occupation of Sea Territory: Requirements for Military Authority and Comparison to Art. 43 of the Hague Convention IV*, *in* Operational Law in International Straits and Current Maritime Security Challenges 255 (Jörg Schildknecht, Rebecca Dickey, Martin Fink & Lisa Ferris eds., 2018).

[73] Benvenisti, *supra* note 41, at 55.

[74] *See* Section 6.3. Friedman argues that in such cases, the occupant must allow the occupied state to continue to administer these activities, or to cooperate with it. *See* Friedman, *supra* note 66, at 19. It is doubtful whether in armed conflict this type of cooperation is feasible.

occupants powers to conduct new activities in continental shelves and EEZs, not least because these are not part of the occupied territory in the strict sense.[75]

2.3.2 Allied Territory

During war, belligerents might acquire control over *allied* territory, having driven the common enemy out. Arguably, the law of occupation would not apply in such cases, since this territory is not hostile, as required in article 42 Hague.[76] Usually, in such situations, the allies would enter into a "civil affairs" agreement which regulates the administration of the territory.[77] A notable historical example is the agreement between the Allies and France, after its liberation in 1944.[78] Yet, when such agreements do not exist, some states posit that rules inspired by the law of occupation could apply by analogy,[79] and some commentators argued that it should apply.[80] However, a more nuanced approach might be required nowadays. Since the control over the territory is not "hostile," it is unclear why the controlling belligerent would need, by default, the vast security powers recognized by the law of occupation. Furthermore, nationals of allied states (co-belligerents) are explicitly excluded from the status of protected persons under GCIV, which *at least* implies that the law of occupation was not envisioned to apply in allied territories.[81] Therefore, at least when individual rights are implicated, the better view is that control over allied territories would be subject to IHRL.[82]

[75] *See id.* at 11–18. We briefly address related questions in Section 6.3.

[76] U.S. Dep't Def., Law of War Manual, 767 (2016) [hereinafter DoD Manual].

[77] *Id.* at 760.

[78] Directives and Agreements in Civil Affairs in France, Aug. 25, 1944, *reprinted in* U.S. Army Judge Advocate General School, Civil Affairs Military Government: Selected Cases and Materials 10 (1958).

[79] DoD Manual, *supra* note 76, at 760; UK War Off., Law of War on Land III 1958, ¶ 499 at 140 [hereinafter Law of War on Land]; HCJ 102/82 Tsemel v. Minister of Def., 37(3) PD 365, ¶ 7 (1983) (Isr.).

[80] Gerhard von Glahn, The Occupation of Enemy Territory: A Commentary on the Law and Practice of Belligerent Occupation 27 (1957).

[81] GCIV, *supra* note 1, art. 4.

[82] Al-Skeini v. United Kingdom, 2011-IV Eur. Ct. H.R. 99, ¶ 135 (recognizing "the exercise of extra-territorial jurisdiction by a Contracting State when, through the consent, invitation or acquiescence of the Government of that territory, it exercises all or some of the public powers normally to be exercised by that Government").

2.4 Occupation by Whom?

Article 42 clearly applies to occupations by single states. Yet, territory can come under the effective control of a range of actors such as coalitions, international organizations, proxies, and even non-state actors (NSAs).

2.4.1 Coalitions

A simple case of an occupation by coalition takes place when states coordinate their war effort yet maintain operational autonomy, and proceed to occupy different parts of their enemy's territory. In such cases, each state is clearly an occupant in the specific territory it controls, irrespective of the fact that a coalition exists.[83]

A more complex situation occurs where several occupants establish a common authority to administer the entire territory. This took place in Iraq, where the CPA was established jointly by the United States, UK, and "coalition partners."[84] The CPA administration was then divided into regional areas, in which coalition members were assigned responsibility; however, decision-making on the macro level was done by the head of the CPA, appointed by the United States.[85] Nonetheless, this did not relieve each coalition member of its separate responsibility as an occupant in the territory it controlled. In *Al-Skeini*, the European Court of Human Rights (ECtHR) treated the UK as an occupant in the areas it controlled, notwithstanding the existence of the CPA, or the fact that the overall command in Iraq was vested in U.S. generals.[86] Furthermore, it is reasonable that in situations where coalition members form a joint administration, they would also be jointly responsible under the law of occupation across the entire territory.[87]

[83] Dinstein, *supra* note 58, at 57.

[84] Letter dated 8 May 2003 from the Permanent Representatives of the United Kingdom of Great Britain and Northern Ireland and the United States of America to the United Nations addressed to the President of the Security Council, U.N. Doc. S/2003/538 (May 8, 2003).

[85] *Al-Skeini*, 2011-IV Eur. Ct. H.R. 99, ¶ 13.

[86] *Id.* ¶ 20, ¶¶ 143–147.

[87] *See* Dinstein, *supra* note 58, at 57; Kristen E. Boon, *The Future of the Law of Occupation*, 46 Can. Y.B. Int'l L. 107, 121 (2008); Christine Chinkin, *The Continuing Occupation?: Issues of Joint and Several Liability and Effective Control*, *in* The Iraq War and International Law 161 (Philip Shiner & Andrew Williams eds., 2008); Stefan Talmon, *A Plurality of Responsible Actors: International Responsibility for Acts of the Coalition Provisional Authority in Iraq*, *id.* at 185; *see generally* André Nollkaemper, Jean d'Aspremont, Christiane Ahlborn, Berenice Boutin, Nataša Nedeski, Ilias Plakokefalos, with collaboration of Dov Jacobs, *Guiding Principles on Share Responsibility in International Law*, 31 Eur. J. Int'l L. 15 (2020).

A further complication in Iraq emanated from the fact that two "multinational divisions" participated in the occupation, and were placed under the command of other coalition members. For instance, the UK was given command of a multinational division in its operations in southeast Iraq.[88] Was the UK the occupant in these areas, the multinational division being only its instrument? And, if not, how are the responsibilities of an occupant distributed within a multinational division? If one state within the division is tasked only with securing humanitarian convoys can it be an occupant?[89]

These questions have yet to be resolved conclusively. Some experts called for a functional approach, according to which in a coalition scenario, the state whose troops effectively control any piece of territory at a given moment would be occupants in that particular area. Others suggested a "task-based" test, in which any state that performs a task normally undertaken by an occupant, would be bound by obligations from the law of occupation relevant to that specific task.[90] These approaches, however, do not provide all the answers, since in multinational settings troop contingents belonging to one state can be placed under the command of another. In such cases, the rules on state attribution should determine where ultimate control of the situation lies.[91]

2.4.2 International Organizations

The situations above differ from cases in which control is exercised by forces belonging not to an ad hoc coalition, but to an international organization which possesses, as such, a distinct international legal personality. In most cases, when international organizations operate in another state, they receive its consent to do so. In the rare case that this is not so, can international organizations be occupants?

As a point of departure, it cannot be the case that the law of occupation is per se inapplicable to international organizations, since otherwise states could circumvent their obligations simply by establishing such

[88] *Al-Skeini*, 2011-IV Eur. Ct. H.R. 99, ¶ 20.
[89] *Compare* Danish Manual, *supra* note 12, at 430.
[90] ICRC, Expert Meeting, *supra* note 7, at 34–35.
[91] Int'l Law Comm'n, Draft Articles on Responsibility of States for Internationally Wrongful Acts, *extract from* the Rep. of the International Law Commission on the work of Its Fifty-third Session, U.N. Doc. A/56/10, arts. 6, 47 (2010) [hereinafter ARSIWA]; *but see* ICRC, Expeet Meeting, *supra* note 7, at 34–35.

organizations.[92] Yet, some have argued that territorial administration by UN forces should be specifically excluded from the law of occupation, inter alia because their legal status is exhausted by their mandates alone.[93] It is unclear, however, why this should be the case. UNSC mandates cannot regulate each and every aspect of an operation. Therefore it is highly unlikely that a mandate would set aside the law of occupation as a whole, even assuming that the UNSC had the power to do so.[94] The better position is that the fact that control is exercised by an international organization—whether the UN or otherwise—does not exclude the application of the law of occupation in addition to the specific mandate, if the conditions of occupation exist. Indeed, a 2021 resolution by the Institut de Droit International provides that the customary law of occupation may apply "by analogy and on a strictly supplementary basis" to forces authorized by a UNSC Chapter VII mandate.[95]

The discussion above is distinct from the question of attribution, and whether in a particular scenario it is the international organization, rather than the individual state, which is the occupant. The question here is reminiscent of the problem of attribution in occupations by coalitions.[96] Nonetheless, it is nowadays clear that the mere existence of an international *authorization* for the operations—such as a UNSC Resolution under Chapter VII—does not negate the attribution of acts to individual states. According to the prevailing standard, acts by state organs would be attributed to an international organization only if they are placed under its effective control.[97]

[92] *See generally*, Daphna Shraga, *The United Nations as an Actor Bound by International Humanitarian Law*, 5 INT'L PEACEKEEPING 64 (1998).

[93] *See* ICRC, EXPERT MEETING, *supra* note 7, at 78.

[94] *Id.* at 34, 82–84; *see also* BENVENISTI, *supra* note 41, at 62–66.

[95] Institut de Droit International, Territorial Administration by the United Nations and Other International Institutions Authorized by the United Nations, art. 11 (Sept. 4, 2021); *see also* Eyal Benvenisti, *The Applicability of the Law of Occupation to UN Administration of Foreign Territory*, *in* STRENGTHENING HUMAN RIGHTS PROTECTIONS IN GENEVA, ISRAEL, THE WEST BANK AND BEYOND 103 (Joseph E. David, Yaël Ronen, Yuval Shany & J.H.H. Weiler eds., 2021); ICRC, EXPERT MEETING, *supra* note 7, at 33–34, 78–81. Usually, international organizations operate with host state consent, which precludes occupation. Some have suggested the law of occupation might be of relevance also in this case by analogy. See *id.* at 84, 86–87.

[96] *See* Section 2.4.2.

[97] R. (Al-Jedda) v. Sec'y of State for Def. [2008] 1 AC 332 (HL) ¶¶ 23–24; Al-Jedda v. the UK, 2011-IV Eur. Ct. H.R. 305 ¶¶ 80–84; Int'l Law Comm'n, Articles on Responsibility of International Organizations, *extract from* the Rep. of the International Law Commission on the Work of Its Sixty-third Session, U.N. Doc. A/66/10, art. 7 (2011). Of course, the many complex doctrinal and normative questions in this context are beyond the scope of this book.

2.4.3 Proxies

A situation of increasing importance concerns occupation by *proxies*. In such cases a belligerent might be considered an occupant although the territory is administered by another actor, if that actor is subject to the belligerent's control. These situations are close to, but analytically distinct from, cases in which an occupant delegates some powers to a subordinate local authority, while retaining ultimate control over the territory. A prime example of the latter case concerns the Turkish presence in Northern Cyprus, which is widely considered an occupation, notwithstanding the establishment of the Turkish Republic of Northern Cyprus in 1983.[98] Another case is Turkey's control over parts of northern Syria since 2016, which is administered through Syrian opposition groups.[99] A similar case concerns Russia's occupation of Luhansk and Donetsk, although it recognized the so-called breakaway republics in 2022.[100] Last, the establishment of the Palestinian Authority in Gaza and the West Bank pursuant to the Oslo Accords, while not a subordinate regime in the full sense, did not relieve Israel of its occupant status.[101]

In "pure" occupation by proxy, conversely, the occupant might exercise little, if any, direct control over the territory, and conducts its affairs through a non-state intermediary. The key question here is the threshold of control over the NSA that would transform the state into an occupant.[102] While there is some debate on the proper legal framework for assessing this question, on most accounts, occupation by proxy is determined by the law on state responsibility, and specifically, the law on attribution.[103] It is beyond the scope of this work to discuss each possible way in which attribution materializes.[104] We focus here on the most pertinent case, in which a state controls or directs an NSA that *itself* controls territory.

[98] *See* Benvenisti, *supra* note 41, at 191–94; Gross, *supra* note 50, at 79–80.

[99] *See* Carlotta Gall, *In Turkey's Safe Zone in Syria, Security and Misery Go Hand in Hand*, N.Y. Times (Feb. 16, 2021), https://www.nytimes.com/2021/02/16/world/middleeast/syria-turkey-erdogan-afrin.html.

[100] OSCE, Report on Violations of International Humanitarian and Human Rights Law, War Crimes and Crimes Against Humanity Committed in Ukraine Since 24 February 2022 18 (Apr. 13, 2022) [hereinafter OSCE Report].

[101] *See, e.g.*, S.C. Res 2334 (Dec. 23, 2016).

[102] *See* Kalandarishvili-Mueller, *supra* note 4, ch. 2.

[103] ARSIWA, *supra* note 91, arts. 4–11. For a critique of this approach, see Kubo Mačák, Internationalized Armed Conflicts in International Law 44–47 (2018).

[104] *See* James Crawford, State Responsibility: The General Part 141–65 (2013).

In general, NSA conduct is not attributed to states, although, in certain cases, states might incur due diligence obligations to prevent it.[105] However, when an NSA is directed or controlled by a state, its conduct will be attributed to the state.[106] Thus, when an NSA that controls territory is directed or controlled by a state, that state can be considered an occupant by proxy. It should be emphasized that in such cases, at least according to the conventional view, it is not that the *NSA* itself becomes an occupant; rather, for the purposes of international obligations, the former is integrated into the state itself, and the latter is considered the occupant, while the NSA is simply its de facto organ.[107]

The threshold of "control" required for state attribution has been controversial, because international courts adopted conflicting standards.[108] In *Nicaragua*, the ICJ held that attribution requires "effective control of the military or paramilitary operations in the course of which the alleged violations were committed."[109] This standard, which requires "effective control" over the specific conduct by NSAs, was repeated by the ICJ in later cases.[110] Notably, in the *Armed Activities* case, it ruled that Uganda was not an occupant by proxy of areas in the DRC, since it did not effectively control the conduct of the groups operating there.[111] According to this standard, however, it is doubtful whether occupation by proxy would ever occur, because once the NSA exercises any form of independent discretion, no attribution would materialize. Furthermore, under this standard, a state would be able to cherry-pick its obligations, by dialing up and down the discretion it allows to an armed group.

For similar reasons, international criminal tribunals have adopted a laxer standard for attribution, known as the "overall control" test. In *Tadić*, the ICTY held that when the NSA is a hierarchical organization, its actions

[105] *See generally* Joanna Kulesza, Due Diligence in International Law ch. 2 (2016).

[106] ARSIWA, *supra* note 91, art. 8.

[107] *See* ICRC, Commentary 2016, *supra* note 9, ¶ 329; Tristan Ferraro, *Determining the Beginning and End of an Occupation Under International Humanitarian Law*, 94 Int'l Rev. Red Cross 133, 158 (2012); Dinstein, *supra* note 58, at 51; for a different view, see Mačák, *supra* note 103, at 228–30; Tom Gal, *Unexplored Outcomes of* Tadić: *Applicability of the Law of Occupation to War by Proxy*, 12 J. Int'l Crim. Just. 59, 60–61 (2014).

[108] Gal, supra note 107, at 61–62.

[109] Military Aid and Paramilitary Activities in and Against Nicaragua (Nicar. v. U.S.A.), Judgment, 1986 I.C.J. Rep. 14, ¶ 115 (June 27).

[110] Application of the Convention on the Prevention and Punishment of the Crime of Genocide (Bosn. & Herz. v. Serb. & Montenegro), Judgment, 2007 I.C.J. Rep. 43, ¶¶ 403–06 (Feb. 26).

[111] *Nicar. v. U.S.A.*, 1986 I.C.J. Rep. 14, ¶¶ 160, 177.

could be attributable to a state where the latter had "a role in organizing, coordinating or planning the military actions of the military group, in addition to financing, training and equipping or providing operational support to that group." This standard is satisfied even in the absence of specific instructions concerning each and every act.[112] The ICC, too, adopted this standard in a string of decisions.[113] In *Ntaganda*, it ruled that since there was no evidence that Uganda exercised overall control over rebel groups in the DRC, the conflict between these groups and the DRC was a non-international one.[114]

Granted, the "overall control" test was usually used to classify armed conflicts as non-international or international (i.e. when a state is fighting an NSA controlled overall by another state). Yet, it seems that this test might equally apply to the identification of a state as an occupant when an armed group under its controls exercises control over territory.[115] Admittedly, this might lead to peculiar results. For instance, if State A exercises overall control over an opposition group in State B, and consequently is considered an occupant, it might incur positive obligations that would possibly require it to send its own forces to the territory. It would be absurd that the law of occupation would impose such a duty of escalation. Arguably in such situations, a functional approach should be adopted, imposing on the occupant by proxy obligations commensurate with its control over the NSA.

Indeed, some ambiguity remains—in particular in the ICTY's jurisprudence—as to whether *for the purposes of occupation by proxy*, an additional test, beyond the overall control test over the NSA, must be satisfied. In *Blaškić*, the ICTY determined that Croatia occupied Bosnian territory, owing to its overall control over the HVO, an NSA.[116] In *Naletilić*, however, the ICTY held that while the overall control test is applicable to the determination whether an international armed conflict exists, "[a] further degree of control is required to establish occupation."[117]

[112] Prosecutor v. Tadić, Case No. IT-94-1-A, Judgment, ¶ 137 (Int'l Crim. Trib. for the Former Yugoslavia July 15, 1999).

[113] Prosecutor v. Lubanga, Case No. ICC-01/04-01/06, Judgment, ¶ 541 (Mar. 14, 2012); Prosecutor v. Katanga, ICC-01/04-01/07, Judgment, ¶ 1178 (Mar. 7, 2014); Prosecutor v. Bemba, ICC-01/05-01/08-3343, Trial Chamber III Judgment, ¶ 130 (Mar. 21, 2016).

[114] Prosecutor v. Ntaganda, ICC-01/04-02/06, Judgment, ¶¶ 727–728 (July 8, 2019).

[115] ICRC, Commentary 2016, *supra* note 9, ¶¶ 330–332; *but see* Mačák, *supra* note 103, at 230.

[116] Prosecutor v. Blaškić, Case No. IT-95-14-T, Trial Chamber Judgment, ¶ 149 (Int'l Crim. Trib.for the Former Yugoslavia Mar. 3, 2000).

[117] Prosecutor v. Naletilić, Case No. IT-98-34-T, Trial Chamber Judgment, ¶ 214 (Int'l Crim. Trib.for the Former Yugoslavia Mar. 31, 2003).

While it is debatable whether a more demanding test would be desirable for occupation by proxy,[118] it is unclear whether this is what was actually meant in *Naletilić*. In its reference to "a further degree of control," the ICTY could have meant two different things: either that for occupation by proxy, the state must exercise further control over the NSA, beyond overall control; or, alternatively, that it was making the rather obvious claim that even when a state is in overall control over the *NSA*, the NSA's effective control over *territory* is additionally needed to establish an occupation.[119]

2.4.4 Territorial Control by NSAs

Even absent attribution to a state, NSAs might gain control over territory. The paradigmatic case is ISIL, which controlled territories in Iraq and Syria from 2014 to 2019. Although ISIL controlled and administered vast territories, it was never recognized as a state.[120] Does the law of occupation, or an analogical framework, apply to such situations?[121] The traditional answer is negative.[122] However, from the standpoint of individuals, the legal status of the armed entity controlling them is secondary at best. From the point of view of ousted governments also, some interests remain the same whether their territory is controlled by another state or by an NSA. As most aspects of territorial control by NSAs are highly contested, we highlight here—by no means in an exhaustive manner—some key dilemmas.[123]

First, the question whether NSAs should be subject to obligations paralleling those of the law of occupation requires accounting for various possible scenarios, each giving rise to different considerations. Territory can be controlled by "external" NSAs, which enter the state from another

[118] *See* Benvenisti, *supra* note 41, at 61–62.

[119] This is supported by the fact that the Tribunal was responding to the prosecutor's argument that "occupied territory means 'any territory under the overall control of a party to the conflict.'" *Naletilić*, Case No. IT-98-34-T, ¶ 211.

[120] *See generally* Tal Mimran, *In a Broken Dream: Lessons from the Rise and Demise of the Self-Declared Caliphate of the Islamic State in Syria and Iraq*, 29 J. Transnat'l L. & Pol'y 77 (2019–20).

[121] While there has been occasional use of the term "occupation" regarding NSAs, it is not clear whether this was in the formal legal sense. *See, e.g.*, Human Rights Committee, Situation of Human Rights in Yemen, Including Violations and Abuses Since September 2014 Report of the Detailed Findings of the Group of Eminent International and Regional Experts on Yemen ¶ 178, U.N. Doc. A/HRC/42/CRP.1 (Sept. 3, 2019).

[122] *See* Danish Manual, *supra* note 12, at 431.

[123] *See generally* René Provost, Rebel Courts: The Administration of Justice by Armed Insurgents (2021).

territory. In such cases, it is easier to envision them as occupants.[124] In other cases, NSAs might gain control over territory in an internal conflict, such as was the case in Ethiopia, where in 2021 the Tigray Defense Forces took control over the Tigray Region.[125] Here, the rationales for considering them as occupants might differ in accordance with the specific circumstances of the conflict.

Furthermore, whether NSAs should be viewed as occupants requires considering whether there is any added value in extending the law of occupation to such scenarios. An alternative could be the de facto application of IHRL in such cases. While, traditionally, IHRL only binds states, there have been many calls to also recognize the human rights obligations of NSAs.[126] If this framework gains acceptance, many obligations imposed by the law of occupation can find parallels under IHRL, including obligations to maintain public order. Even the conservationist principle can be read into the obligation under IHRL to respect the right to self-determination.[127] The IHRL route might be preferable policywise, if one seeks to impose obligations on NSAs without necessarily granting them the powers explicitly recognized by the law of occupation.[128] Nonetheless, one clear benefit of the occupation framework is that in contrast to IHRL,[129] it is well established that NSAs indeed possess international legal personality for the purpose of IHL, when they are parties to an armed conflict.[130]

124 *See* Adam Roberts, *What Is a Military Occupation?*, 55 Brit. Y.B. Int'l L. 249, 292–93 (1984).

125 *See* Declan Walsh, *After Sudden Defeat, Captured Ethiopian Soldiers Are Marched to Prison*, N.Y. Times (June 2, 2021), https://www.nytimes.com/2021/07/02/world/africa/tigray-ethiopia-soldiers-captured.html.

126 *See* Human Rights Committee, Report of the Special Rapporteur on Extrajudicial, Summary or Arbitrary Executions on Armed Non-State Actors: The Protection of the Right to Life, U.N. Doc. A/HRC/38/44 (June 5, 2018); Daragh Murray, Human Rights Obligations of Non-State Armed Groups (2016); Katharine Fortin, The Accountability of Armed Groups Under Human Rights Law (2017); Andrew Clapham, Human Rights Obligations of Non-State Actors (2006); Yaël Ronen, *Human Rights Obligations of Territorial Non-State Actors*, 46 Cornell Int'l L.J. 21 (2013); Jan Arno Hessbruegge, *Human Rights Violations Arising from Conduct of Non-State Actors*, 11 Buff. Hum. Rts. L. Rev. 21 (2005).

127 ICCPR, *supra* note 13, art. 1(1).

128 And we reserve here the question whether under de facto application of IHRL, NSAs would be able to derogate from such obligations in order to exercise security powers.

129 ICRC, International Humanitarian Law and the Challenges of Contemporary Armed Conflicts—Recommitting to Protection in Armed Conflict on the 70th Anniversary of the Geneva Conventions (2019), 44 [hereinafter ICRC, Challenges of Contemporary Armed Conflicts].

130 Common Article 3 to the Geneva Conventions; APII, *supra* note 15, art. 1. This is not the case with IHRL, where the mere capacity of NSAs to be bound remains a controversial issue. *See* Murray, *supra* note 126, chs. 2–5; Fortin, *supra* note 126, at ch. 6.

Unfortunately, IHL does not give clear guidance on territorial control by NSAs. The law of occupation expressly treats only states as de jure occupants.[131] Additionally, the law of NIAC itself does not *explicitly* contain elements that parallel the law of occupation.[132] It does not elaborate on territorial control; it deals mainly with negative obligations;[133] and it consciously refrains from directly granting powers to NSAs.

Still, IHL is not *entirely* silent on this issue. The law of NIAC continues to apply when NSAs control territory, at least as long as the armed conflict persists.[134] Indeed, the mere application of APII is *contingent* upon such control.[135] Furthermore, virtually all of the negative obligations enshrined in the law of NIAC—such as those contained in the Fundamental Guarantees regime of article 4 APII—mirror similar prohibitions that apply to occupants.[136] Additionally, some *positive* obligations—reminiscent of those found in the law of occupation—also apply to territorial administration by NSAs. This is most notably the case toward children, who "shall receive education,"[137] and wounded, sick, and shipwrecked civilians in the territory that must be *provided* with medical care.[138] While the general obligation to maintain law and order is absent from the law of NIAC, it is possible to argue—inspired by the ICTY's approach in the *Tadić* case—that since IHL imposes nowadays similar humanitarian obligations in IAC and NIAC, the "essence" of the obligations under the law of occupation must apply also to territorial control by NSAs.[139] The ICRC suggests a similar route, arguing

[131] Hague IV applies only to "Contracting powers." Convention (IV) respecting the Laws and Customs of War on Land and its annex: Regulations concerning the Laws and Customs of War on Land, art. 1, Oct. 18, 1907, 187 C.T.S. 227 [hereinafter Hague IV]. Relevant provisions under GCIV apply only to High Contracting Parties (states); *see also* ICRC, Challenges of Contemporary Armed Conflicts, *supra* note 129, at 42. However, in the past, a recognition of belligerency or insurgency could result in some limited obligations to rebels that held territories. *See* Fortin, *supra* note 126, at 90–107. These doctrines have largely disappeared from practice. *See* Eliav Lieblich, International Law and Civil Wars: Intervention and Consent, ch. 7 (2013).

[132] ICRC, Challenges of Contemporary Armed Conflicts, *supra* note 129, at 43.

[133] *See, e.g.*, Common Art. 3(1)(a)–(c); APII, *supra* note 15, arts. 4(1)–(2), 13–17.

[134] ICRC, Challenges of Contemporary Armed Conflicts, *supra* note 129, at 42–43.

[135] APII, *supra* note 15, art. 1(1).

[136] *See* Sandesh Sivakumaran, The Law of Non-International Armed Conflict 530–31 (2012).

[137] APII, *supra* note 15, art. 4(3)(a).

[138] *Id.* art. 7.

[139] Prosecutor v. Tadić, Case No. IT-94-1-A, ¶¶ 126–127 (Int'l Crim. Trib. for the Former Yugoslavia Oct. 2, 1995).

for a "pragmatic approach" which recognizes the de facto responsibilities of NSAs in territories they control, in accordance with their capacities.[140]

Establishing IHL-based negative or positive *obligations* on NSAs which control territory, does not solve, however, the question of their powers. While far from being universally agreed, the issue might be less controversial concerning powers to act in favor of the local population. As Sivakumaran notes, international law already recognizes the legal effect of acts of unrecognized governments, when they benefit individuals (the *Namibia* exception). The same logic applies by extension to acts by NSAs.[141] Furthermore, since there is no reason that NSAs would enjoy *broader* powers than states, and considering the principle of self-determination, it makes sense that their powers would be limited by the obligation to respect the status quo ante.

Beyond these powers, should international law also recognize the power of NSAs to adopt *security* measures available to occupants, such as setting up courts, enacting penal legislation, powers to detain, or to requisition property?[142] Can NSAs lawfully manage natural resources?[143] Absent such powers, many of these acts would not only be prohibited under the territorial state's domestic criminal law, but might also amount to war crimes. This question ties into a broader dilemma in IHL, between its traditional reluctance to equate between states and NSAs, and the need to incentivize NSAs to comply with their obligations by granting them at least *some* rights and powers.[144]

140 ICRC, Challenges of Contemporary Armed Conflicts, *supra* note 129, at 42–44; *see also* Ximena Galvez Lima, *Covid-19 Vaccination Centers in ANSA-Controlled Areas*, Geneva Call (Mar. 4, 2021), https://www.genevacall.org/covid-19-vaccination-centers-in-ansa-controlled-areas/.

141 Sivakumaran, *supra* note 136, at 530–31; Namibia Opinion, ¶ 125.

142 *See, e.g.*, Rosie Good, *War Crimes Charges Brought for Seizure of Property in Non-International Armed Conflict*, GPIL (July 11, 2019), https://gpil.jura.uni-bonn.de/2019/07/war-crimes-charges-brought-for-seizure-of-property-in-non-international-armed-conflict/. In this German case, the indictment claimed that living in a home requisitioned by ISIL in Syria could be a "war crime against property." However, it is also implied that NSAs *can* seize property if it is "imperatively demanded by the necessities of the armed conflict." *See also* Michael Börsch, Press Release Nr. 21/2021, Mutter von fünf Kindern wegen mitgliedschaftlicher Beteiligung an der Terrororganisation "IS" verurteilt, Justiz-Online (July 1, 2021), https://www.olg-duesseldorf.nrw.de/behoerde/presse/archiv/Pressemitteilungen_aus_2021/20210701_PM02_FadiaS/index.php.

143 *See* Chapter 6.

144 James G. Stewart, Corporate War Crimes: Prosecuting the Pillage of Natural Resources 21–22 (2010), *cited in* Sivakumaran, *supra* note 136, at 531; for a critique of IHL's traditional approach to NSAs, see Frédéric Mégret, *From "Savages" to "Unlawful Combatants": A Postcolonial Look at International Humanitarian Law's "Other"* in International Law and Its Others 265 (Anne Orford ed., 2006).

In terms of the *lex lata*, IHL indeed imposes due process obligations during NIAC, and regulates conditions of detention.[145] Whether these can be read to *authorize* parties to NIACs to establish courts, to enact penal provisions, or to detain individuals has been a subject of much debate. The alternative view is that these provisions only *limit* such activities, but do not provide direct authorization for them. This broader discussion is beyond the scope of this book.[146]

In our particular context, the question has arisen whether Common Article 3(d), which prohibits "the passing of sentences and the carrying out of executions without previous judgment pronounced by a regularly constituted court," permits, or even *requires*, the establishment of such courts by NSAs which control territories.[147] The Stockholm District Court grappled with this question in 2018.[148] The defendant, Haisam Sakhanh, was tried for war crimes due to his involvement in the execution of seven Syrian soldiers, captured by a Syrian armed group in 2012.[149] Sakhanh argued that no violation had occurred, since the execution followed a death sentence imposed by a legitimate court as required by Common Article 3.[150] Specifically, he claimed that the soldiers were convicted for grave acts which were already crimes under Syrian law, which also provided for capital punishment in such cases. The sentence, he maintained, was passed by a judicial council formed by the Free Syrian Army, an NSA, which was staffed by former regime judges.[151]

The Court ruled that Common Article 3's reference to a "regularly constituted court" is not limited to state courts, as the provision mainly concerns ensuring respect for fundamental procedural guarantees. Accordingly, it concluded that NSAs may establish courts under Common Article 3, for two purposes: to maintain law and order, and to keep discipline among their own forces.[152] Quite creatively, the Court imposed two additional

[145] *See* Common Art. 3(d); APII, *supra* note 15, arts. 5–6.

[146] *See* Sivakumaran, *supra* note 136, at 301–03; ICRC, Challenges of Contemporary Armed Conflicts, *supra* note 129, at 46.

[147] *Compare* Alejandro Chehtman, *Occupation Courts,* Jus Ad Bellum *Considerations, and Non-State Actors: Revisiting the Ethics of Military Occupation*, 21 Legal Theory 18, 37–43 (2015).

[148] Tingsrätten i Stockholm [TR] 2017-02-16 case no. 3786-16 (Swed.), *translated in* 16 J. Int'l Crim. Just. 403 (2018).

[149] Specifically, Sakhanh was charged with a violation of Common Article 3 of the Geneva Conventions, *id.* at 404–06.

[150] *Id.* at 406.

[151] *Id.* at 408.

[152] *Id.* at 413–14.

conditions: that NSA courts apply existing (or substantively similar) penal law—since only states can enact penal legislation;[153] and that they be staffed by judges or judicial officials that served before the conflict.[154] In the case at hand, the Court rejected Sakhanh's factual claims, holding that there were no convincing evidence that a trial took place at all.[155]

Notably, the Court refrained from drawing direct analogies from the law of occupation.[156] Ultimately, its approach is both reminiscent of, yet differing from, the principles of the law of occupation. The recognition that NSAs can establish courts to maintain law and order directly evokes the powers and duties of occupants. The requirement that NSAs apply existing law is reminiscent of the conservationist principle; yet as it was phrased by the Court, it is more limiting than the law of occupation, since occupants can indeed promulgate new penal laws. The same applies to the requirement that NSA courts be staffed by existing judges. This is indeed based on conservationist logic, but is more restrictive since—as we shall see—occupants can in fact appoint military judges. Ultimately, it can be said that the Court treated NSAs as underprivileged occupants.

2.5 Conditions for Occupation

2.5.1 Actual or Potential Exercise of Authority

Occupation requires the existence of foreign *authority* in the territory. The term "authority," however, is far from clear—both because of the inherent vagueness of the term itself, and the particular phrasing of article 42 Hague. It is clear that formal declarations by states alone do not solve this problem. While occupants sometimes issue formal proclamations that a territory is occupied, the beginning of occupation ultimately requires the *existence* of authority as provided for in article 42.[157]

[153] *Id.* at 414.
[154] *Id.*
[155] *Id.* at 416–24.
[156] *See* Jonathan Somer, *Opening the Floodgates, Controlling the Flow: Swedish Court Rules on the Legal Capacity of Armed Groups to Establish Courts*, EJIL: TALK! (Mar. 10, 2017), https://www.ejiltalk.org/opening-the-floodgates-controlling-the-flow-swedish-court-rules-on-the-legal-capacity-of-armed-groups-to-establish-courts/.
[157] VON GLAHN, *supra* note 80, at 40–44; *see, e.g.*, CPA Regulation No. 1, The Coalition Provisional Authority, CPA/REG/16 May 2003/01 (May 16, 2003), *reprinted in* 2 STEFAN

A key difficulty, in this context, concerns the interpretation of article 42's second sentence, providing that occupation exists only "where such authority has been established *and* can be exercised" (emphasis added). Does this sentence imply cumulative conditions, requiring both the formal establishment of authority, and the de facto ability to carry it out (hereinafter, the *cumulative approach*)? Or, conversely, is authority merely a factual term, fulfilled once territory is controlled? Both interpretations are problematic. If the formal establishment of authority is required, a belligerent could actually control territory, while circumventing the duties imposed on occupants simply by not establishing a formal authority. If, however, authority is factual only, then the phrase "has been established" become redundant.

The history of article 42 reveals that these ambiguities resulted from the conflicting interests of the negotiating parties. The formula found in article 42 was first conceived in the Brussels Declaration of 1874.[158] At the time, occupation was considered a favorable status. It entailed many powers, did not impose burdensome obligations, and was a prelude to possible conquest.[159] Accordingly, potential occupants—at the time, mainly Russia and Germany—preferred a low threshold for occupation, that would allow them to exercise powers as occupants at the earliest possibility.[160] The potentially occupied states, however, were mainly concerned that powerful states would prematurely—and without actually controlling territory—declare that territories were occupied; and accordingly would treat resisting individuals as criminals liable to execution (rather than as participants in a *levée en masse*, who were entitled to POW status).[161]

These states—for instance, Belgium, the Netherlands, Switzerland, and France—argued that occupation would require not only driving out the defending forces, but also that the invader actually take over the civil aspects of the administration.[162] In other words, they wished to rule out the possibility of occupation without actual exercise of administration ("paper occupation").[163]

Talmon, The Occupation of Iraq: The Official Documents of the Coalition Provisional Authority and the Iraqi Governing Council 2 (2013).

[158] Project of an International Declaration concerning the Laws and Customs of War art.1, Aug. 27, 1874, 69 B.F.S.P. 1059 [hereinafter Brussels Declaration].

[159] *See* Section 1.1.

[160] Benvenisti, *supra* note 41, at 45.

[161] Doris Appel Graber, The Development of the Law of Belligerent Occupation, 1863–1914: A Historical Survey 24–26 (1949).

[162] Benvenisti, *supra* note 41, at 45.

[163] *Compare* Graber, *supra* note 161, at 56.

The resulting ambiguity, which ultimately made its way into article 42, reflects a compromise. As mentioned, the phrases "has been established" and "can be exercised" could be understood as cumulative requirements, ensuring that occupation is not only formally declared, but contains an element of true administrative control—while also maintaining a degree of ambiguity to satisfy powerful states.[164] However, recall that nowadays, the interests at the basis of the law of occupation have been inversed. Since today, occupation entails many positive obligations and annexation is prohibited, occupants might be tempted to advance an argument not anticipated by the framers of article 42: that although they control territory, the law of occupation does not apply—for instance, because they have not established a formal administration.

Perhaps for this reason, the mainstream contemporary view is that occupation requires *effective control* over territory, which in turn spawns a presumption concerning the *ability*—and therefore duty—to administer it.[165] For example, in the *Hostages* case at Nuremberg, German officers were accused of committing crimes in occupied territories.[166] It was crucial for the Tribunal to determine whether the relevant territories were occupied, since the criminality of some of the conducts hinged on their taking place under occupation. Although there is some ambiguity in the ruling, the Tribunal concluded that "to the extent that the occupant's control is maintained and that of the civil government eliminated, the area will be said to be occupied."[167] Although there are different positions on this issue in military manuals,[168] most commentators understand this conclusion as implying

[164] Benvenisti, *supra* note 41, at 45–46.

[165] For the development of the term "effective control," see ICRC, Commentary 2016, *supra* note 9, ¶ 301 n.158.

[166] U.S. v. List, Case No. 47: The Hostages Trial, VIII United Nations War Crimes Comm'n, Law Reports of Trials of War Criminals 34 (U.S. Military Tribunal, Nuremberg).

[167] *Id.* at 57. Ambiguity remains because the ruling also states that occupation "presupposes" "the establishment of an administration." *Id.* at 55.

[168] For a survey of manuals, see Vaios Koutroulis, Le Début et la Fin du Droit de L'occupation 48 (2010). The British Military Manual of 1958 explicitly states that although article 42 Hague implies the actual establishment of a military administration, what is required is "first, that the legitimate government should, by the act of the invader, be rendered incapable of publicly exercising its authority within the occupied territory; secondly, that the invader should be in a position to substitute his own authority for that of the legitimate government." Law of War on Land, *supra* note 79, ¶ 530. Newer manuals take different approaches. For instance, the 2016 U.S. DoD Manual requires that the occupant take "measures to establish its authority." DoD Manual, *supra* note 76, at 738, 739. The 2016 Danish Manual is more equivocal. On the one hand, it holds that occupation "calls for more qualified control, including control of the territory's civilian administration." Danish Manual, *supra* note 12, 435. On the other hand, it offers several "factors" that determine whether an occupation exists, including those that allude to *potential* establishment of administration. The Danish Manual concludes

that once a belligerent is in physical control of territory, it would be presumed to be in position to administer it, and hence it would be considered occupied—whether or not such an administration has actually been established.[169] This is indeed the better view, considering the object and purpose of the modern law of occupation, namely, to extend protection to all persons under control of a hostile army.[170] Otherwise, armed forces could control territory while creating a legal black hole in term of responsibilities.

A pertinent case adopting the better approach is the HCJ's *Tsemel* case.[171] During Israel's invasion of Lebanon in 1982, Israeli forces took control over significant parts of the country, and detained suspected militants in a facility in Lebanon (*Ansar*). Several lawyers petitioned the Court, arguing that the detainees had been denied access to counsel, and that the basis for their detention had not been disclosed. In response, the state claimed, inter alia, that "no Israeli military administration was established" in Lebanon and therefore—although it maintained some vagueness on this issue—GCIV did not apply there de jure.[172] The Court rejected this reasoning and held that what matters was the "potential to replace the authorities of the previous government, not whether it [the state] did so in fact." Accordingly, it ruled, detainees in *Ansar* were protected by GCIV.[173]

This makes the ruling of the ICJ in *DRC v. Uganda* an outlier. There, the DRC argued that Uganda occupied parts of its territory following its invasion in 1998.[174] The main implication being that if Uganda indeed occupied territory, it would be responsible not only for direct violations of the law, but also for not exercising due diligence to protect civilians against violations by others.[175] Uganda responded that in most areas "there [was] no Ugandan military administration in place" and that local administration "was run by the Congolese themselves."[176] The ICJ's majority seemingly returned to the *cumulative approach*, holding that an occupation requires that authority

ambiguously that "[i]n the vast majority of cases, occupation occurs locally when the armed forces of the territorial State are driven out by the advance of other military forces." *Id.*

[169] *See, e.g.*, von Glahn, *supra* note 80, at 28; Dinstein, *supra* note 58, at 51–53; Benvenisti, *supra* note 41, at 47–49; *See* ICRC, Commentary 2016, *supra* note 9, ¶ 304.

[170] Wall Opinion ¶ 95.

[171] HCJ 102/82 Tsemel v. Minister of Def., 37(3) PD 365 (1983) (Isr.).

[172] *Id.* ¶ 3.

[173] *Id.* ¶ 7.

[174] Armed Activities on the Territory of the Congo (Dem. Rep. Congo v. Uganda), Judgment, 2005 I.C.J. Rep. 168, ¶ 167 (Dec. 19) [hereinafter *DRC v. Uganda*].

[175] *Id.* ¶ 178.

[176] *Id.* ¶ 170.

was "in fact established and exercised": meaning that foreign forces "had substituted their own authority for that of the Congolese Government."[177] It accordingly held that Uganda's appointment of a governor in one area (the Ituri district) was clearly "evidence" that it established and exercised authority as an occupant.[178] In other areas it ruled that the DRC did not provide specific evidence that such authority was exercised.[179]

Several observations, however, might temper this ruling. First, the majority's approach was heavily criticized by Judge Kooijmans, who opined that "[a]s long as it [Uganda] effectively occupied the locations which the DRC Government would have needed to re-establish its authority, Uganda had effective, and thus factual, authority."[180] Second, it is unclear whether the ICJ actually applied the *cumulative approach* to the merits, or conversely that its ruling was driven by the DRC's failure to present sufficient evidencethat the said territories were occupied.[181] In this context, the appointment of a governor in Ituri was viewed, in the ruling, as *evidence* for authority, not a precondition for it.[182] Further support for these doubts is found in the qualification by the majority, that for the purpose of authority to materialize, it would be irrelevant "whether or not Uganda had established a structured military administration of the territory occupied."[183]

A case in point concerns the U.S. presence in al-Tanf in southeastern Syria. Originally established to assist local forces against ISIL, the U.S. maintained its presence there even after ISIL was largely defeated, in order to control potential Iranian supply routes to the area and beyond. In addition to its garrison in the area, the U.S. kept, in 2019, a 55-kilometer "exclusion zone" in which it claimed a right to strike any approaching forces, including those belonging to the Syrian government.[184] This de facto protection from regime forces prompted tens of thousands of Syrians to escape into the exclusion zone, crowding in the Rukban refugee camp. Humanitarian aid to the camp, however, was effectively blocked both by the Syrian regime and

[177] *Id.* ¶ 173.
[178] *Id.* ¶¶ 175–76.
[179] *Id.* ¶ 177.
[180] *Id.* Separate Opinion of Judge Kooijmans, 306, ¶ 49.
[181] *Id.* ¶ 177.
[182] *Id.* ¶ 176.
[183] *Id.* ¶ 173.
[184] Lara Seligman, *U.S. Considering Plan to Stay in Remote Syrian Base to Counter Iran*, Foreign Policy (Jan. 25, 2019, 12:47 PM), https://foreignpolicy.com/2019/01/25/us-considering-plan-to-stay-in-remote-syrian-base-to-counter-iran-tanf-pentagon-military-trump/.

neighboring Jordan.[185] Nonetheless, the United States argued that aiding the camp was the responsibility of the Syrian regime and Russia which supported it. In July 2019, a U.S. official argued that if the United States provided such aid, it would effectively admit to being an occupant in Syria.[186] This argument seems to reflect the approach that occupation requires actual—rather than potential—establishment of authority, and exposes its obvious shortcomings. To the extent that the United States was in a position to administer Rukban, it was under positive duties—deriving from the law of occupation—to aid civilians there.[187]

A similar question has arisen concerning the U.S. control of oil fields in northern Syria since the late 2010s. This control, too, was justified by the United States as part of the anti-ISIL effort, and in this case, also, the United States had not established an occupation administration. Perhaps surprisingly, the German government declared that because of the absence of a formal administration, the United States was not an occupant.[188] This view suffers from the same predicament discussed above: it seems absurd that the application of the law of occupation's rules on natural resources can be circumvented simply by not establishing an administration in the area.[189]

2.5.2 Quality and Quantity of Control

2.5.2.1 Physical Presence?

What constitutes control for the purpose of the law of occupation? In other words, when can it be said that a belligerent is in a position to administer the territory? This issue can be divided into two sub-questions: one qualitative, concerning the means and methods of control; and the other quantitative, concerning the scope of control. Underlying the discussion of both sub-questions is a basic dilemma concerning occupation: Should the law

[185] Robert Ford & Carolyn O'Connor, *U.S. Has Legal and Moral Responsibility to Protect Civilians at Rukban in Syria*, Just Security (Aug. 12, 2019), https://www.justsecurity.org/65773/u-s-has-legal-and-moral-responsibility-to-protect-civilians-at-rukban-in-syria/.

[186] *Id.*

[187] *Id.*

[188] *See* Stefan Talmon, *German Government on Foreign Troop Presence in Syria*, GPIL (Feb. 17, 2020), https://gpil.jura.uni-bonn.de/2020/02/german-government-on-foreign-troop-presence-in-syria/.

[189] *See* Eliav Lieblich, *Germany Goes 19th Century with New Statement on Law of Occupation—On Status of US Forces in Syria*, Just Security (Feb. 19, 2020), https://www.justsecurity.org/68714/germany-goes-19th-century-with-new-statement-on-law-of-occupation-on-status-of-us-forces-in-syria/.

of occupation be triggered in a binary fashion, and apply as a whole, once a certain threshold is crossed? Or, rather, should obligations from the law of occupation be triggered functionally, and apply in a piecemeal fashion, whenever and to the extent that persons are affected by foreign forces?[190]

Concerning the qualitative aspect, recall that one of the three preconditions for occupation is that the hostile army is *physically present* in the territory. On the traditional view, at least in order to first establish an occupation—contra, perhaps, to maintaining it—physical presence requires deploying troops on the land, or "boots on the ground." In contrast, aerial or naval power alone would not suffice.[191] The "boots on the ground" requirement was easily understandable in the past, when effective control was synonymous with control over land.[192] Today, the key justification for this approach might be its relative clarity. Otherwise, it is fair to ask whether states that utilize technology to exercise disaggregated elements of control from afar should be considered virtual or "cyber-occupants,"[193] or, at least, be subject to occupation-like duties concerning these specific control functions.[194] Yet, as we shall see, while such an approach has received some support concerning the *end* of occupation, this has been less so for the *beginning* of occupation. However, the reasons for this possible asymmetry remain undertheorized.

2.5.2.2 Between Hostilities and Occupation?

Assuming that boots on the ground are required for occupation, a longstanding question concerns the distinction between the phase of hostilities—when invading forces encounter active resistance—and that of occupation, in which some stability is envisioned. Can some elements of the law of occupation apply immediately when invading foreign forces encounter—or exercise power over—civilians, or, rather, is it required that hostilities subside first? The view requiring a clear-cut distinction between the phases was traditionally dominant,[195] and some still argue for such an approach. Cuyckens, for example, argues that blurring the lines would only cause legal uncertainty, would impose impractical duties on forces during

[190] *Compare* Gross, *supra* note 50, at 123–35.
[191] ICRC, Expert Meeting, *supra* note 7, at 17.
[192] *Compare* von Glahn, *supra* note 80, at 28–29.
[193] Benvenisti, *supra* note 41, at 53–55.
[194] *See* Gross, *supra* note 50, ch. 2.
[195] *See* U.S. v. List, Case No. 47: The Hostages Trial, VIII United Nations War Crimes Comm'n, Law Reports of Trials of War Criminals 34, 55 (U.S. Military Tribunal, Nuremberg); von Glahn, *supra* note 80, at 28; for a critique, see Benvenisti, *supra* note 8, at 933.

active hostilities, and that in any case, extending the law of occupation to the invasion phase is unnecessary, since at this stage, individuals are protected by the general rules of IHL and perhaps IHRL.[196]

The official commentary on GCIV of 1952, written by Pictet, advanced a different view. Pictet argued that GCIV applies to all protected persons that fall into the hands of a hostile army,[197] and therefore, the term "occupation" under GCIV should accommodate all interactions between a foreign army and the civilian population. According to the "Pictet Theory," "[t]here is no intermediate period between ... the invasion phase and the inauguration of a stable regime of occupation."[198] Occupation, to Pictet, is not a binary position but a construct in which the extent of obligations follows the breadth of control. Some obligations could apply even to a single patrol behind enemy lines; while others require a more extensive and stable presence in the territory. In this way, Pictet hoped to ensure that "[n]o loophole is left."[199] In this sense, Pictet was clearly a harbinger of the functional approach to occupation.

In doctrinal terms, Pictet's approach bifurcated between occupation of territory as defined in article 42 Hague, and "occupation of individuals," so to speak, which triggers GCIV, in accordance with article 4 of the Convention, which defines protected persons as those who find themselves "in the hands" of the enemy.[200] This approach has some support in international jurisprudence. The Pictet theory was adopted, almost word for word, by the ICTY in its *Naletilić* ruling,[201] and was reflected, to an extent, by the Ethiopia–Eritrea Claims Commission in its *Aerial Bombardment* award.[202] It has also been applied by the OSCE Expert Group on Ukraine concerning Ukrainian territories controlled by Russia after its invasion in 2022.[203]

[196] Cuyckens, *supra* note 50, at 54–59; *see also* Marten Zwanenburg, *Challenging the Pictet Theory*, 94 Int'l Rev. Red Cross 30 (2012); Dinstein, *supra* note 58, at 43–48.

[197] GCIV, *supra* note 1, art. 4.

[198] ICRC, Commentary on IV Geneva Convention 60 (Jean S. Pictet ed. 1958) [hereinafter ICRC, Commentary 1958].

[199] *Id.* at 60–61; *see also* Marco Sassòli, *A Plea in Defence of Pictet and the Inhabitants of Territories Under Invasion: The Case for the Applicability of the Fourth Geneva Convention During the Invasion Phase*, 94 Int'l Rev. Red Cross 42 (2012).

[200] ICRC, Commentary 1958, *supra* note 198, at 60.

[201] *Naletilić*, Case No. IT-98-34-T, ¶¶ 203–208, 220–222.

[202] Eritrea–Ethiopia Claims Commission—Partial Award, Western Front, Aerial Bombardment—Eritrea's Claim 3, XXVI (Part VIII) UN Reports of International Arbitral Awards 291, ¶ 27 (2005); *see also* Gross, *supra* note 50, at 76.

[203] OSCE Report, *supra* note 100, at 7–8.

Taken seriously, the "in the hands" test, as applied to individuals, could perhaps be extended to situations beyond actual physical contact with troops.[204] It is possible to envision situations in which individuals are in the hands of an enemy through drones, cyber operations, and in the future, perhaps, through autonomous weapons systems. Arguably, therefore, the neat distinction between the stage of hostilities and effective control through boots on the grounds might be substituted by a test that looks at the actual exercise of power in the territory.[205]

Notably, the 2016 commentary on the Geneva Conventions is more reserved on this issue than Pictet. It first argues that the only definition of occupation is found in article 42 Hague, while the Geneva Conventions only piggyback on this definition. The implications must be that article 4 GCIV alone does not establish "occupation of individuals."[206] However, the 2016 commentary concedes that this "does not mean that certain rules of the law of occupation cannot be applicable during the invasion phase."[207]

At the end of the day, a distinction between the phases might yield odd results. For example, if no occupation-like duties apply during the invasion stage, it would be unclear to what extent a unit that takes over a home during hostilities, would be required, under IHL, to provide food for the residents, beyond merely not interfering in its provision.[208] Recognizing these gaps, even the conservative 2016 U.S. DoD Manual notes that "as a matter of policy," U.S. forces would apply the law of occupation, to the extent possible, "to areas through which U.S. forces are passing, and even on the battlefield."[209]

It is precisely here that significant work is needed on the interaction between the law of occupation and IHRL. Since it is widely accepted that IHRL continues to apply during armed conflict, it could be said that even if the law of occupation does not apply during the invasion stage, equivalent obligations—to respect and ensure rights—might stem from IHRL. However, some jurisprudence cast doubts over this possibility. As ruled by the ECtHR, in *Georgia v. Russia (II)*, jurisdiction for the purpose of the application of the ECHR does not materialize in the stage of active combat "in a context of chaos."[210] Yet this reasoning was

204 Benvenisti, *supra* note 8, at 947.
205 *Id.* at 949.
206 ICRC, Commentary 2016, *supra* note 9, ¶¶ 296–99.
207 *Id.* ¶ 300.
208 GCIV, *supra* note 1, art. 55.
209 DoD Manual, *supra* note 76, at 734.
210 Georgia v. Russia (II), App. No. 38263/08 ¶ 137 (Jan. 21, 2021).

heavily criticized in partially dissenting opinions as inconsistent with previous case law,[211] and is in tension with the view of the UN Human Rights Committee, according to which jurisdiction can be triggered extraterritorially wherever effects on rights are "direct and reasonably foreseeable."[212]

2.5.2.3 Scope of Control

Even after hostilities subside, there still remains a question concerning the scope of control required to establish an occupation. In essence, similar questions arise in relation to the ending of occupation, which is addressed in the next section in more detail. In general, it is accepted that the fact that the belligerent does not maintain presence in every inch of the territory at all times does not rule out an occupation. Beyond this rather obvious statement, this question is especially pertinent in situations where some armed resistance to the occupation remains, or begins after occupation has been established. Here, too, it is clear that the mere existence of resistance in a certain area within the territory does not mean that the latter was not occupied.[213] If, however, this resistance amounts to a fully formed armed conflict it would be difficult to argue that *at least* in the areas under the resistance's control, the occupant's obligations remain unaltered.

It seems that the accepted standard in such situations examines the effort required by the occupant to assume complete control over the resisting areas. In the *Hostages* case, the Nuremberg Tribunal ruled that although, during Germany's occupation of Greece and Yugoslavia, Partisans occasionally controlled some areas, these remained occupied since "the Germans could at any time they desired assume physical control" over them.[214] A similar standard asks whether the occupant can "within a reasonable time, send detachments of troops to make its authority felt" in the

[211] *Id.* Joint Partly Dissenting Opinion of Judges Yudkivska, Wojtyczek, and Chanturia; Marko Milanovic, Georgia v. Russia No. 2: *The European Court's Resurrection of* Bankovic *in the Contexts of Chaos*, EJIL: Talk! (Jan. 25, 2021), https://www.ejiltalk.org/georgia-v-russia-no-2-the-european-courts-resurrection-of-bankovic-in-the-contexts-of-chaos/.

[212] Human Rights Committee, General Comment No. 36 on Article 6 of the International Covenant on Civil and Political Rights, on the Right to Life, U.N. Doc. CCPR/C/GC/36, ¶ 63 (Oct. 30, 2018) [hereinafter GC 36].

[213] Adam Roberts, *The End of Occupation: Iraq 2004*, 54 Int'l & Comp. L.Q. 27, 34 (2005).

[214] U.S. v. List, Case No. 47: The Hostages Trial, VIII United Nations War Crimes Commission, Law Reports of Trials of War Criminals 34, 56 (U.S. Military Tribunal, Nuremberg).

relevant area.[215] Of course, the key question here is the exact content of this standard. Arguably, if in order to "assume physical control" or to "make its authority felt," the occupant must engage in full-blown hostilities, this standard will not be satisfied.[216] As a general rule, it could be argued that an area would be occupied if the occupant is capable of making its *administrative and law-enforcing authority* felt there, without resorting to hostilities.[217] An example for such a situation could be the status of Israel in "Area A" in the West Bank, which is subject to the Palestinian Authority's civil and security jurisdiction under the Oslo Accords.[218] Still, Israel frequently carries out arrests and other activities in this area without the need to resort to hostilities.[219]

Of course, this standard is complicated nowadays. It is quite possible that in a certain situation, an occupant would be able to make *some* law-enforcing authority felt, while having to fight to make other elements of control felt. For instance, it might be required to fight its way into an area for the purposes of detaining a person, yet it could, from a far, make its administrative authority felt by controlling energy and telecommunications there. It seems perfectly reasonable that, in such cases, the full duties of occupation would only apply to the latter elements.

2.5.3 Lack of Consent

The last requirement for occupation is that the control is nonconsensual. In general, if the foreign force receives the consent of the territorial state, it cannot be said to be "hostile," as required by article 42 Hague.[220] In such cases, the status and role of the foreign force would be circumscribed by the

215 ICRC, Commentary 2016, *supra* note 9, ¶ 316; DoD Manual, *supra* note 76, at 738–39; von Glahn, *supra* note 80, at 29.

216 Benvenisti, *supra* note 41, at 51.

217 For the distinction between law enforcement and hostilities, *see, e.g.*, ICRC, Expert Meeting: The Use of Force in Armed Conflicts, Interplay Between the Conduct of Hostilities and Law Enforcement Paradigms 8–9 (Gloria Gaggioli ed., 2013).

218 The Israeli–Palestinian Interim Agreement on the West Bank and the Gaza Strip (Oslo II) art. XIII, Isr.–PLO, Sept. 28, 1995.

219 Amira Hess & Jack Khoury, *Israel Demolishes 70 Homes in Palestinian-Controlled East Jerusalem Neighborhood*, Haaretz (July 25, 2019), https://www.haaretz.com/israel-news/.premium-israel-begins-demolition-of-homes-in-palestinian-controlled-east-j-lem-neighborhood-1.7547258.

220 *See* Mačák, *supra* note 103, at 33–34; *compare* Kyo Arai, *Between Consented and Uncontested Occupation*, 51 Isr. L. Rev. 365 (2018).

terms of the consent for its presence, sometimes defined in status of forces agreements (SOFAs).[221] Of course, the ability to rely on consent for the purpose of excluding or terminating the application of the law of occupation provides for a major loophole. Historically, states invoked consent in dubious circumstances, to circumvent both the prohibition on the use of force and the law of occupation.[222]

Consent can interact with the law of occupation in two instances. When it is granted prospectively, it excludes occupation to begin with. However, when it is granted *under* occupation, the question of consent merges with the issue of occupation's ending. Presumably, such consent can be expressed by the ousted sovereign in a peace agreement, or by a new indigenous government to which authority has been transferred.[223] Therefore, the discussion here should be read in conjunction with our next section, addressing the end of occupation.

To exclude an occupation, consent must be valid, and extended by a competent entity. Very generally speaking, consent must be free, and must be granted by a legitimate government, however defined. Of course, consent by local authorities or opposition groups would not suffice to negate occupation. Beyond these general statements, the legality and limits of consent to foreign military presence is one of the most contentious questions in international law.[224]

Perhaps the most suspect situation, in this context, is when consent is invoked retroactively, *after* the belligerent has already taken control over the territory. This is because both the notions of free consent, and of the existence of a legitimate government, are exceedingly difficult to ascertain under occupation.[225] This tactic was successfully deployed by U.S.-led coalitions in Afghanistan and Iraq, in which consent by transitional governments was

[221] *See, e.g.*, Agreement on the Withdrawal of the United States Forces from Iraq and the Organization of Their Activities During Their Temporary Presence in Iraq, U.S.–Iraq, Nov. 17, 2008, S. EXEC. DOC. 09–6 (2009); *see generally* DIETER FLECK, THE HANDBOOK OF THE LAW OF VISITING FORCES (2d ed. 2018).

[222] *See* Eliav Lieblich, *The 1956 Soviet Intervention in Hungary*, *in* INTERNATIONAL LAW ON THE USE OF FORCE: A CASE-BASED APPROACH 48 (Tom Ruys, Olivier Corten & Alexandra Hofer eds., 2018); Statement by Members of the International Law Association Committee on the Use of Force, JUST SECURITY (Mar. 4, 2022), https://www.justsecurity.org/80454/statement-by-members-of-the-international-law-association-committee-on-the-use-of-force/ (concerning Russia in Ukraine).

[223] BENVENISTI, *supra* note 41, at 56; for historical examples, see Roberts, *supra* note 213, at 29–30.

[224] *See generally* LIEBLICH, *supra* note 131; ERIKA DE WET, MILITARY ASSISTANCE ON REQUEST AND THE USE OF FORCE (2020).

[225] ICRC, EXPERT MEETING, *supra* note 7, at 29.

generally viewed as sufficient to relieve the coalitions from the burden of occupation. However, in these cases, the problems of retroactive consent were mitigated, to an extent, by UNSC resolutions that validated this consent.[226] A less successful case has been Russia's invocation of the consent of a generally unrecognized secessionist government to justify its annexation of Crimea in 2014.[227] In this case, subsequent UNGA resolutions persisted in viewing Crimea as occupied territory.[228]

Situations in which consent to foreign presence is granted immediately after or during active hostilities are similarly suspect.[229] For example, it is difficult to argue that the agreement between NATO and Serbia, following the Kosovo campaign, in which Serbia pledged to withdraw its forces from Kosovo and to accept the deployment of the NATO-led force (KFOR), was based on genuine consent.[230] This can also be implied from the agreement's one-sided nature, as it imposed a multitude of obligations on Serbia, with scant explicit obligations on the other party, and designated KFOR's commander as the "final authority to interpret" the agreement.[231] Indeed, the fact that the deployment of KFOR was conditioned on a Chapter VII resolution by the UNSC, demonstrates that even NATO did not seriously view Serbia's consent as sufficient.[232]

In any case, where consent is invoked when one party controls the other—as might be the case in occupation—attention should be given to the ICJ's approach in the *Chagos Islands Opinion*. There, the ICJ held that "it is not possible to talk of an international agreement, when one of the parties to it … was under the authority of the latter."[233] This statement, however, was qualified, as the Court added that in such situations "heightened scrutiny should be given to the issue of consent."[234] This implies that genuine consent is not entirely excluded in situations of control, but that,

[226] *See* S.C. Res. 1386 (Dec. 20, 2001) (on Afghanistan); S.C. Res. 1546 (June 8, 2004) (regarding Iraq); ICRC, Expert Meeting, *supra* note 7, at 22–23.

[227] *See* Christian Marxsen, *The Crimea Crisis, An International Law Perspective*, 74 ZaöRV 367 (2014).

[228] *See, e.g.*, G.A. Res. 73/194 (Dec. 17, 2018).

[229] *See also* our discussion of armistices etc. in Section 2.5.3.

[230] Military–Technical Agreement between the International Security Force (KFOR) and the Governments of the Federal Republic of Yugoslavia and the Republic of Serbia from 9 June 1999, art. 1(2), June 15, 1999, U.N. Doc. S/1999/682.

[231] *Id.* art. 4.

[232] *See id.* art. 1(2).

[233] Legal Consequences of the Separation of the Chagos Archipelago from Mauritius in 1965, Advisory Opinion, 2019 I.C.J. Rep. 95, ¶ 172 (Feb. 25).

[234] *Id.*

for understandable reasons, a higher bar for its demonstration would be required.

Arguably, if the occupant claims that it has transferred authority while remaining in the territory, and then invokes the consent of the local authorities, occupation would be terminated only when at hand is an indigenous government, endorsed by the local population through a transparent transitional process (such as a referendum), and which receives a fair amount of international recognition.[235] It is clear, in this context, that establishing a subordinate regime—whether as part of an interim arrangement or for any other reason—cannot be construed as a transfer of authority.[236] When determining whether a regime is subordinate, some analogy can be drawn from the jurisprudence of the ECtHR. Primarily in the context of Turkey's control over Northern Cyprus, and Russia's control over South Ossetia and Abkhazia, the Court examined not only the strength of the states' military presence, but also whether their "military, economic and political support for the local subordinate administration provides it with influence and control over the region."[237]

Importantly, even where consent given to a foreign presence is valid, it can be withdrawn by the host state. If the foreign state refuses and remains in the territory, and assuming that other conditions for occupation are fulfilled, it can acquire the status of an occupant. That was possibly the case in the DRC in 1998, when the former withdrew its consent to the Ugandan presence in its territory, but the latter refused to comply.[238] Another example followed the January 2020 killing of Iranian General Qassem Soleimani by U.S. forces present in Iraq, without the latter's consent.[239] Iraq condemned the strike as an aggression against it, and as "a flagrant violation of the terms under which United States forces are present in the country."[240] The Iraqi parliament called on the government to withdraw its consent to

[235] *See* BENVENISTI, *supra* note 41, at 56.

[236] For instance, the fact that following the Oslo Accords, a Palestinian Authority was established in the West Bank and Gaza, has not relieved Israel from the status of an occupant. *See* HCJ 1661/05 Hof Azza Regional Council v. the Knesset, 59(2) PD 481, ¶ 10 (2005) (Isr.).

[237] *See, e.g.*, Georgia v. Russia (II), App. No. 38263/08 ¶¶ 164–175 (Jan. 21, 2021).

[238] *DRC v. Uganda* ¶¶ 49–53.

[239] Permanent Rep. of the U.S. to the U.N., Letter dated Jan. 8, 2020 from the Permanent Rep. of the United States of America to the United Nations addressed to the President of the Security Council, U.N. Doc. S/2020/20 (Jan. 9, 2020).

[240] Permanent Rep. of Iraq to the U.N., Identical letters dated Jan. 6, 2020 from the Permanent Rep. of Iraq to the United Nations addressed to the President of the Security Council, U.N. Doc. S/2020/15 (Jan. 6, 2020).

the presence of U.S. forces.[241] The immediate response by the United States was negative.[242] Ultimately, no official request of withdrawal was made, and the question, of course, is whether these dynamics already imply coercion by the United States.[243]

Three more points are in order. First, consent cannot be implied merely from nonresistance by the territorial state. Historical examples for such cases can be found in WWII, in which Germany encountered no significant resistance when it invaded Denmark, which recognized Germany's clearly overwhelming force. Similarly, Bohemia and Moravia were also occupied without resistance.[244] In order to preempt claims that such territories are not occupied, Common Article 2(2) emphasizes that GCIV applies even if occupation "meets with no armed resistance."[245] The rationale is clear: the fact that a state cannot resist, or otherwise chooses not do so, cannot serve to deprive it from title nor its population from the protections of the law of occupation.[246]

Second, a ceasefire, an armistice, or any other type of interim agreement in which belligerents agree to cease active hostilities although foreign forces still occupy parts of their territories do not alone constitute consent to the foreign presence. They merely represent consent by states to a *process* aiming to bring about the end of the conflict; but in the interim stage, foreign presence in their territories cannot be considered consensual, and to the extent that control is exercised, their territories remain occupied.[247]

Third, another complexity concerning the relations between consent and occupation stems from article 47 GCIV. Article 47 provides that protected persons cannot be deprived of their rights, "in any case or in any manner,"

[241] W.J. Hennigan & Kimberly Dozier, *Iraqis Push for U.S. Troop Withdrawal in Symbolic Vote*, Time (Jan. 5, 2020, 4:11 PM), https://time.com/5759101/iraqi-parliament-vote-for-us-withdrawal/.

[242] Karen DeYoung, Louisa Loveluck, and Mustafa Salim, *Trump Administration Refuses to Heed Iraq's Call for Troop Withdrawal*, Wash. Post (Jan. 11, 2020, 1:52 AM), https://www.washingtonpost.com/world/middle_east/iraq-asks-united-states-to-set-up-mechanism-for-troop-withdrawal/2020/01/10/794058ea-32f8-11ea-971b-43bec3ff9860_story.html.

[243] *See* Sajad Jiyad, *Iraq Still Might Force the United States Out*, War on the Rocks (Jan. 29, 2020), https://warontherocks.com/2020/01/iraq-still-might-force-the-united-states-out/.

[244] *See* ICRC, Commentary 2016, *supra* note 9, ¶ 286.

[245] Wall Opinion ¶ 95.

[246] ICRC, Commentary 2016, *supra* note 9, ¶ 289.

[247] Von Glahn, *supra* note 80. A historical example is the post–WWI Rhineland occupation, instituted by the Armistice Agreement of 11 November, 1918. *See* Ernst Fraenkel, Military Occupation and the Rule of Law: Occupation Government in the Rhineland, 1918–1923 6–8 (1944). Another example is the Israel–Syria Disengagement Agreement of 1974, after which Israel remained the occupant in the Golan Heights.

inter alia due to "any agreement concluded between the authorities of the occupied territories" and the occupant.[248] On an extreme reading, article 47 excludes any termination of occupation by consent, not only by a regime established under occupation, but by a government that still enjoys independence in other parts of the territory. This, however, has its own costs: it would be difficult to conclude peace agreements involving territorial concessions by the occupied state, if negotiations take place while the territories are still occupied.[249] The better view is to read article 47 as referring to the rights of protected persons *during* occupation, which cannot be waived, and not to occupation writ large—that can be ended by genuine agreement.[250]

2.6 The End of Occupation

2.6.1 Symmetrical, Asymmetrical, Binary, and Functional Approaches

When does occupation end, and consequently, both the obligations and powers deriving from it cease? Similar to what was observed concerning the beginning of occupation, formal declarations by occupants are not determinative.[251] Beyond this, much remains controversial. On one view—which we call "the symmetrical approach"—the requirements for the end of occupation mirror those of its beginning.[252] According to this approach, if foreign forces are no longer physically present in the territory, if they are present but not in a position to exercise effective control, or if their presence becomes consensual, occupation is terminated in a binary manner.[253]

Although the symmetrical position is conceptually simple, applying it is a thorny task, not least because the difficulties here mirror those that complicate establishing that occupation exists to begin with.[254] In some cases, the UNSC, by exercising its "epistemic authority," can validate that

[248] GCIV, *supra* note 1, art. 47.

[249] *Compare* Dinstein, *supra* note 58, at 135; *but see* Kirsten Schmalenbach & Alexander Prantl, *How to End an Illegal War?*, Völkerrechtsblog (Apr. 21, 2022), https://voelkerrechtsblog.org/how-to-end-an-illegal-war/.

[250] *See* the examples given in ICRC, Commentary 1958, *supra* note 198, at 274–75.

[251] ICRC, Expert Meeting, *supra* note 7, at 27–28.

[252] Benvenisti, *supra* note 41, at 56.

[253] ICRC, Expert Meeting, *supra* note 7, at 30; *see also* Yuval Shany, *Faraway, so Close: The Legal Status of Gaza After Israel's Disengagement*, 8 Y.B. Int'l Humanitarian L. 369 (2005).

[254] ICRC, Expert Meeting, *supra* note 7, at 27.

occupation has ended.[255] An easy case is when the UNSC recognizes that an occupant has withdrawn its forces, as was acknowledged—albeit in a presidential statement—after Israel left South Lebanon in 2000.[256] A more controversial situation, however, occurs when the UNSC recognizes that power has been transferred to local authorities, as was the case in 2004 in Iraq.[257] In Resolution 1546, the UNSC endorsed the Interim Government of Iraq as a sovereign authority, and held that once it takes power, and the CPA ceases to exist, the "occupation will end."[258] Notably, this was not made contingent on any withdrawal of foreign forces from Iraq.[259] Resolution 1546, essentially, made a determination that the Interim Government was a sovereign body, and that the foreign presence in Iraq was now based on its consent. Debatable as this conclusion was, the majority view is that the UNSC is competent to make such determinations.[260]

The symmetrical position, however, is not uncontested. Some argue for *asymmetry* between the beginning of occupation and its end. Dinstein argues, for example, that while "boots on the ground" are a precondition to establish occupation, "[o]nce belligerent occupation commences, the degree of effective control can wane or wax."[261] To Scobbie, the end of occupation should be determined by the fulfillment of normative criteria, namely the right to self-determination.[262] Others, such as Gross, maintain an asymmetric approach, yet criticize binary approaches concerning the end of occupation, and advance a *functional* approach instead. According to the latter, obligations from the law of occupation would apply to the elements of control actually maintained by the occupant, even if it withdraws its troops.[263] Yet, all asymmetrical or functional approaches need to explain

[255] On epistemic authority, see Michael Zürn, Martin Binder, and Matthias Ecker-Ehrhardt, *International Authority and Its Politicization*, 4 INT'L THEORY 69, 86 (2012).

[256] Press Release, Security Council, Security Council Endorses Secretary-General's Conclusion on Israeli Withdrawal from Lebanon as of 16 June, U.N. Press Release SC/6878 (June 18, 2000).

[257] *See* Roberts, *supra* note 213, at 38–44.

[258] S.C. Res. 1546, ¶¶ 1–2 (June 8, 2004).

[259] *Id.* preamble.

[260] *See* ICRC, EXPERT MEETING, *supra* note 7, at 29; Robert Kolb, *Occupation in Iraq Since 2003 and the Powers of the UN Security Council*, 90 INT'L REV. RED CROSS 29 (2008). Remarkably, the post–WWI British occupation of Iraq was deemed to have ended in a comparable manner. Norman Bentwich, *Mandated Territories: Palestine and Mesopotamia (Iraq)*, 2 BRIT. Y.B. INT'L L. 48, 50 n.1 (1921–22).

[261] DINSTEIN, *supra* note 58, at 301.

[262] Iain Scobbie, *An Intimate Disengagement: Israel's Withdrawal from Gaza, the Law of Occupation and Self-Determination*, 11 Y.B. ISLAMIC & MIDDLE E. L. ONLINE 3, 6–7 (2004).

[263] GROSS, *supra* note 50, ch. 2; ICRC, COMMENTARY 2016, *supra* note 9, ¶¶ 309–313.

why the same tests should not apply also to the *beginning* of occupation, or of occupation-like duties, perhaps as suggested by the Pictet theory.[264]

2.6.2 The Case of Gaza as an Example

An especially difficult situation arises when states remove their "boots on the ground" from occupied territory, but continue to exercise some elements of authority there. The most pertinent example concerns the Gaza Strip, which Israel occupied in 1967. It is in this context that most contemporary debates on the end of occupation take place.

In September 2005, Israel withdrew its military and civilian settlements from Gaza, and redeployed its armed forces around the Gaza–Israel fence (the "disengagement"). In 2007, Hamas, a Palestinian armed group, took control over the territory. Since the disengagement—and more forcefully after Hamas took over—Israel argues that it lacks "effective control" over Gaza, and consequently, bears no positive obligations toward the population. Rather, it claims, since it is engaged in an ongoing armed conflict with armed groups in Gaza, only the law on the conduct of hostilities applies.[265]

However, even after the disengagement, Israel retained significant control over life in Gaza. For example, and while some of these aspects of control ebb and flow, Israel has retained complete control over the air and maritime areas of Gaza; it maintains—along with Egypt—strict control over the passage of goods and persons from and to Gaza; it controls Gaza's population registry; and Gaza is highly dependent on Israel for energy.[266] Moreover, Israel routinely deploys in Gaza means that are not legally available in non-occupied territories, such as delineating the fishing zones inside Gaza's territorial waters, or spraying herbicide to enforce its "no-go zones."[267]

In 2008, the HCJ issued its *Bassiouni* ruling. At hand was whether, and to what extent, Israel could restrict the supply of electricity and fuel to Gaza, which is, essentially, a question of the existence of positive obligations

[264] *See* Section 2.5.2.2.

[265] *See, e.g.*, Israel Ministry of Foreign Affairs, The 2014 Gaza Conflict: Factual and Legal Aspects ¶¶ 45–48 (2015).

[266] *See* Gisha, Scale of Control: Israel's Continued Responsibility in the Gaza Strip, ch. 2 (2011).

[267] *See* Michael Schaeffer Omer-Man, *Israel Spraying Herbicides Inside Gaza Violates International Law, Rights Groups Say*, +972 Magazine (Jan. 9, 2019), https://972mag.com/gaza-israel-herbicides-intl-law/139591/.

toward Gaza. The Court endorsed the state's view that Israel no longer had "any effective capability … of enforcing order and managing civilian life in the Gaza Strip"—and that therefore, the territory was not occupied.[268] However, the Court stated, without elaborating, that Israel incurred some obligations toward Gaza that stemmed from its control over the border crossings; from the "situation that was created" by its control over Gaza for decades; and from the fact that Gaza was almost completely dependent on Israel for electricity.[269]

Either by virtue of the "waxing and waning" nature of Israel's effective control over life in Gaza, or because of the elements of control described above, many international bodies and commentators claim that Israel remains under obligations from the law of occupation concerning Gaza.[270] Yet, these positions mostly concede that many government functions in Gaza are exercised by Hamas. Concerning these functions, Israel cannot make its "authority felt" absent significant hostilities. Accordingly, if the law of occupation were to apply binarily to Gaza, this might result in an absurd obligation on Israel to send troops to ensure public order there.[271]

For this reason, most positions on Gaza reveal the emerging acceptance of a nonbinary view on the end of occupation. Dinstein, for instance, argues that Gaza remains occupied.[272] Yet, he also concedes that post-disengagement, "Israel's responsibilities in Gaza have shrunk dramatically."[273] Comparably, the functional approach to occupation, as suggested by Gross, gained much ground in the context of Gaza. On this view, obligations stemming from the law of occupation continue to apply to elements of

[268] HCJ 9132/07 Al-Bassiouni v. Prime Minister of Israel, Nevo Legal Database, ¶ 12 (Jan. 30, 2008) (Isr.); *see also* 1 The Public Commission to Examine the Maritime Incident of 31 May 2010: The Turkel Commission Rep. ¶¶ 45–47 (2010); for comparable positions, see Hanne Cuyckens, *Is Israel Still an Occupying Power in Gaza?* 63 Neth. Int'l L. Rev. 275 (2016); *see also* Eyal Benvenisti, *The International Law of Prolonged Sieged and Blockades: Gaza as a Case Study*, 97 Int'l L. Stud. 969 (2021).

[269] HCJ 9132/07 *Al-Bassiouni*, ¶ 12.

[270] *See, e.g.*, Human Rights Council, Rep. of the Detailed Findings of the Independent International Commission of Inquiry on the Protests in the Occupied Palestinian Territory, U.N. Doc. A/HRC/40/CR.P.2, 22–24 (Mar. 18, 2019) [hereinafter Human Rights Council Rep.]; Dinstein, *supra* note 58, at 296–303; Mustafa Mari, *The Israeli Disengagement from the Gaza Strip: An End of the Occupation?* 8 Y.B. Int'l Hum. L. 356 (2005). Even those arguing that Gaza is not occupied cite different sources of positive obligations that might apply to the situation, such as IHRL or "general law of obligations." *See* Yuval Shany, *The Law Applicable to Non-Occupied Gaza: A Comment on* Bassiouni v. The Prime Minister of Israel, 42 Isr. L. Rev. 101 (2009).

[271] ICRC, Expert Meeting, *supra* note 7, at 29.

[272] Dinstein, *supra* note 58, at 301.

[273] *Id.* at 302.

control which Israel still exercises there.[274] This approach has been adopted, for instance, by the ICRC and by a UN Commission, which held that Israel's obligations toward Gaza are "commensurate with the degree to which it exercises control."[275]

Moreover, even if one adopts the symmetric model, thereby accepting that the disengagement ended the occupation in Gaza, this does not mean that Israel is entirely free from some obligations toward Gaza that originate from the law of occupation. Such obligations might arise under the law of *post-occupation*. According to this view, when an occupant unilaterally terminates its occupation, but the territory remains dependent on it, the enduring elements of dependence must be analyzed in light of the law of occupation. This is because the occupant, during its occupation, is bound to create the conditions that would allow independence after its withdrawal. If it fails to do so, it cannot evade its responsibilities ex post.[276]

[274] GROSS, *supra* note 50, at 204–47.

[275] Human Rights Council Rep., *supra* note 270, ¶¶ 66–67.

[276] Eyal Benvenisti, *The Law on the Unilateral Termination of Occupation*, *in* A WISER CENTURY? JUDICIAL DISPUTE SETTLEMENT, DISARMAMENT AND THE LAWS OF WAR 100 YEARS AFTER THE SECOND HAGUE PEACE CONFERENCE 371 (Thomas Giegerich & Ursula E. Heinz eds., 2009); Benjamin Rubin, *Disengagement from the Gaza Strip and Post-Occupation Duties*, 42 ISR. L. REV. 528, 550–58 (2009).

PART 2

THE SCOPE OF THE OCCUPANT'S POWERS AND OBLIGATIONS

3

Maintaining Public Order and Life in Occupied Territories

General Issues and Specific Obligations

Part 1 addressed general concepts and frameworks relating to the law of occupation. In Part 2, we move to analyze in more detail occupants' powers and obligations. In this chapter, we take a general look at the two main provisions which delineate the scope of powers and obligations possessed by the occupant: article 43 Hague and article 64 GCIV. Specifically, we focus on the basic tension inherent in these provisions: that between the conservationist principle and the occupant's duty to further the welfare of the local population. After discussing articles 43 and 64 generally, we discuss how the principles that they enshrine are reflected in the legislative, administrative, and judicial powers of the occupant. The chapter ends with an analysis of some specific obligations established by the law of occupation.

3.1 Article 43 Hague

3.1.1 General Issues

Once an occupation is established, article 43 Hague is triggered:

> The authority of the legitimate power having in fact passed into the hands of the occupant, the latter shall take all the measures in his power to restore, and ensure, as far as possible, public order and safety, while respecting, unless absolutely prevented, the laws in force in the country.[1]

[1] There is a discrepancy between the binding French text of article 43 and the English translation. The binding French text reads "l'ordre et la vie publics" ("public order and life") rather than "public order and safety." Yoram Dinstein, The International Law of Belligerent Occupation 100 (2d ed. 2019). We use both interchangeably.

Article 43, being the source of the occupant's legal obligations and powers, constitutes the foundational norm of the law of occupation. It also serves a quasi-constitutional role, by delimiting these powers. Article 43 reflects the three interests protected by the law of occupation: those of the absent sovereign (by requiring that the occupant respect the laws in force); those of the local population (the obligation to ensure public order and safety); and the security of the occupying forces (as part of the public order and safety).[2] Importantly, article 43 is an exhaustive norm: it requires the occupant to act as a trustee for these interests, and these interests *only*. It cannot, therefore, act in the occupied territory to further its own national, economic, and political interests in the wider sense. Ultimately, the powers and obligations under article 43 encompass almost every aspect of governance in occupied territories.[3] Naturally, we cannot touch upon each one of these possible aspects. We confine our analysis, therefore, to the most general issues delineating the occupant's scope of authority.

Some of the duties and powers relating to public order and safety are further detailed in specific provisions in Hague IV and GCIV.[4] Concerning theses specific provisions, article 43 acts as a statement of general principles. The specific rules simultaneously reflect the principles enshrined in article 43 and are interpreted in light of them.[5] Additionally, article 43 can be an *independent* source of powers and obligations concerning issues not addressed explicitly in other provisions. Unsurprisingly, this makes article 43 susceptible to a wide array of competing claims, both by occupants and those seeking to challenge them.

Two further general observations are in order. First, by referring to the duty to take all measures "to restore, and ensure" public order and safety, article 43 establishes the positive duties at the core of the law of occupation. Note, that the obligation to "ensure" these interests, requires both that the

[2] *See* Eyal Benvenisti, The International Law of Occupation 69 (2d ed. 2012).

[3] *See, e.g.*, Tallinn Manual 2.0 on the International Law Applicable to Cyber Operations 546–49 (Michael N. Schmitt ed., 2d ed. 2017).

[4] For example, Convention (IV) relative to the Protection of Civilian Persons in Time of War art. 56, Aug. 12, 1949, 6 U.S.T. 3516, 75 U.N.T.S. 287 [hereinafter GCIV] details the obligations of occupying powers in relation to public health. *See* Marco Longobardo, *The Duties of Occupying Powers in Relation to the Prevention and Control of Contagious Diseases Through the Interplay Between International Humanitarian Law and the Right to Health*, 55 Vand. J. Transnat'l L. 757 (2022).

[5] *Compare* Protocol Additional to the Geneva Conventions of 12 August 1949, and relating to the Protection of Victims of International Armed Conflicts (Protocol I) art. 48, June 8, 1977, 1125 U.N.T.S. 3 [hereinafter API] which outlines the "basic rule" of distinction, and followed by several detailed rules.

occupant act to promote them, and also that it exercise due diligence to protect them against third parties.[6] This due diligence requirement is implied in the reference, in article 43, to measures that are "in his [the occupant's] power."[7]

Second, article 43 is a source both of obligations *and* powers. In this context, it is helpful to distinguish between two types of powers recognized by article 43. The first are those necessary to fulfill the occupant's obligations toward the local population. The second type are powers that relate, conversely, to the operational necessities of the occupant ("security needs"). The phrase "public order and safety" has been generally understood to encompass both types of powers.[8] Of course, as the understanding of the "public order" powers granted by article 43 widens, the scope of the conservationist principle must become narrower.

3.1.2 The "Local Population"

When considering the occupant's positive obligations, a preliminary question concerns the identity of the "local population" toward which the occupant's trusteeship applies. Article 43 Hague refers to the "public" in the territory, while articles 44–45 Hague mention the "inhabitants." GCIV, however, introduces the category of "protected persons," toward which special obligations apply. The definition of protected persons is complex.[9] Importantly, protected persons are individuals who find themselves "in the hands" of an occupant "of which they are not nationals." Further excluded are nationals of neutral or co-belligerent states, if their state has diplomatic relations with the occupant.[10] Dinstein, accordingly, identifies

[6] Dinstein, *supra* note 1, at 100–01; Armed Activities on the Territory of the Congo (Dem. Rep. Congo v. Uganda), Judgment, 2005 I.C.J. Rep. 168, ¶ 178 (Dec. 19).

[7] *See also* Marco Longobardo, *The Relevance of the Concept of Due Diligence for International Humanitarian Law*, 37 Wisc. Int'l L. J 44, 48, 73–76 (2019).

[8] Dinstein, *supra* note 1, at 101–05.

[9] *See* Elizabeth Salmón, *Who Is a Protected Civilian?*, *in* The 1949 Geneva Conventions: A Commentary 1135 (Andrew Clapham, Paola Gaeta & Marco Sassòli eds., 2015).

[10] GCIV, *supra* note 4, art. 4. *See* analysis in Dinstein, *supra* note 1, at 69–71; Salmón, *supra* note 9, at 1145–47. According to art. 73 of API, *supra* note 5, stateless persons or refugees who fled to the occupied territory before the beginning of hostilities, are protected persons for the purpose of GCIV. Beyond this protection, the occupant would also be bound by international refugee law, and supplemental protections of non-refoulement as found in various IHRL treaties. Convention relating to the Status of Refugees, July 28, 1951, 189 U.N.T.S. 137.

a "discrepancy" between the obligations owed toward persons in both categories—inhabitants of the territory at large versus protected persons.[11]

Systematically comparing between the protections afforded to protected persons and other persons under the law of occupation is beyond the scope of this book. Importantly, the advent of "fundamental guarantees" under API[12] and the application of IHRL during occupation have arguably leveled the field in terms of the protection afforded to all individuals. However, the question remains whether the special status of protected persons under GCIV affects the interpretation of the "public" to which obligations are owed under article 43 Hague. Crucially, does the public in article 43 encompass also *non*-protected persons in occupied territories, such as nationals of the occupant? If so, may the occupant further *their* interests, even if these clash with those of protected persons? Unsurprisingly, this question was raised concerning Israeli settlers in the West Bank. In several decisions, the HCJ ruled that the duty to "ensure public order and safety" does not only encompass local Palestinians, but *all* of the population in the territory, *including* Israeli settlers.[13] Therefore, the HCJ authorized many times measures intended to further their interests.[14]

These rulings, however, cannot be understood divorced from the context of the Israeli occupation, where Israel refuses to acknowledge the de jure application of GCIV and accordingly of the prohibition on transferring its civilians into the territory.[15] It should be stressed that although the duty to maintain public order and safety requires the occupant to ensure the safety of non-protected persons in the territory—such as tourists, refugees, merchants—this duty cannot be used to circumvent specific prohibitions, such as the prohibition on settlements.

In its *Settlements Regularization Law* case, the HCJ somewhat tempered its position. Although it repeated its view that Israeli settlers are part of the local population for the purpose of article 43 Hague, it stressed that the duty to further the welfare of the local population applies primarily to protected persons, as defined in article 4 GCIV. Accordingly, the Court ruled that the military commander of the West Bank cannot expropriate Palestinian

[11] DINSTEIN, *supra* note 1, at 69.

[12] API, *supra* note 5, art. 75.

[13] *See, e.g.*, HCJ 2150/07 Abu Safiyeh v. Minister of Def., 63(3) PD 331 ¶ 20 (2009) (Isr.).

[14] *See, e.g.*, HCJ 10356/02 Hess v. IDF Commander in the West Bank, 58(3) PD 443 (2004) (Isr.); *see also* David Hughes, *Moving from Management to Termination: A Case Study of Prolonged Occupation*, 44 BROOK. J. INT'L. L 109, 144–45 (2018).

[15] *See* Section 2.2.2.

property for the benefit of Israeli settlers alone.[16] While this ruling does not alleviate the problem of circumvention mentioned above, it is notable for reading-in the status of protected persons into the interpretation of article 43 Hague, emphasizing that the former are the primary beneficiaries of the trusteeship obligations enshrined in the article.[17] This makes sense because if article 43 aims to protect self-determination, it must give precedence to the collective interests of the people entitled to self-determination in the particular territory.

3.1.3 The Conservationist Principle between Laissez-Faire, the Welfare State, and Neoliberalism

The positive duties and powers recognized in article 43 are limited by the requirement to respect, "unless absolutely prevented, the laws in force in the country." This is the source of the conservationist principle, the rationale of which was detailed in Chapter 1.[18] While the article refers to the *laws* in force, it must be understood broadly, to encompass the general status quo ante in the territory. For example, long-term changes in infrastructure enacted by administrative decisions are also covered by this principle, even if they do not require changing the local law.[19]

The scope of the obligation to respect the status quo ante is perhaps the most difficult question of the law of occupation. Ultimately, it is this obligation that distinguishes occupation from sovereignty. Unsurprisingly, the phrase "unless absolutely prevented" has been central in the debate on article 43 ever since the negotiations on its drafting.[20] The main problem arises from its ambiguity. Does the phrase "unless absolutely prevented" mean unless *physically* prevented? If this were the case, the phrase would

[16] *See* HCJ 1308/17 Silwad Municipality v. The Knesset ¶¶ 69–70, 79, Nevo Legal Database (June 9, 2020) (Isr.).

[17] *See* Tamar Hostovsky Brandes, *Constitutional Adjudication of International Law Violation: The Israeli Supreme Court's Invalidation of the Settlement Regularization Law*, VERFASSUNGSBLOG (June 14, 2020), https://verfassungsblog.de/constitutional-adjudication-of-international-law-violations/.

[18] *Compare* GERHARD VON GLAHN, THE OCCUPATION OF ENEMY TERRITORY: A COMMENTARY ON THE LAW AND PRACTICE OF BELLIGERENT OCCUPATION 96 (1957).

[19] *Compare* HCJ 393/82 Jam'iat Iscan Al-Ma'almoun v. IDF Commander of Judea and Samaria, 37(4) PD 785, ¶ 27 (1983) (Isr.).

[20] BENVENISTI, *supra* note 2, at 90.

apply in very few situations, since an occupant would rarely be physically prevented from respecting local laws.[21] Conversely, does it refer to being "absolutely prevented" normatively, meaning, in light of competing legal or moral interests? If the latter is true, which competing interests are relevant? Is it ultimately the good of the local population that should have the upper hand on the law in force, or rather military necessity?[22] Perhaps, "unless absolutely prevented" should refer to the occupant's international obligations, for example, as enshrined in IHRL?[23] Of course, if the phrase is construed in a limiting manner, article 43 would give precedence to the interests of the ousted sovereign over the immediate interests of the local population.[24] Notably, during the drafting of article 43, military necessity was viewed as the only consideration that could "absolutely prevent" respect of the local law; however, such a limiting view was never implemented in practice.[25]

A stringent interpretation of the conservationist principle was understandable in the 19th century, when the principle was first conceived. Back then, wars were generally short, and—relatively speaking— mostly did not implicate lives of civilians. Many governments, at least in the West, operated under the assumption of laissez-faire, which implied minimal intervention in the market, beyond the protection of property. Both of these characteristics supported a limiting understanding of the conservationist principle: since wars—and occupations—were short, and did not significantly affect civilian life, there was no need to enact significant changes in the territories; and since the state was not deeply involved in the market, such changes were not expected to begin with.[26]

Yet, these basic assumptions were already under considerable strain by the end of the 19th century. In this context, several mutually reinforcing factors should be noted. First, at least in Europe, laissez-faire gradually gave way to the welfare state. The assumption that the occupant can slip into the "night-watcher" role of the ousted sovereign and that beyond ensuring

[21] An interesting historical example of a situation of physical inability concerns the British occupation of Palestine in 1917, where the Ottomans, in their withdrawal, took away the land registers. *See* Norman Bentwich, *The Legal Administration of Palestine Under the British Military Occupation*, 1 Brit. Y.B. Int'l L. 139, 140 (1920–21).

[22] *Compare* Benvenisti, *supra* note 2, at 90–91.

[23] *Compare id.* at 92.

[24] *Id.* at 69.

[25] Dinstein, *supra* note 1, at 120; Benvenisti, *supra* note 2, at 91.

[26] *See id.* at 70; *see* Ernst H. Feilchenfeld, The International Economic Law of Belligerent Occupation 13, 17 (1942); Julius Stone, Legal Controls of International Conflict: A Treatise on the Dynamic of Disputes and War-Law 729 (1954).

basic security, "the machine will run itself," could no longer be sustained. Maintaining public order now required active involvement in a wide variety of aspects.[27] The problem is that as much as the occupant is expected to be actively involved in public policy decisions in occupied territories, the potential for conflicts of interest, abuse, and exploitation widens.

Second, the rise of the Washington Consensus and neoliberalism at the end of the 20th century added a new twist to these dynamics: states were now expected to "reform" in order to access the global economy, inter alia through trade liberalization, privatization, and deregulation.[28] Modern occupants could now invoke article 43 in order to justify such reforms.[29]

A third pressure on the conservationist principle flowed from the extension of the law of occupation beyond Europe. When non-western states became international legal subjects in the early 20th century, their territories were now potentially subject to the law of occupation, rather than to immediate conquest. This new legal encounter required western occupants to respect the status quo ante of ousted sovereigns which they considered inferior. Unsurprisingly, this too contributed to the weakening of the conservationist principle. The Ottoman Empire is a case in point. Being recognized as a "non-Christian" yet fully sovereign international person,[30] its territories taken during WWI were generally considered occupied. When Britain took Palestine from the Ottoman Empire in 1917, it was explicitly designated "Occupied Enemy Territory South," subject to the international law of occupation.[31] Yet, the general British view was that Palestine was now relieved from "Turkish misrule."[32] While the local laws generally remained in force, "every department of government ... has been reformed," in order to bring "British Justice" to the country.[33]

In sum, developments in political economy and in the nature of conflicts, along with occupants' perception of local law as inferior, pushed for a more flexible reading of the conservationist principle. A pertinent example for

[27] Benvenisti, *supra* note 2, at 78–79; HCJ 393/82 Jam'iat Iscan Al-Ma'almoun v. IDF Commander of Judea and Samaria, 37(4) PD 785, ¶ 18 (1983) (Isr.).

[28] *See, e.g.*, John Williamson, *A Short History of the Washington Consensus*, 15 L. & Bus. Rev. of the Americas 7, 9–10 (2009).

[29] We discuss this in Chapter 6. The imposition of trade liberalization reforms is by no means new. *See, e.g.*, 1 Lassa Oppenheim, International Law: A Treatise § 103 (2d ed. 1912).

[30] *Id.* at § 102.

[31] Bentwich, *supra* note 21, at 139.

[32] *Id.*

[33] *Id.* at 140–41.

this process can be found in the HCJ's ruling, as early as 1972, that "whenever the laws in force in occupied territories do not allow the military administration to fulfill its obligations towards the local inhabitants, this amounts to absolute prevention, which in turn permits the administration to change these laws."[34]

3.2 Enter Article 64 GCIV: Continuity or Change?

The pressures on the conservationist principle are reflected in article 64 of GCIV, which supplements article 43 Hague:

> The penal laws of the occupied territory shall remain in force, with the exception that they may be repealed or suspended by the Occupying Power in cases where they constitute a threat to its security or an obstacle to the application of the present Convention.
>
> Subject to the latter consideration and to the necessity for ensuring the effective administration of justice, the tribunals of the occupied territory shall continue to function in respect of all offences covered by the said laws.
>
> The Occupying Power may, however, subject the population of the occupied territory to provisions which are essential to enable the Occupying Power to fulfil its obligations under the present Convention, to maintain the orderly government of the territory, and to ensure the security of the Occupying Power, of the members and property of the occupying forces or administration, and likewise of the establishments and lines of communication used by them.

The plain language of article 64 focuses on penal laws and criminal tribunals in occupied territory, and the penal authority of the occupant.[35] Yet, its underlying rationales, the object and purpose of GCIV, and its drafting

[34] HCJ 337/71 The Christian Association for Holy Places v. Minister of Def., 26(1) PD 574 ¶ 11 (1972) (Isr.).

[35] Von Glahn, *supra* note 18, at 115.

history, lead to the conclusion that article 64 has wider implications.[36] Several takeaways should be pointed out.

First, article 64 clarifies the hierarchy between the local law and the international law of occupation. The article provides that laws in force can be changed where they constitute "an obstacle to the application" of GCIV. This implies that from the international legal standpoint, GCIV should trump the laws in force in the territory. This makes sense. Just as a state cannot rely on its *own* domestic law to circumvent its international obligations,[37] it cannot rely on the domestic law of the occupied territory to escape its duties under the law of occupation.[38] This clarification is highly important, since relying on local laws to override the law of occupation can provide a significant loophole. For example, Israel has argued for decades that it can lawfully demolish homes of Palestinian militants in the West Bank on the basis of a British emergency regulation from 1945, which remains in force in the territory.[39] As the "local law," the argument goes, the regulation applies in the territory notwithstanding the Geneva Conventions.[40] Article 64, however, rules out this interpretation.[41]

The second key feature of article 64 is its possible relaxation of the conservationist principle. Recall, that article 43's language implies the stringent demand that existing law be respected "unless absolutely prevented." Article 64 GCIV, conversely, recognizes the suspension of local laws if they are a "threat" to the occupant's security; and allows new laws to be enacted "which are essential . . . to maintain the orderly government." Although this phrasing requires that new laws be "essential" to fulfill their purposes, it provides the occupant with a comparatively wide margin of discretion.[42]

[36] Yutaka Arai-Takahashi, *Law-Making and the Judicial Guarantees in Occupied Territories*, *in* Clapham et al., *supra* note 9; Hans-Peter Gasser, *Protection of the Civilian Population*, *in* The Handbook of International Humanitarian Law 237, 286 (Dieter Fleck ed., 2d ed. 2008).

[37] *See*, respectively, Vienna Convention on the Law of Treaties of 1969, art. 27, May 23, 1969, 1155 U.N.T.S. 331 [hereinafter VCLT]; Int'l Law Comm'n, Draft Articles on Responsibility of States for Internationally Wrongful Acts, *extract from* the Rep. of the International Law Commission on the work of Its Fifty-third Session, U.N. Doc. A/56/10 (2010).

[38] *See* Dinstein, *supra* note 1, at 123–26.

[39] Defence (Emergency) Regulations, reg. 119, 1945, Palestinian Gazette, supp. 2, 1055, 1089.

[40] *See* HCJ 434/79 Sahwill v. IDF Commander of the Judea and Samaria, 34(1) PD 464 (1979) (Isr.); to be sure, Israel argues alternatively that GCIV also allows such actions. Meir Shamgar, *The Observance of International Law in the Administered Territories*, 1 Isr. Y.B. Hum. Rights 262, 275–76 (1971); *but see* Eliav Lieblich, *House Demolitions 2.0*, Just Security (Dec. 18, 2015), https://www.justsecurity.org/28415/house-demolitions-2-0/.

[41] *See* Dinstein, *supra* note 1, at 125–26.

[42] *See* Marco Sassòli, *Legislation and Maintenance of Public Order and Civil Life by Occupying Powers*, 16 Eur. J. Int'l L. 661, 670–71 (2005).

Ultimately, article 64 enumerates clearly the three legitimate objectives of legislation—and by extension, of all administrative actions—under occupation: legislation essential for *security* purposes; legislation essential to fulfill obligations under GCIV; and legislation essential for the "orderly government of the territory."[43]

Notwithstanding the textual differences between article 43 Hague and article 64 GCIV, many commentators maintain that article 64 simply offers a more precise phrasing of the principles already present in article 43, and affects neither the scope of the occupant's powers nor the limitations imposed by the conservationist principle.[44] However, to argue that article 64 GCIV adds nothing to article 43 Hague requires a quite permissive reading of the latter. If this permissive view of article 43 is adopted, it could be said that article 64 GCIV did not, in fact, significantly change the scope of the occupant's powers, but rather reflected the existing broad interpretation of article 43.

If this is true, what remains of the conservationist principle? The answer depends, to an extent, on the duration of the occupation, and is in any case capped by the prohibition on "transforming" the occupied territory or bringing about de facto annexation. We discuss these issues in Chapter 4.

3.3 Welfare of the Local Population or Self-Interest? Possible Yardsticks

The previous section demonstrated that article 64 CCIV reflects the longstanding trend to interpret article 43 flexibly. As a point of departure, the status quo ante should be maintained, but change is generally permissible if the measure is essential to interests recognized as legitimate under the law of occupation. This raises a basic problem: How can an external observer distinguish between genuine measures, and those that are merely self-interested?

One test for distinguishing between genuine and self-interested actions is to ask whether the occupant would adopt comparable means in its own territory. Dinstein calls this the "litmus test."[45] The problem is that this test

[43] *Compare* Dinstein, *supra* note 1, at 122–28.
[44] *See id.* at 121; Hanne Cuyckens, Revisiting the Law of Occupation 145–51 (2017).
[45] *See* Dinstein, *supra* note 1, at 132–33; *compare* Russel Buchan, *International Community and the Occupation of Iraq*, 12 J. Confl. & Sec. L. 37, 55 (2007).

assumes a baseline of similarity between the territories. Usually, the material differences between them would actually call for different measures. In other cases, the fact that the occupant adopts similar measures in its own territory can be evidence of de facto annexation, or of attempts of economic integration that would not benefit the local population.[46]

It seems that there is no satisfactory test to address this problem. A possible adjustment to the litmus test would be to ask, as a thought experiment, whether the occupant would have adopted the same measures *if its own citizens were to be affected.*[47] Yet, this test is quite contingent. Some governments are self-interested also when acting domestically.[48] Feilchenfeld, for his part, offered a slightly different test: in the context of the occupant's tax powers, he suggested that, at least in prolonged occupation, tax modification would be possible when "the lawful sovereign would … have found it necessary to modify tax legislation."[49] This test presumes that a measure would be genuine if the territory's sovereign would have taken it itself. Yet, this standard can harm the local population, in cases where the ousted sovereign disregards its people. Others suggest that local participation in the occupant's decision-making would be the best yardstick for its measures.[50] However, local participation cannot be the *only* yardstick, since the local population might refuse to participate in such processes, and this alone cannot relieve the occupant of its obligations. Some experts suggest that international mechanisms are best to assess the occupant's actions, but it is far from clear which mechanisms should do so and in what capacity.[51] Last, another possible test could be that to the extent that new legislation conforms to relevant international standards, it would be presumed genuine—and conversely, where there is deviation from these standards, the occupant would be under a stringent duty to justify them.[52] But this requires that

[46] *See* Benvenisti, *supra* note 2, at 92–93; Theodor Meron, *Applicability of Multilateral Conventions to Occupied Territories*, 72 Am. J. Int'l L. 542, 550 (1978); Adam Roberts, *Prolonged Military Occupation: The Israeli-Occupied Territories Since 1967*, 84 Am. J. Int'l L. 44, 94 (1990); *see also* debate in Tristan Ferraro, ICRC, Expert Meeting, Occupation and Other Forms of Administration of Foreign Territory 74–75 (2012) [hereinafter ICRC, Expert Meeting].

[47] *Compare* Avishai Margalit & Michael Walzer, *Israel: Civilians & Combatants*, 56 N.Y. Rev. Books 1 (2009).

[48] *Compare* Adil Ahmad Haque, Law and Morality at War 161–62 (2017).

[49] Feilchenfeld, *supra* note 26, at 49.

[50] ICRC, Expert Meeting, *supra* note 46, at 76.

[51] *Id.* at 76–77.

[52] For similar arrangements in other context, see, e.g., Agreement on Technical Barriers to Trade art. 2(4), Apr. 12, 1979, 1186 U.N.T.S. 276; International Health Regulations art. 43, July 25, 1969, 764 U.N.T.S. 3.

clear international standards exist. It seems therefore that the test for the genuineness and necessity of measures must remain contextual.

3.4 Welfare of the Local Population and Nondiscrimination

A related question is whether the occupant's positive obligations toward the local population require the conditions in the occupied territory to be equalized with this those in the occupying state. Arguably, such a standard could be derived from IHRL duties of nondiscrimination.[53]

Although this seems compelling on its face, a demand for equality between the territories cannot be the general baseline for the law of occupation. Decisions about resource allocation change between societies, and many times, equalizing conditions would require the occupant to transform the territory.[54] If the conservationist principle is to have any effect, the law of occupation cannot be understood to impose such an absolute obligation.

Nonetheless, this conclusion should not be taken at face value. Arguably, a duty to equalize the conditions between the territories might be desirable in cases of de facto annexation. If an occupant decides to treat the territory as its own, then it seems that it cannot have it both ways: it should extend to the local population similar benefits enjoyed by its own.[55] Furthermore, if it unlawfully transfers its own citizens to the territory, it cannot invoke difference of nationality to justify preferential treatment of its own citizens within the territory. To the extent that the occupant provides to settlers conditions equivalent to those in its own territory, this naturally affects its obligations toward protected persons also.[56]

[53] *See, e.g.*, Sari Bashi, *Human Rights in Indefinite Occupation: Palestine*, CARDOZO J. INT'L & COMP. L. (2020).

[54] We discuss taxation in Section 7.1.1.

[55] *Compare* ACRI, ONE RULE, TWO LEGAL SYSTEMS: ISRAEL'S REGIME OF LAWS IN THE WEST BANK (2014), https://law.acri.org.il/en/wp-content/uploads/2015/02/Two-Systems-of-Law-English-FINAL.pdf; Ariel Zemach, *The Emerging Right of West Bank Palestinians to Israeli Citizenship*, 42 U. PENN. J. INT'L L. 271 (2020); Itamar Mann & Yael Berda, *Annexation or Not, It's Time All Palestinians Under Israeli Control Had the Right to Vote*, NEWSWEEK (May 21, 2020) https://www.newsweek.com/annexation-west-bank-right-vote-1505494.

[56] *Compare* HCJ 168/91 Murcus v. Minister of Def., 45(1) PD 467, 470–71 (1991) (Isr.). In this case, the HCJ ruled that owing to nondiscrimination obligations, once the military commander decided to distribute protective gear against possible chemical attacks from Iraq to Israeli settlers, it was obliged to distribute them also to Palestinians. This question has arisen

3.5 The Legislative, Administrative, and Judicial Powers of the Occupant

Having discussed the general scope of the powers of the occupant in relation to the conservationist principle, we now take a closer look at the occupant's legislative, administrative, and judicial powers.

3.5.1 Legislative and Administrative Powers: General Issues

In general, the occupant has the power to legislate in the occupied territory, and to make administrative decisions. The power to make administrative decisions can either derive from the local law—in which case the occupant acts in place of the ousted executive—or derived from new legislation by the occupant.[57] The distinction between legislation and administrative decisions is not really consequential under occupation. In occupation, both are ultimately adopted in an authoritarian manner by the military commander. Although the military commander might be expected to respect its own laws when it acts in its executive capacity, the executive and legislative powers in occupation are vested in the same entity.[58] Therefore, all powers under occupation are "administrative" in nature.

Article 64 GCIV mentions three types of legislative actions: repealing local laws; suspending them; or enacting new provisions. In practice, all three actions change the legal status quo ante, and therefore there is limited value in discussing them separately. Nevertheless, an interesting question arises concerning the difference between "repealing" and "suspending" local laws. The former connotes a permanent change, while the latter envisions temporariness. In effect, however, there is little difference between these measures. This is because the occupant does not have a clear legal

again concerning Israel's policy not to provide Covid-19 vaccines to West Bank Palestinians. *See* Eyal Benvenisti, *Israel Is Legally Obligated to Ensure the Population in the West Bank and Gaza Strip Are Vaccinated*, Just Security (Jan. 7, 2021), https://www.justsecurity.org/74091/israel-is-legally-obligated-to-ensure-the-population-in-the-west-bank-and-gaza-strip-are-vaccinated/.

[57] *See* HCJ 69/81 Abu Aita v. Commander of the Judea and Samaria Area, 37(2) PD 197 ¶ 11(b) (1983) (Isr.).

[58] *Compare id.*

authority nor practical ability to repeal a law—or, for that matter, to make any change in local law—that would survive post-occupation.[59] In legal terms, once occupation ends, the power of its legislation is annulled, and, in practical terms, whether occupation legislation would be maintained is a matter for the returning sovereign to decide.[60] Still, it is quite common that, post-occupation, states and their courts maintain actions taken lawfully by the occupant. This could be either for the sake of legal continuity, or because such measures conferred rights on third parties.[61]

Concerning legislative powers, a distinction was traditionally made between constitutional norms, statutes, and administrative regulations. While the occupant was deemed restricted in its powers to change or suspend the first two, much more freedom was assumed in relation to regulations.[62] Two rationales can explain this. One is that regulations are of less importance in the overall legal structure of the occupied territory, and therefore changing them is less intrusive.[63] However, this reasoning seems outdated in an era in which, in many states, vast fields of governance are subject to executive regulation.[64] The second rationale relates to democracy or self-determination: arguably, changing or suspending constitutional norms or legislation is a deeper intrusion into the will of the local population. While this makes sense, it is also quite contingent. Whether constitutional or legislative norms indeed reflect the will of the people depends on the specific regime. Furthermore, the mere establishment of an occupation administration alters—even if temporarily—the constitutional structure in the territory, as the military commander becomes the supreme authority.[65] In sum, while it seems that some consideration must be given to the formal location of the norm in the normative hierarchy, what matters more is the function

[59] *Compare* Dinstein, *supra* note 1, at 121.

[60] *But see* Felice Morgenstern, *Validity of the Acts of the Belligerent Occupant*, 28 Brit. Y.B. Int'l L. 291, 298–99 (1951).

[61] *Id.* at 296–98; Tristan Ferraro, *Enforcement of Occupation Law in Domestic Courts: Issues and Opportunities*, 41 Isr. L. Rev. 331, at 351–52.

[62] Von Glahn, *supra* note 18, at 99.

[63] *Id.*

[64] *See, e.g.*, Richard H. Pildes & Cass R. Sunstein, *Reinventing the Regulatory State*, 62 U. Chicago L. Rev. 1 (1995).

[65] For example, the Coalition Provisional Authority promulgated that "Regulations and Orders issued by the Administration shall take precedence over all other laws." CPA Regulation No. 1, The Coalition Provisional Authority, CPA/REG/16 May 2003/01 (May 16, 2003), *reprinted in* 2 Stefan Talmon, The Occupation of Iraq: The Official Documents of the Coalition Provisional Authority and the Iraqi Governing Council 2 (2013).

of the change enacted by the occupant: that is, the extent to which it affects the life of the local population, or creates an irreversible situation.

Another important issue is whether the laws in force in the territory are static or dynamic. In other words, are the laws "frozen," so to speak, at the moment of occupation, or does the ousted sovereign—to the extent that it continues to operate outside of the occupied territory—maintain the power to legislate in the occupied part of its territory? The same question arises concerning new precedents by courts in the non-occupied parts of the territory. This question has two distinct implications: first, whether new legislation in the non-occupied area *binds the occupant*, as part of the laws in force in the territory. The second is whether, if the occupant disregards these new laws, the returning sovereign can apply them *retroactively*.[66] While the first issue relates to the scope of suspension of sovereignty in occupied territories, the second mostly concerns the legitimate expectations of individuals in relation to their own sovereign.[67] We focus here on the first issue, since it is more saliently a problem of the law of occupation.

The traditional approach was that the ousted sovereign could not legislate or decree in the occupied territory.[68] For example, the Belgian government-in-exile prohibited, in 1916, trading between Belgian and German citizens. Yet, the Belgian–German Mixed Arbitral Tribunal held, in 1922, that a trade contract between Belgians and Germans could not have been invalidated before the liberation of Belgium in 1918, because the ousted sovereign could not decree in occupied territories.[69] In the same vein, Israel has frozen the Jordanian legislation in the West Bank as it was in June 1967.[70]

In parallel, however, a more flexible approach has emerged during and since WWII. Some prominent commentators now began to argue that generally the ousted sovereign's new laws apply in the occupied territories, as long as they do not conflict with the occupant's lawful powers.[71] Arguably,

[66] For a ruling that adopts this view, see Ammon v. Royal Dutch Co., 21 I.L.R. 25, 27 (Federal Tribunal, Switz. 1954).

[67] *Compare* Benvenisti, *supra* note 2, at 105; *see also* European Commission for Democracy Through Law, *Opinion on the Law of Occupied Territories of Georgia*, CDL-AD (2009) 15 (Mar. 17, 2009), ¶ 24, https://www.venice.coe.int/webforms/documents/default.aspx?pdffile=CDL-AD(2009)015-e [hereinafter *Opinion on the Law of Occupied Territories of Georgia*].

[68] Von Glahn, *supra* note 18, at 34.

[69] *Id.* at 35.

[70] Israel never conceded that Jordan was a lawful sovereign to begin with. *See* Shamgar, *supra* note 40, at 263–67.

[71] *See* Arnold D. McNair, *Municipal Effects of Belligerent Occupation*, 57 L.Q. Rev. 33, 73 (1941).

this would be in line with the interest to grant the local population, through its government in the non-occupied part of the territory, more input into the administration of their affairs.[72] This question arose in the Second Circuit, in the 1953 case of *Netherlands v. Federal Reserve Bank of New York*.[73] Upon its occupation of the Netherlands, Germany ordered Jews to deposit all negotiable assets, including securities, in a certain office. Some of the bonds deposited were then transferred to other entities or sold. The case at hand dealt with bonds that ended up in the hands of an American, who was made to deposit them at the Federal Reserve due to a violation of federal foreign funds regulations.[74] The Netherlands claimed that it was entitled to the bonds based on a decree ordered by its government-in-exile during the occupation, in which it assumed protective temporary title over such properties.[75] The Second Circuit ruled for the Netherlands, based on a trend it identified, in which several courts gave effect to legislation of governments-in-exile in occupied territories. As the Court reasoned, new legislation might apply, as long as it does not amount to "hostile measures aimed at combating the occupant" and hampering its "legitimate" rule.[76] Yet, the Court was able to refrain from committing to a general view on the legislative power of the ousted sovereign, because, in this case, the German order was clearly contrary to article 46 Hague, which prohibits confiscation.[77] It is therefore difficult to entangle the recognition of the government-in-exile's legislative powers in this case, from the unlawful act at hand.

A more recent case seems to adopt a comparable approach. In October 2008, Georgia enacted the Law on the Occupied Territories of Georgia, which annulled "all legislative and administrative acts issued by the *de facto* authorities in Abkhazia and South Ossetia" controlled by Russia. The law also restricted access to the territories and prohibited economic activities, such as real estate transactions, if they were inconsistent with Georgian law.[78] The Venice Commission, in its opinion on this law, refrained from opining on the validity of the ousted sovereign's laws in the occupied territories, but its approach resembled that of the Court in the *Netherlands* case. The Commission held that generally Georgian law should not hinder

[72] *Compare* Benvenisti, *supra* note 2, at 247.
[73] State of the Netherlands v. Federal Reserve Bank of New York, 201 F.2d 455 (2d. Cir. 1953).
[74] *Id.* at 456.
[75] *Id.* at 459–60.
[76] *Id.* at 462.
[77] *Id.* at 370.
[78] *Opinion on the Law of Occupied Territories of Georgia*, *supra* note 67.

Russia in fulfilling its duties toward the occupied population.[79] Yet, it implied that if real estate transactions in the territory contravened existing Georgian law, they might also run counter to Russia's duty to respect the law in force. Because such transactions would be violations of international law by the occupant, Georgia could annul them.[80] Yet, this case is of limited general value, because both Abkhazia and South Ossetia are recognized by Russia as breakaway states, and therefore not administered as occupied territories. Under these circumstances, the Georgian law seems to respond to the attempted secession of the territories, rather than to measures undertaken under the law of occupation.

Concerning the continuing power of courts, it is common for occupants to abolish the resort or appeal to superior courts located in the non-occupied portions of the territory. This has been done by Israel, concerning the Jordanian Court of Cassation, and also by the Allies in certain areas in WWII.[81] But this does not mean that local courts in the occupied territories, which continue to operate, are per se prevented from applying new interpretations or precedents adopted by such superior courts.

In sum, it seems reasonable that new laws of the ousted sovereign would be presumed valid in the occupied territories, unless undermining the *lawful* administration by the occupant. This might seem dramatic at first glance, but considering the general relaxation of the conservationist principle, it is not necessarily so. After all, if the new laws (or rulings, for that matter), would be deemed contrary to the interests outlined in article 64 GCIV, the occupant would be able to repeal or suspend them anyway.[82]

A related question concerns the subjection of the occupant, in its legislative and administrative actions within the occupied territories, to treaties which bind the sovereign. We address this issue briefly in Chapter 6.[83]

An interconnected question concerns the occupant's powers to negotiate treaties with third parties on behalf of the occupied territory. It seems that since the occupant is empowered to legislate in the territory there is also no a priori bar that the occupant *as such* enter into treaties with third parties. It should be emphasized, however, that this would only be possible if these treaties comply with the requirements

[79] *Id.* ¶ 18.
[80] *Id.* ¶ 22.
[81] Benvenisti, *supra* note 2, at 217, n.89; Raja Shehadeh, The West Bank and the Rule of Law 18 (1980).
[82] *Compare* Benvenisti, *supra* note 2, at 247.
[83] *See* Section 6.1.5.

of article 43 Hague—including the conservationist principle—and, perhaps, when such treaties promote global community interests such as the reduction of pollution, the fight against pandemics, and so forth.[84] Additionally, treaties entered into by the occupant must acknowledge the occupied status of the territory, and not be used to further annexationist policies.[85]

A complex question is whether such treaties continue to bind the returning sovereign post-occupation. It seems that as a point of departure, the answer is negative. The occupant cannot bind the ousted sovereign, and third parties must be well aware that they have entered into an agreement with a temporary administrator, and accordingly have no legitimate expectation that the sovereign would respect them.

3.5.2 Administrative Occupation Law?

Assuming the scope of the occupant's legislative and administrative power is agreed upon, questions still arise concerning its decision-making. Does the law of occupation impose on occupants—when legislating or making ad hoc decisions—administrative law-like obligations? Procedurally, these can entail, for example, transparency, hearing rights, and participation rights; substantively, they might subject decisions to reasonableness and proportionality standards.

Such obligations might be particularly relevant when the occupant takes security measures against individuals, an issue we address in Chapter 5. As we shall see, the power to take some of these measures is explicitly limited by administrative law-like obligations.[86] Here we ask another question: Is an occupant bound by such principles in general?

Admittedly, neither article 43 Hague nor article 64 GCIV expressly subject decision-making to such standards. Yet, there are at least five ways in which such standards might still apply. Two ways ascend from domestic law. *First*, such principles may stem from the local law. Arguably, if the occupant is required to respect the local law in general, then it must also respect the local administrative law—at least when executing local laws.

[84] Benvenisti, *supra* note 2, at 84.

[85] Case C-104/16 P, Council of the E.U. v. Front Polisario, ECLI:EU:C:2016:973, ¶¶ 86–99 (Dec. 21, 2016), https://curia.europa.eu/juris/liste.jsf?language=en&num=C-104/16.

[86] *See, e.g.*, GCIV, *supra* note 4, arts. 78, 65.

Second, the occupant's own administrative law principles might apply personally to state agents, even when acting extraterritorially.[87]

The other ways in which administrative law obligations can apply during occupation descend from international law. The *third* way is by recognizing principles of administrative law as general principles of international law, to be read into occupation law.[88] The *fourth* way is through the parallel application of IHRL, to the extent that the latter encompasses administrative law-like obligations.[89] *Fifth*, such norms can apply if we understand all sovereigns—whether occupants or not—as bound by other-regarding obligations, which entail accountability in decision-making.[90]

However, general principles of administrative law are notoriously vague, which may facilitate occupants' ability to utilize the legitimating power of these principles, without significantly limiting themselves in practice.[91] A case in point is the HCJ's *Planning Commissions* case.[92] In 1971, the military commander in the West Bank enacted an order on planning, abolishing the local planning commissions mandated by Jordanian law.[93] The order established new commissions without any requirement of local Palestinian membership.[94] The petitioners argued that the order contradicted articles 43 Hague and 64 GCIV, both because of the lack of Palestinian representation, and since its real aim was to facilitate Israeli settlements.[95] Following the petition, the military administration adopted a "participation procedure" according to which at the early planning stages, a "preliminary meeting" with local Palestinians would take place, in which their views

[87] This has notably been the approach of the HCJ in a multitude of cases. For a critical analysis *see* Adam Shinar, *Israel's External Constitution: Friends, Enemies and the Constitutional/Administrative Law Distinction*, 57 VA. J. INT'L L. 735 (2018).

[88] *See, e.g.*, HCJ 2056/04 Beit Sourik Village Council v. The Government of Israel, 58(5) PD 807 ¶¶ 36–37 (2004) (Isr.).

[89] *See* Eva Brems & Laurens Lavrysen, *Procedural Justice in Human Rights Adjudication: The European Court of Human Rights*, 35 HUM. RTS. Q. 177 (2013).

[90] Eyal Benvenisti, *Sovereign as Trustees of Humanity: On the Accountability of States to Foreign Stakeholders*, 107 AM. J. INT'L L. 295, 300 (2013).

[91] *See* Martti Koskenniemi, *Occupied Zone—"A Zone of Reasonableness"?* 41 ISR. L. REV. 13 (2008).

[92] HCJ 5667/11 Dirat-Rif'aya Village Council v. Minister of Def., Nevo Legal Database (June 9, 2015) (Isr.) [hereinafter *Planning Commissions* case]

[93] Order on Planning of Cities, Villages and Buildings (Judea & Samaria) (No. 418), 5731–1971; Planning of Cities, Villages and Building Law, no. 79 of 1966 (Jordan).

[94] *Id.* §§ 2(2), 2(4), 4(a).

[95] *Planning Commissions* case, ¶ 2. It should be noted that at the time of the petition, the planning order was in place only in Area C of the West Bank, where Israel maintains full civil control in accordance with the Oslo Accords.

will be heard, and after which reservations could be submitted.[96] However, this procedure did not mandate including Palestinians in the commissions themselves. The HCJ rejected the petition.[97] While it conceded that planning in the West Bank should reflect administrative law principles such as transparency and participation, it qualified that due to the "complex" situation in the area and the "adversarial" relationship between Israel and the Palestinians these principles cannot entail full participation.[98] It therefore held that the participation procedure was satisfactory, provided that it would be implemented genuinely.[99] The use of administrative law in this case both obscured the real issue—the allocation of land to settlements—and provided legitimating language through the participation procedure.

3.5.3 Courts, Judiciary, and Public Officials

The law of occupation envisions a "double-tiered" court system in occupied territories.[100] The first consists of the existing courts, whether civil or criminal, which operate in accordance with local law. In general, the occupant should allow these courts to continue to function,[101] while respecting their independence.[102]

Notably, if a local court system does not exist or ceases to function altogether, the occupant might be obliged to establish such courts—or at least a comparable system of dispute resolution, in accordance with local customs—as part of its general obligation to maintain public order.[103] For example, when the Ottoman Empire lost Palestine to Britain in WWI, it withdrew most of its administration from the territory—including judges. Courts were therefore reestablished by the British occupant.[104] An interesting question is whether the occupant is empowered to establish *new*

[96] *Id.* ¶ 9
[97] *Id.* ¶ 21
[98] *Id.* ¶ 22.
[99] *Id.* ¶¶ 25–26.
[100] DINSTEIN, *supra* note 1, at 145; VON GLAHN, *supra* note 18, at 112.
[101] GCIV, *supra* note 4, art. 64 refers to tribunals, but this obligation must apply, *mutatis mutandis*, also to civil courts.
[102] Convention (IV) relative to the Protection of Civilian Persons in Time of War, Geneva, 12 August 1949, art. 54, *in* ICRC, COMMENTARY ON IV GENEVA CONVENTION 60 (Jean S. Pictet ed., 1958) [hereinafter ICRC, COMMENTARY 1958].
[103] VON GLAHN, *supra* note 18, at 111.
[104] Bentwich, *supra* note 21, at 140. This also took place when Israel occupied Gaza in 1967. *See* DINSTEIN, *supra* note 1, at 146.

"local" courts, addressing new subject matter, even if a court system is already in place. This has been done by the CPA in Iraq, and also by Israel in the West Bank.[105] Whether this is lawful under the law of occupation is a sub-question of the scope of the conservationist principle.

Many questions arise concerning the continuing operation of local courts.[106] One perplexing issue is whether the occupant is required to subject itself to the jurisdiction of local courts, to the extent such jurisdiction exists in local law. This question can concern the occupant's commercial transactions in the territory (*acta jure gestionis*) or its public acts (*acta jure imperii*).[107] Concerning the former, the traditional view has been that owing to its "military supremacy" and "alien character," the occupation administration cannot be sued in local courts, even concerning simple contractual interactions.[108] However, nowadays, even foreign states are not immune from such jurisdiction,[109] and access to justice is a recognized human right.[110] Therefore, it seems hardly compatible with the occupant's trusteeship obligations to exempt itself from local jurisdiction in such cases.

A much more difficult question concerns local courts' power to review the occupant's public actions, such as legislation or administrative acts.[111] For example, if, according to local law, international law enjoys supremacy over domestic law, a local court might attempt to invalidate an occupant's

[105] The CPA established a new Central Criminal Court; Israel established municipal courts for violations of municipal by-laws. Dinstein, *supra* note 1, at 146.

[106] In the context of Israel and the Palestinian territories, see generally Michael Karayanni, Conflicts in a Conflict: A Conflict of Laws Case Study on Israel and the Palestinian Territories (2014).

[107] *See generally* Alexander Orakhelashvili, *Jurisdictional Immunity of States and General International Law—Explaining the* Jus Gestionis *v.* Jus Imperii *Divide*, *in* The Cambridge Handbook of Immunities and International Law 105 (Tom Ruys, Nicolas Angele & Luca Ferro eds., 2019).

[108] Von Glahn, *supra* note 18, at 108.

[109] *See* Jurisdictional Immunities of the State (Germany v. Italy: Greece Intervening), Judgment, 2012 I.C.J. 99 ¶¶ 60–61 (Feb. 3).

[110] *See generally* Access to Justice as a Human Right (Francesco Francioni ed., 2007).

[111] Not to mention civil or criminal jurisdiction over the occupant's officials. Usual practice in international territorial administrations confers on members of these administrations complete immunity in local courts. *See* Steven R. Ratner, *Foreign Occupation and International Territorial Administration: The Challenges of Convergence*, 16 Eur. J. Int'l L. 695, 716 (2005). It is clear that occupants would invoke the same immunity. Israel specifically excluded claims against its own forces from the civil jurisdiction of the local courts in the occupied territories. Benvenisti, *supra* note 2, at 217. The Oslo Accords also make clear that Palestinian courts have no jurisdiction over Israeli officials. *See* Israeli–Palestinian Interim Agreement on the West Bank and the Gaza Strip (Oslo II), Annex IV, Isr.–PLO., Sept. 28, 1995.

act that contravenes the law of occupation.[112] Furthermore, in cases where the occupant executes the local law acting in its administrative capacity, a local court might subject it to administrative review. Of course, such attempts are likely to put into sharp relief the inherently tense relations between the occupant and the local authorities. During WWI and WWII, some courts attempted to exercise such powers, while others have been reluctant for both legal and practical reasons.[113]

An interesting case is the ruling of the Ramallah Court of Appeals, a Palestinian/Jordanian Court, in the *Al Jabari* case of 1968.[114] Following the occupation, many Palestinian lawyers refused to appear in the local courts as a measure of protest. The military commander, in response, permitted Israeli lawyers to replace them. A local court in Hebron refused to give effect to the commander's order, and prevented an Israeli lawyer from appearing in a case, ruling that the occupant was not competent to make such changes in the local law.[115] On appeal, the Ramallah Court reversed the ruling. It conceded that the occupant can change local law only "if such measures are imperative"; but that local courts are not competent to review such decisions.[116]

Ultimately, while it is possible to defend a legal construction that recognizes local courts' power to review public acts by the occupant,[117] it is unlikely that such review would be effective. In particular, local decisions reviewing the occupant's actions might be quashed by new legislation by the occupant or ignored altogether.[118]

In practice, where occupants allow claims against the occupation administration—whether in civil or public issues—these are usually relegated to their own judicial or quasi-judicial bodies. Historically, and depending on subject matter, the authority to hear claims against occupants was delegated to military courts in the occupied territory; to special claims

[112] *See* Morgenstern, *supra* note 60, at 301.

[113] *See* Ferraro, *supra* note 61, at 346–49; Ernst Fraenkel, Military Occupation and the Rule of law: Occupation Government in the Rhineland, 1918–1923 207–24 (1944).

[114] Al-Ja'bari v. al Awiwi (Ramallah Court of Appeals, 17 June 1968), 42 I.L.R. 484, 486–87 (1971).

[115] Case (DC Hebron) 44/67 (Feb. 5, 1968); *see also* Yehuda Z. Blum, *The Missing Reversioner: Reflections on the Status of Judea and Samaria*, 3 Isr. L.R. 279, 279–80 (1968).

[116] *Al-Ja'abari*, 42 I.L.R. 486.

[117] *See* Morgenstern, *supra* note 60, at 307; von Glahn, *supra* note 18, at 109–10; *compare* Ferraro, *supra* note 61, at 347–50.

[118] *See* Fraenkel, *supra* note 113, at 209.

commissions;[119] to specific mechanisms established by the occupant;[120] or to the occupant's domestic courts.[121]

The second tier of the court system in occupied territories comprises military courts established by the occupant. The primary role of such courts is the adjudication of security offenses *enacted by the occupying power*.[122] We discuss military courts in Chapter 5.

The law of occupation also addresses the status of local judges (as well as that of public officials in general). Yet, article 54 GCIV, which regulates this issue, is somewhat ambiguous. On the one hand, it provides that the occupant "may not alter the status of public officials and judges . . . should they abstain from fulfilling their functions for reasons of conscience." On the other, the article qualifies in paragraph 2, that the prohibition "does not affect the right of the Occupying Power to remove public officials from their posts." Read together, this seems to mean that the occupant may remove judges or public officials unless its sole reason to do so is their conscientious refusal. A further ambiguity is found in the fact that Paragraph 2, which permits the removal of public officials, does not mention judges explicitly. While some take for granted that this includes the power to remove judges,[123] some argue that the failure to refer to judges implies that they cannot be removed by the occupant.[124]

Unfortunately, these issues do not exhaust the complications arising from article 54. The article does not only prohibit altering the status of conscientiously refusing public officials or judges; it also rules out sanctions or

[119] Von Glahn, *supra* note 18, at 113; in relation to the Occupied Palestinian Territories, see Order Concerning Claims (Judea & Samaria) (No. 271) 5728–1968.

[120] In Iraq, rights of appeal were established in some CPA orders. *See, e.g.*, CPA Order No. 6, Eviction of Persons Illegally Occupying Public Building ¶ 3, CPA/ORD/8 June 2003/06 (June 28, 2004), *reprinted in* Talmon, *supra* note 65, at 10; CPA Order No. 14, Prohibited Media Activity ¶ 6, CPA/ORD/10 June 2003/14 (June 12, 2003), *reprinted in id.* 99.

[121] In Israel, on civil issues *see, e.g.*, § 5A, Civil Wrongs Law (Liability of the State), 5712–1952, LSI 6 147 (Isr.); on public issues, see Eli Nathan, *The Power of Supervision of the High Court of Justice over Military Government*, *in* Military Government in the Territories Administered by Israel 1967–1980—Legal Aspects 109 (Meir Shamgar ed., 1982); Yuval Shany, *Rule of Law De Jure and/or De Facto?: Shamgar and the International Law of Belligerent Occupation*, *in* Strengthening Human Rights Protections in Geneva, Israel, the West Bank and Beyond 179 (Joseph E. David, Yaël Ronen, Yuval Shany & J.H.H. Weiler eds., 2021).

[122] GCIV, *supra* note 4, arts. 64, 66.

[123] ICRC, Commentary 1958, *supra* note 102, at 60; Dinstein, *supra* note 1, at 147.

[124] Gasser, *supra* note 36, at 290, *cited in* Arai-Takahashi, *supra* note 36, at 1430.

"measures of coercion" against them. Simultaneously, however, paragraph 2 does not preclude compelling at least some public officials to work, either for the needs of the army of occupation, or for those of the local population.[125] It seems therefore that article 54 must be understood as providing a conscientious refusal exception to the occupant's general power to compel public officials to work.

Taken as a whole, it is reasonable that article 54—consistent with the general spirit of the law of occupation—requires that public officials and judges maintain their positions as part of the status quo ante, and could be removed and nominated only in fulfillment of the occupant's trusteeship duties, and as a point of departure in accordance with the procedures of the local law.[126]

3.6 Specific Obligations toward the Local Population and the Duty to Cooperate with Local Authorities

Article 43 Hague establishes the occupant's general powers and obligations to act in favor of the local population, and grants it quite significant discretion while doing so. Later treaties, however, structure this discretion in several aspects, by clarifying the occupant's obligations in specific instances. These provisions are meant to ensure a basic minimum for the welfare of the local population, and in particular the most vulnerable parts of it, and to ensure other basic interests that occupants might neglect or abuse. It is beyond the scope of this book to provide a comprehensive analysis of each of these obligations. Here, we discuss such obligations briefly, as well as the obligation, occasionally required, to cooperate with local authorities in discharging them.

[125] Article 54 references art. 51 for this purpose. Article 51 excludes, namely, work that amounts to taking part in military operations.

[126] *Compare* ICRC, COMMENTARY 1958, *supra* note 102, art. 54; Katharine Fortin, *Abducting Dissent: Kidnapping Public Officials in Occupied Ukraine*, ARTICLES OF WAR (Mar. 22, 2022), https://lieber.westpoint.edu/kidnapping-public-officials-occupied-ukraine/; OSCE, Report on Violations of International Humanitarian and Human Rights Law, War Crimes and Crimes Against Humanity Committed in Ukraine Since 24 February 2022 18–19 (Apr. 13 2022).

3.6.1 Specific Obligations: Children, Essential Needs, Humanitarian Access, Cultural Property, and Gender

GCIV and API impose positive obligations and protections relating to children.[127] Chiefly, GCIV provides that the occupant must facilitate, with the cooperation of the local authorities, care and education for children.[128] This duty is expanded, in API, to a general negative duty of "special respect" for children, and positive duties to protect them against "any form of indecent assault" by third parties and to provide them with any "care and aid they require."[129] Furthermore, detained children must be held separately from adults, and enjoy special protection against the death penalty.[130] Indeed, some of the provisions relating to the protection of children under occupation are quite general. These provisions are therefore complemented by the Convention on the Rights of the Child.[131]

An arrangement of particular importance concerns the positive obligations of the occupant in relation to essential needs. During armed conflict, a belligerent is not required to *provide* the needs of civilians on the other side. Rather, its duty is *not to interfere* with humanitarian relief by third parties.[132] If, however, a territory is occupied, this negative duty transforms into a *positive* duty to provide. In this context, the law of occupation imposes positive obligations to ensure the food, medical supplies, clothing, means of shelter, and other supplies essential to the survival of the local population.[133] Furthermore, the occupant is under a duty, to the fullest extent of the means available, to maintain hospitals and to ensure—with the cooperation of local authorities—public health.[134] These general duties are complemented with rights enshrined under the ICESCR,[135] and the rules

[127] *See* DINSTEIN, *supra* note 1, 197–201.

[128] GCIV, *supra* note 4, art. 50.

[129] API, *supra* note 5, art. 77(1).

[130] *Id.* arts. 77(4), 77(5).

[131] Convention on the Rights of the Child, Nov. 20, 1989, 1577 U.N.T.S. 3. *See also* Legal Consequences of the Construction of a Wall in the Occupied Palestinian Territory, Advisory Opinion, 2004 I.C.J. Rep. 136 ¶ 112 (July 9) [hereinafter Wall Opinion]. *See* CRC, Concluding observations on the second to fourth periodic reports of Israel, adopted by the Committee at its sixty-third session (27 May–14 June 2013), CRC/C/ISR/CO/2-4 (July 4, 2013).

[132] GCIV, *supra* note 4, art. 23; API, *supra* note 5, arts. 70(1), 70(5).

[133] GCIV, *supra* note 4, art. 55; API, *supra* note 5, art. 69.

[134] GCIV, *supra* note 4, art. 56; API, *supra* note 5, arts. 14(1), 15(3); in the context of Covid-19, see Longobardo, *supra* note 4.

[135] International Covenant on Economic, Social and Cultural Rights, Dec. 16, 1966, 993 U.N.T.S. 3. The ICJ held, in the Wall Advisory Opinion, that the ICESCR indeed applies in occupied territories. Wall Opinion ¶ 112.

of global health law, including the International Health Regulations.[136] The occupant is also required to assist local civil defense organizations.[137]

The question on negative versus positive humanitarian obligations has been pertinent concerning the Gaza Strip. Owing to its position that Gaza is not occupied, Israel claims that it only bears negative obligations in relation to the population.[138] Approaches that view Gaza as occupied territory, whether on binary or functional grounds, result in positive duties to ensure the population its essential needs. For example, this has been the legal basis for most of the calls on Israel to provide Covid-19 vaccines to Palestinians in both the West Bank and Gaza.[139]

Importantly, the fact that the occupant is the de facto authority in the territory, and is bound by the positive duties discussed above, does not permit it to exclude humanitarian assistance by third parties. Thus, the occupant must allow and facilitate humanitarian access and relief consignments by third-party states and humanitarian organizations, if the population is "inadequately supplied."[140] In general, the occupant cannot divert such relief consignments,[141] and must allow their distribution by impartial humanitarian actors.[142] Importantly, the occupant cannot rely on relief actions by third parties to evade its own responsibilities.[143]

The issue of third-party relief has created some tensions between Israel and the EU. Based on its view that Palestinians are inadequately supplied, the EU, as well as its separate states, provide humanitarian funding for Palestinians, and other kinds of humanitarian aid.[144] However, Israel has frequently demolished EU-funded projects in the West Bank, arguing that they were illegal structures under local planning laws. The EU argues, in

[136] International Health Regulations, *supra* note 52. *See also* Longobardo, *supra* note 4, at 4.

[137] API, *supra* note 5, art. 63. Civil defense organizations are defined *id.* art. 61.

[138] HCJ 9132/07 Al-Bassiouni v. Prime Minister of Israel, Nevo Legal Database, ¶ 12 (Jan. 30, 2008); *see* discussion in Section 2.5.

[139] *See, e.g.*, *Israel: Provide Vaccines to Occupied Palestinians*, Human Rights Watch (Jan. 17, 2021), https://www.hrw.org/news/2021/01/17/israel-provide-vaccines-occupied-palestinians [hereinafter *Vaccines*, Human Rights Watch] *compare* Eyal Benvenisti, *Israel Is Legally Obligated to Ensure the Population in the West Bank and Gaza Strip Are Vaccinated*, Just Security (Jan. 7, 2021), https://www.justsecurity.org/74091/israel-is-legally-obligated-to-ensure-the-population-in-the-west-bank-and-gaza-strip-are-vaccinated/ (arguing that this duty emanates from Israel's prolonged blockade of Gaza).

[140] GCIV, *supra* note 4, art. 59. *See also* API, *supra* note 5, arts. 69(2), 71.

[141] Unless in cases of "urgent necessity" and in the interest of the occupied population, with the consent of a Protecting Power (or its substitute). *See* GCIV, *supra* note 4, art. 60.

[142] *Id.* art. 61(1).

[143] *Id.* art. 60.

[144] European Civil Protection and Humanitarian Aid Operations: Palestine (Sept. 23, 2021), https://ec.europa.eu/echo/where/middle-east/palestine_en.

turn, that such demolitions are unlawful under international law.[145] While it is clear that humanitarian aid should conform with the law in force in the occupied territory, this must be subject to the general principle that the law is applied for the benefit of the local population, and not for internationally unlawful reasons such as construction of settlements. In such cases, it would be difficult to argue that third parties must respect the occupant's restrictions on humanitarian projects.

A particularly detailed arrangement exists concerning cultural property. The occupant must act positively to safeguard the cultural property in the occupied territory, and cooperate with local authorities, whether against destruction, removal, or transfer of such property.[146] Last, while GCIV and API contain several provisions relating to the protection of women, these are quite general, and the law of occupation's dearth of specific positive obligations in the field of gender protection—including in relation to LGBTQ rights—can indeed be criticized.[147] However, in this case also, IHRL obligations stemming from CEDAW and other relevant international norms on gender can impose further obligations on the occupant, giving content to the general norms of the law of occupation.[148]

3.6.2 Cooperation with National and Local Authorities

Some provisions imposing specific obligations on the occupant require that these be discharged with the cooperation of national and local authorities.

[145] *See* Euro-Med Monitor, Squandered Aid, Israel's Repetitive Destruction of EU-Funded Projects in Palestine (Mohammed Shehada, Catherine Charrett & Dina Asaad eds., 2016); *Joint Stake-out by the Current and Former EU Members of the Security Council, and Norway and the UK*, France ONU (Feb. 26, 2021), https://onu.delegfrance.org/middle-east-we-reiterate-our-call-on-israel-to-halt-demolitions-and.

[146] Convention for the Protection of Cultural Property in the Event of Armed Conflict art. 5, May 14, 1954, 249 U.N.T.S. 215; Second Protocol to the Hague Convention of 1954 for the Protection of Cultural Property in the Event of Armed Conflict art. 9, March 26, 1999, 2253 U.N.T.S. 172; *see also* Dinstein, *supra* note 1, at 215–17; U.S. Dep't Def., Law of War Manual, 790–92 (2016) [hereinafter DoD Manual].

[147] *See* GCIV, *supra* note 4, art. 27(2); API, *supra* note 5, art. 76; *see also* Fionnuala Ní Aoláin, *Gendering the Law of Occupation: The Case of Cyprus*, 27 Minn. J. Int'l L. 107 (2018); *see generally* Noelle Quenivet, *Special Rules on Women*, *in* Clapham et al., *supra* note 9, 1271; Judith Gardam, *Women, Human Rights and International Humanitarian Law*, 38 Int'l Rev. Red Cross 421(1998).

[148] Convention on the Elimination of All Forms of Discrimination against Women, Dec. 18, 1979, 1249 U.N.T.S. 1.

This is notably the case with the working of educational and care institutions for children[149] and the maintenance of public health.[150] The requirement of cooperation might suggest that in these specific cases, the burden of responsibility is shared between the occupant and local authorities. According to Pictet, the cooperation requirement means that the occupant alone is not "responsible for the whole burden of organizing hospitals and health services and taking measures to control epidemics."[151]

The meaning of the cooperation requirement has arisen in the context of Israel's refusal to take responsibility for vaccinating Palestinians in the West Bank against Covid-19. Israel's main argument was that public health was the responsibility of the Palestinian Authority, in accordance with the Oslo Accords.[152] However, this bilateral agreement cannot derogate from the law of occupation, owing to the non-derogation clause in article 47 GCIV.[153] Beyond that, the duty to cooperate does not absolve the occupant from the ultimate responsibility, if the local authorities cannot discharge their obligations. Rather, it is primarily a duty to approach the local authorities, consult with them, and offer cooperation before acting unilaterally if needed.

The latter interpretation is strengthened when contextualizing the duties to cooperate. These duties are enshrined in relation to children's education and public health and hygiene, aspects which often touch upon sensitive and traditional values in a given society. The requirement to seek the cooperation of the local authorities in these fields can be understood as primarily meant to prevent external intervention in sensitive issues. This understanding is augmented by the fact that GCIV provides, beyond the cooperation requirement, that in adopting health measures the occupant shall consider "the moral and ethical susceptibilities of the population."[154] Granted, these provisions can be criticized as enshrining patriarchal and gendered norms. However, this background serves to highlight that the duty of cooperation is mostly about the need to consult with local authorities, not about transferring responsibility.

[149] GCIV, *supra* note 4, art. 50.

[150] *Id.* art. 56.

[151] ICRC, Commentary 1958, *supra* note 102, at 313.

[152] *See* TOI Staff, *High Court Petition Demands Israel Supply West Bank, Gaza with Virus Vaccines*, Times of Israel (Mar. 25, 2021), https://www.timesofisrael.com/high-court-petition-demands-israel-supply-west-bank-gaza-with-virus-vaccines/.

[153] *See* Section. 2.5.3; *Vaccines*, Human Rights Watch, *supra* note 139.

[154] GCIV, *supra* note 4, art. 56(3).

4
Maintaining Public Order in Occupied Territories
Prolonged and Transformative Occupation

This chapter continues discussing the scope of the occupant's powers in light of the conservationist principle. It deals with two general issues: the effect of time over these powers ("prolonged occupation"); and the question whether, in certain cases, the occupant can significantly transform the institutional and physical situation in the territory in a permanent manner ("transformative occupation").

The two share some similarities. Prolonged and transformative occupations might overlap, since many transformative occupations will be prolonged, and many prolonged occupations will ultimately become transformative. Furthermore, both occupations, as legal doctrines, run the risk of facilitating the entrenchment of occupation and the occupant's interests.[1] However, the concepts should remain analytically distinct. Prolonged occupation refers to the temporal scope of the occupation and its effects over the occupant's powers. Transformative occupation, conversely, refers to the *policies* of the occupation.

4.1 Prolonged Occupation

4.1.1 Occupation and Time: The Concept and Predicaments of Prolonged Occupation

Recall that the law of occupation requires that the occupant restore and ensure public order and safety, while respecting the status quo ante.[2] In

[1] *See* Aeyal Gross, The Writing on the Wall: Rethinking the Law of Occupation 38 (2017).

[2] Convention (IV) respecting the Laws and Customs of War on Land and its annex: Regulations concerning the Laws and Customs of War on Land art. 43, Oct. 18, 1907,

parallel, although the law of occupation envisions temporariness, it does not provide an explicit cap on the duration of occupation.[3] Likewise, there is no clear guidance in the relevant treaties concerning the effect of time over the occupant's powers and obligations, or over its discretion when promoting them.[4]

It is clear that as occupation is prolonged, the tensions between the occupant's trusteeship obligations and the conservationist principle become more pronounced. On the one hand, from the point of view of the interests of the local population, freezing the legal, economic, and infrastructural situation pre-occupation becomes less tenable as time passes.[5] However, as time passes, occupation challenges more the same ideas of self-determination that the law of occupation claims to protect.[6] Additionally, the occupant becomes more entangled in the territory, accentuating the conflicts between the occupant's own interests and its trusteeship obligations.[7] The passage of time therefore pulls in two opposite directions: it pushes for wider powers, while simultaneously making such changes more intrusive in terms of self-determination, and more suspect in their motivations.

These dynamics have led to much preoccupation with *prolonged occupation*, and the manner in which it affects occupants' powers and obligations.[8] It should be emphasized that prolonged occupation is not a distinct legal category. Rather, the passage of time might affect the internal balance between the interests protected by the law of occupation.[9] This change of

187 C.T.S.227 [hereinafter Hague IV]; Convention (IV) relative to the Protection of Civilian Persons in Time of War art. 64, Aug. 12, 1949, 6 U.S.T. 3516, 75 U.N.T.S. 287 [hereinafter GCIV]; *see* Chapter 3.

[3] Regarding the possible illegality of indefinite occupation, see Sections 1.4.3–1.4.4.

[4] Eyal Benvenisti, The International Law of Occupation 244 (2d ed. 2012). In relation to article 6(3) GCIV see Section 1.4.3.

[5] *Compare* Adam Roberts, *Prolonged Military Occupation: The Israeli-Occupied Territories Since 1967*, 84 Am. J. Int'l L. 44, 45 (1990), *with* David Hughes, *Moving from Management to Termination: A Case Study of Prolonged Occupation*, 44 Brook. J. Int'l. L 109, 130–48 (2018).

[6] As well as on rights in general. *See, e.g.*, Fionnuala Ní Aoláin, *The Gender of Occupation*, 45 Yale J. Int'l L. 335 (2020).

[7] *See* HCJ 2056/04 Beit Sourik Village Council v. The Government of Israel, 58(5) PD 807 ¶ 27 (2004) (Isr.).

[8] *See* sources cited in Vaios Koutroulis, *The Application of International Humanitarian Law and International Human Rights Law in Situations of Prolonged Occupation: Only a Matter of Time?* 94 Int'l Rev. Red Cross 165, 171 nn.27–28 (2012).

[9] Roberts, *supra* note 5, at 51; Hanne Cuyckens, Revisiting the Law of Occupation 112 (2017); Koutroulis, *supra* note 8, at 170.

balance can be supplemented by increased obligations under IHRL, stemming from the entrenchment of control in the territory.[10]

The attempt to define the exact point in time when an occupation becomes "prolonged" has been labeled by Roberts a "pointless quest."[11] Roberts suggested, for pure methodological reasons, that such occupations are those lasting more than five years, and extending beyond the period of active hostilities.[12] The HCJ applied the reasoning of prolonged occupation as early as 1972, five years after the onset of occupation.[13] While article 6(3) of GCIV distinguishes between occupations lasting less and more than one year after "the general close of military operations," it has possibly fallen into *desuetude*.[14] Arguably, the definition of prolonged occupation should not be a bright-line rule, but a functional one: perhaps, as any case in which the needs of the local population have changed significantly since the occupation began, and because of this, a tension between these needs and the conservationist principle emerges.[15]

While the paradigmatic case of prolonged occupation is Israel's occupation of the Palestinian territories,[16] other cases include, for example, the allied occupations of Germany and Japan after WWII;[17] South Africa's occupation of Namibia;[18] Turkish occupation of Northern Cyprus; Morocco's occupation of Western Sahara;[19] and Russia's occupation of Crimea.[20] However, only in the case of the Palestinian territories and Iraq have the occupants admitted, even if partially, that they are bound by the law of occupation. Therefore, we will naturally focus on these examples.

[10] *Id.* at 194–200 and the sources cited therein.

[11] Roberts, *supra* note 5, at 47; *see* also Koutroulis, *supra* note 8, at 168–69.

[12] Roberts, *supra* note 5, at 47.

[13] HCJ 337/71 Christian Association for Holy Places v. Minister of Def., 26(1) PD 574 ¶ 8 (1972) (Isr.).

[14] *See* Chapter 1; *compare* Iain Scobbie, *International Law and the Prolonged Occupation of Palestine*, SSRN (May 20, 2015), https://papers.ssrn.com/sol3/papers.cfm?abstract_id=2611130, *with* Roberts, *supra* note 5, at 55–57, and Koutroulis, *supra* note 8, at 173.

[15] *Compare with* Gross, *supra* note 1.

[16] *See* Roberts, *supra* note 5; Hughes, *supra* note 5.

[17] Roberts, *supra* note 5, at 48–49.

[18] *Id.* at 49–50.

[19] *Id.* at 50.

[20] *See generally* Robin Geiß, *Russia's Annexation of Crimea: The Mills of International Law Grind Slowly But They Do Grind*, 91 Int'l L. Stud. 425, 444–47 (2015).

4.1.2 The Doctrine of "Prolonged Occupation": Widening the Occupant's Discretion and The Perils of Doing So

It is widely accepted that the prolongation of occupation might result in increased discretion and powers for the occupant in some aspects, and limitations in others.[21] The common approach is that the passage of time allows the occupant more discretion to change the *status quo ante for the benefit of the local population*, while the justification for sweeping security measures decreases.[22] As mentioned above, there are inherent tensions within this notion. While there is appeal in the idea that the territory should not be "frozen" as time passes, the concept is troublesome absent parallel recognition of local participation rights, particularly where the occupant's interests are entangled in the territory.[23] Furthermore, one should consider the critical insight that the need for "development" as time passes is certainly not a neutral concept, and can in itself be viewed as an imposition of a certain ideology of governance.[24]

The HCJ's frequent deployment of the prolonged occupation doctrine, throughout the years, demonstrates these dynamics. Some of the doctrine's earliest invocations could seem quite benign, but, as the decades passed, the doctrine allowed the interests of the occupant to be accorded a central role. Several cases, throughout the decades, demonstrate this trend. In the *Christian Association* case of 1972, the Court allowed amendments to the local law on labor disputes—rejecting local employers' claim that these contradict the conservationist principle—on the reasoning that in prolonged occupation "the occupant's obligation towards the local population

[21] Roberts, *supra* note 5, at 53; Koutroulis, *supra* note 8, at 186.

[22] *See* Tristan Ferraro, ICRC, Expert Meeting: Occupation and Other Forms of Administrations of Foreign Territory 72–74 (2012) [hereinafter ICRC, Expert Meeting]. *See also* Albert Leurquin, *The German Occupation in Belgium and Article 43 of The Hague Convention of the 18th October 1907*, 1 Int. L. Notes 55 (1916); *cited in* Edmund H. Schwenk, *Legislative Power of the Military Occupant Under Article 43 Hague Regulations*, 54 Yale L. J. 393, 399 (1945); Doris Appel Graber, The Development of the Law of Belligerent Occupation, 1863–1914: A Historical Survey 290 (1949); Ernst H. Feilchenfeld, The International Economic Law of Belligerent Occupation 49 (1942).

[23] *See* David Kretzmer & Yaël Ronen, The Occupation of Justice: The Supreme Court of Israel and the Occupied Territories ch. 8 (2d ed. 2021); *see also* Gross, *supra* note 1, at 46–51.

[24] *See generally* Sundhya Pahuja, Decolonising International Law: Development, Economic Growth and the Politics of Universality (2011).

even obliges it to change the law, since the needs of society change as time passes."[25]

In the *Arjoub* case of 1988, the Court ruled that although the law of occupation does not require establishing a military court of appeal in occupied territories, as time passes and "life returns to normal," the military justice system should not "continue to symbolize war [and] temporariness" and resemble more "a fair and perfect legal system."[26] While requiring the establishment of a separate appellate court might seem compelling, the reference to the need to avoid the semblance of temporariness, demonstrates the danger of conflation between prolongation and permanency.

Other applications of the prolonged occupation doctrine highlight the entanglement of interests that it facilitates. The *Value Added Tax (VAT)* case is pertinent.[27] Soon after the occupation began, Israel took various steps to economically integrate the territories with Israel.[28] When Israel introduced VAT in its own territory in 1976, it simultaneously introduced it in the occupied territories.[29] Rejecting petitioners' arguments that this would only serve Israeli interests, the HCJ cited the passage of time as broadening the occupant's powers to ensure public order, including through economic integration.[30] This ruling was criticized as facilitating "economic annexation" through the prolonged occupation doctrine.[31] Furthermore, as integration often serves the interests of the economically stronger occupant, the ruling demonstrates how the doctrine of prolonged occupation can serve to blur the line between the interests of the occupant and those of the local population.

A ruling that simultaneously serves as a landmark case on prolonged occupation and further demonstrates the growing entanglement of interests in such situations is the *Jam'iat Iscan* case of 1983.[32] The military commander decided to expropriate private Palestinian land near Ramallah, in order to build

[25] HCJ 337/71 Christian Association for Holy Places v. Minister of Def., 26(1) PD 574 ¶ 8 (1972) (Isr.).

[26] HCJ 87/85 Arjoub v. IDF Commander of Judea and Samaria et al., 42(1) PD 353, 365 ¶ 15 (1988) (Isr.).

[27] HCJ 69/81 Abu Aita v. Commander of the Judea and Samaria Area, 37(2) PD 197 (1983) (Isr.). We return to this case in Chapter 6, when we discuss economic integration under occupation.

[28] Benvenisti, *supra* note 4, at 224–27.

[29] *Abu Aita*, 37(2) PD ¶ 2.

[30] *Id.* ¶¶ 50(e), 52.

[31] Benvenisti, *supra* note 4, at 242–43.

[32] HCJ 393/82 Jam'iat Iscan Al-Ma'almoun v. IDF Commander of Judea and Samaria, 37(4) PD 785 (1983) (Isr.).

a highway. It claimed that the highway would connect between Palestinian cities, but crucially also between central Israel and Jerusalem, through the West Bank.[33] The landowners argued that the highway was meant to serve the transportation needs of Israel itself, rather than local needs. Alternatively, they claimed, the occupant could not make permanent and far-reaching changes in the territory, such as building highways.[34] The state conceded that the road would also benefit Israelis, but argued that this benefit was secondary to its primary purpose of serving the local population. It also invoked the doctrine of prolonged occupation, claiming that the military administration was required to develop the territory's outdated road system.[35]

The Court ruled that a road cannot be built solely as a "service road" for the benefit of the occupant state *only*, but must reflect the "best interest of the local population."[36] Having accepted with no significant challenge that Israel's civilian needs were not the motivation for the plan, it moved to discuss whether the military administration may carry out infrastructural projects.[37] While in short-term occupation, it ruled, "military-security needs reign supreme," in prolonged occupation "the needs of the local population receive extra validity."[38] These needs, as time passes, are in constant motion, and therefore "the power of the military government extends to taking all necessary measures to ensure growth, change and development,"[39] including to making permanent infrastructural investments.[40] It further ruled that the good of the local population *itself* calls for development cooperation between the military administration and external elements, *including the occupying state*.[41] Importantly, the court did not consider the immense Israeli interests in the road as casting doubt on its alleged primary purpose to serve the local population.[42] It also did not consider the "cooperation" between the military administration and the occupying state as warranting extra scrutiny.[43]

[33] *Id.* ¶¶ 1–3.
[34] *Id.* ¶¶ 7–8.
[35] *Id.* ¶¶ 5–6.
[36] *Id.* ¶ 13.
[37] *Id.* ¶¶ 14, 16.
[38] *Id.* ¶ 22.
[39] *Id.* ¶ 26.
[40] *Id.* ¶ 27.
[41] *Id.* ¶ 28.
[42] Indeed, decades later, the road mainly serves Israelis travelling from central Israel to Jerusalem. Gross, *supra* note 1, at 49.
[43] Under similar reasoning, the HCJ permitted the expropriation of property for the purpose of building a fast rail between Tel Aviv and Jerusalem, parts of which ran through the

Ultimately, the prolonged occupation doctrine was deployed in a manner that almost explicitly moved the occupant's own interests to center stage.[44] In the *Quarries* case, at hand was the legality of Israeli-owned quarries in the West Bank, which were licensed by the military administration and transferred virtually all of their production to Israel, while paying fees and royalties to the military administration.[45] The petitioners argued that the quarrying did not serve the local population. Rather, because the minerals were transferred to Israel or its settlements, and the profits were mainly enjoyed by Israeli companies, the quarries promoted the financial interests of Israel.[46] The state argued primarily that the status of quarries had been settled under the Oslo Accords and alternatively that the quarries served the best interest of the area. Especially in prolonged occupation, it claimed, an "interpretive adjustment" of article 43 was needed to prevent "economic stagnation."[47] Concerning the latter argument, the Court ruled that the prolongation of the occupation requires adjusting law "to the reality on the ground," including to the need to maintain economic relations between the occupied territory and the occupying state.[48] In view of the prolonged occupation, it held, the quarries actually benefit the local population: some minerals are sold to Palestinians; royalties are used by the military administration within the territory; the quarries employ Palestinians and regularly contract with local service providers.[49] Ultimately, the language of prolonged occupation enabled moving Israeli needs to the center:[50] while the quarries might provide *some* benefits to the local economy, these are at best secondary and were in no way the dominant objective of the occupant's actions.[51]

West Bank. *See* HCJ 281/11 Head of Beit Icsa Council v. Minister of Def., Nevo Legal Database (June 9, 2011) (Isr.).

[44] For a similar critique, see, e.g., Micheline Deeik & Asem Khalil, *Prolonged Occupation Under International Humanitarian Law*, BIRZEIT U. WORKING PAPERS SERIES IN LEGAL STUD. (5/2020).

[45] HCJ 2164/09 Yesh Din v. IDF Commander in the West Bank, Nevo Legal Base (Dec. 26, 2011) (Isr.). We discuss in detail the issue of natural resources in Chapter 6.

[46] *Id.* ¶¶ 3, 9.

[47] *Id.* ¶¶ 4, 8–9.

[48] *Id.* ¶ 10.

[49] *Id.* ¶¶ 12–13.

[50] *See also* David Kretzmer, *The Law of Belligerent Occupation in the Supreme Court of Israel*, 94 INT'L REV. RED CROSS 207, 222 (2012).

[51] Yet, the Court did not explicitly adopt a "dominant objective" test. *Compare* HCJ 281/11 Head of Beit Icsa Council v. Minister of Def., Nevo Legal Database ¶ 27 (June 9, 2011) (Isr.) *with* KRETZMER & RONEN, *supra* note 23, at 147–55.

Last, even the notion that prolonged occupation requires lenience in security measures has not played a significant role in practice. In the *Warrants* case of 2021, petitioners challenged the legality of the IDF's practice of conducting "searches" in Palestinian homes without judicial warrants. As they claimed, this practice was unlawful under the parallel application of the law of occupation and IHRL. This interpretation, they claimed, was merited also when considering the duration of the occupation and the adverse effects of this longstanding practice.[52]

The Court held that no explicit requirement for judicial warrants prior to home searches exists under either IHL or IHRL (which it declined to apply de jure). It further held that GCIV's requirements of humane treatment were upheld by the military order that stipulated the conditions for such searches.[53] The claim that prolonged occupation itself calls for a more lenient approach was rejected by one justice, holding that time alone "does not diminish the military commander's duty to maintain the security of the area and to prevent terror attacks."[54] Another suggested that due to the prolongation of the occupation and the infringement of rights caused by entry into homes, the military commander should consider enshrining the procedure and conditions for searches in security legislation—rather than in operational orders.[55] None of the justices accepted that prolonged occupation requires adopting due process protections similar to those applying in Israel, or, for that matter, to Israeli settlers in the West Bank.[56]

4.1.3 The Doctrine of "Prolonged Occupation": Increased Participation Rights?

As demonstrated above, the passage of time might not only serve to justify wider interventions in the status quo ante. It also deepens the possible infringement of the right to self-determination, and intensifies conflicts of interest. To alleviate these problems, it is reasonable that in parallel to the wider powers entailed by prolonged occupation, the doctrine should also

[52] HCJ 2189/20 Hamid v. IDF Commander in the West Bank, Nevo Legal Database ¶¶ 4–7 (Sept. 1, 2021) (Isr.) (Justice Vilner).
[53] *Id.* ¶ 21 ¶¶ 26–34.
[54] *Id.* ¶ 4 (Justice Vogelman).
[55] *Id.* (Justice Elron).
[56] *Id.* ¶¶ 36–37 (Justice Vilner), ¶ 5 (Justice Vogelman).

require local participation in decision-making.[57] In terms of legal sources for such obligations, participation rights can be read into article 43, as an integral part of the trusteeship duties of the occupant. Additionally, and similar to the case of the applicability of administrative law principles during occupation, participation rights can be strengthened by the parallel application of IHRL.[58]

This notion has some support.[59] Roberts argued that in prolonged occupation the occupant must give greater weight tothe will of the local population.[60] Others argue that, as time passes, the occupant is less justified to restrict self-rule, for example by suspending municipal elections.[61] But participation might go beyond noninterference in municipal elections. Arguably, in prolonged occupation, the law of occupation should encourage local participation across the board.[62] Such participation can take the form of delegation of powers to local officials; of consultation with local representatives prior to the adoption of important initiatives; of establishing joint administrative agencies, and so forth.[63]

For example, during the initial stages of the occupation of Iraq, the CPA "recognized" the Governing Council of Iraq,[64] established pursuant to UNSC Resolution 1483, which called for the formation of "an Iraqi interim administration."[65] Formally, the CPA resolved to "consult and coordinate" with the Governing Council "on all matters involving the temporary governance of Iraq."[66] A much earlier example is the acquiescence of the Allies, in 1919, for Germany's appointment of a "Reichskommissar" for the Allied-occupied Rhineland, that served as a quasi-ambassador for Germany in the territory. The Reichskommissar mediated between the local population and

[57] *But see* HCJ 5667/11 Dirat-Rif'aya Village Council v. Minister of Def., Nevo Legal Database (June 9, 2015) (Isr.).

[58] *See* Section 3.5.2.

[59] ICRC, Expert Meeting, *supra* note 22, at 75–76.

[60] Roberts, *supra* note 5.

[61] *See* Moshe Drori, *Municipal Elections in Occupied Judea and Samaria*, 9 Isr. L. Rev. 97, 100–01 (1974).

[62] Benvenisti, *supra* note 4, at 247.

[63] *Id.*; Emma Playfair, *Playing on Principle? Israel's Justification for Its Administrative Acts in the Occupied West Bank*, *in* International Law and the Administration of Occupied Territories: Two Decades of Israeli Occupation of the West Bank and Gaza Strip 205 (Emma Playfair ed., 1992).

[64] CPA Regulation No. 6, Governing Council of Iraq, ¶ 1 CPA/REG/13 July 2003/06 (July 13, 2003).

[65] S.C. Res. 1483, ¶ 9 (May 22, 2003).

[66] CPA Reg. No. 6, Governing Council of Iraq, ¶ 2(1).

administrative agencies and the occupants; and the occupants' orders were presented for its examination before enactment.[67]

Nonetheless, it is quite possible that the local population would refuse to participate in such procedures, for fear of normalization and legitimation of the occupation. But this does not affect the occupant's possible obligation to genuinely offer such participation. It also should be stressed that while prolonged occupation might require increased local participation, local participation in itself cannot be used to legitimate the prolonging of occupation.

An interesting question is whether in extreme cases of prolonged occupation, the occupant must not only grant the occupied population participation rights in the occupation administration, but must also grant it rights within the occupant's *own* political system, namely through voting rights. Some commentators have made such an argument. It seems that such an obligation, to that extent that it exists, would not stem directly from the law of occupation but from the right to self-determination or IHRL, and could only be valid—and we cannot exhaust this question here—in cases where the occupation amounts to de facto annexation, either because the occupant does not intend to end the occupation or because it treats the territory as its own.[68]

4.2 Transformative Occupation

4.2.1 Definition and Modalities

As with prolonged occupation, there is no formal legal category of transformative occupation.[69] Roberts, who coined the term, defined the concept as a situation where in the name of advancing "a more democratic and peaceful state," the occupant introduces fundamental changes to the constitutional, social, economic, and legal order.[70] This definition includes

[67] *See* Ernst Fraenkel, Military Occupation and the Rule of law: Occupation Government in the Rhineland, 1918–1923 111–16 (1944).

[68] *See* Ariel Zemach, *The Emerging Right of West Bank Palestinians to Israeli Citizenship*, 42 U. Penn. J. Int'l L. 271 (2020); Itamar Mann & Yael Berda, *Voting as a Vehicle for Self-Determination in Palestine and Israel*, 100 Tex. L. Rev 941 (2022).

[69] Cuyckens, *supra* note 9, at 114.

[70] Adam Roberts, *Transformative Military Occupation: Applying the Laws of War and Human Rights*, 100 Am. J. Int'l L. 580, 581 (2006).

both a quantitative ("fundamental changes") and qualitative ("a more democratic") element. While analytically, transformative occupation does not require a specific motivation, it is true that many cases of such occupations—for example, the mandate system, post–WWII Germany, and post-2003 Iraq—were formally portrayed as promoting liberal values. This, however, does not exclude the possibility of what Fox calls "non-liberal transformations," where transformation seeks to *restrict* individual rights and self-determination.[71] While, as we shall see, there is debate on the lawfulness of the former, it is clear that transformations which fall under the "dark side of this category"[72] would be unlawful. Of course, the challenge would be to distinguish between these categories. It is unsurprising, therefore, that the idea of transformative occupation has been criticized as a cover for annexation,[73] imperialism,[74] or dictatorship.[75]

Indeed, the idea of transformative occupation runs counter to the conservationist principle, and also to self-determination, which enshrines the right of the people to freely determine their political fate. The basic dilemma of transformative occupation, however, is that self-determination can push toward the opposite conclusion: If the occupant is bound to respect self-determination and basic rights, how can it be expected to uphold regimes that contravene these ideals?[76] Be that as it may, to the extent that transformative occupation is possible, it can only result in the relaxation of the conservationist principle. It cannot relax the occupant's trusteeship obligations and allow it to exploit the territory.

Transformative occupation is legally distinct from cases where an occupant transfers power back to an independent local government, yet remains in the territory "in support" of it.[77] If the transfer of power was genuine, and the consent to the previous occupant's presence was valid, changes enacted

[71] Gregory H. Fox, *Transformative Occupation and the Unilateralist Impulse*, 94 Int'l Rev Red Cross 237, 245 (2012).

[72] Gross, *supra* note 1, at 45.

[73] *Id.* at 38–51.

[74] *See* Kerry Rittich, *Occupied Iraq: Imperial Convergences*, 31 Leid. J. Int'l L. 479 (2018); Matthew Craven, *The Tyranny of Strangers: Transformative Occupations Old and New*, 9 London Rev. Int'l L. 197 (2021); Ralph Wilde, International Territorial Administration: How Trusteeship and the Civilizing Mission Never Went Away 324–26 (2008).

[75] Nehal Bhuta, *The Antinomies of Transformative Occupation*, 16 Eur. J. Int'l L. 721 (2005).

[76] *See* Fox, *supra* note 71, at 241.

[77] As was in post-2004 Iraq. *See* Section 2.5.3.

by the new government are not instances of transformative occupation in the strict sense, since there is no longer an occupation.

In the next sections, we analyze different legal arguments that were presented for transformation of territories. As we shall see, some are more tenable than others. Generally, it seems that absent UNSC authorization, it is difficult to square the massive changes involved in full-scale transformative occupation with the basic notions of the law of occupation.

4.2.2 Reading Transformative Powers into Article 43 Hague

Arguments for transformative occupation sometimes rely on norms internal to the law of occupation. Such an argument would be that, for instance, as time passes, the good of the local population requires significant changes in the territory, overriding the conservationist principle.[78] This view is reminiscent of the HCJ's application of the prolonged occupation doctrine. It is in this sense that there is a significant overlap between the doctrines of prolonged and transformative occupation.

Of course, an immediate question concerns the upper limits of transformation, even if it is accepted that in prolonged occupation significant changes can be made. In the jurisprudence of the HCJ, two limitations seem to emerge. One is where transformation amounts to de facto annexation. In the *Mara'abe* case, the Court ruled that no measures—in this case, constructing "a separation fence" in the West Bank—can be undertaken for annexationist purposes.[79] In practice, mainly due to the HCJ's apprehension from ruling on the legality of the settlements, this upper limit has not been effective. In the *Jam'iat Iscan* case, the Court advanced another limit to transformation, according to which "substantive changes of a permanent character to the political, administrative or judicial institutions" of the territory cannot be made "other than in extraordinary cases such as where existing institutions contravene, in content, the principles of basic justice and morality."[80]

[78] *Compare* Michael N. Schmitt & Charles H.B. Garraway, *Occupation Policy in Iraq and International Law*, 9 J. INT'L PEACEKEEPING 27 (2005), *cited in* CUYCKENS, *supra* note 9, at 118.

[79] HCJ 7957/04 Mara'abe v. Prime Minister of Israel, 60(2) PD 477 ¶ 15 (2005) (Isr.).

[80] HCJ 393/82 Jam'iat Iscan Al-Ma'almoun v. IDF Commander of Judea and Samaria, 37(4) PD 785 ¶ 23 (emphasis added) (1983) (Isr.).

On this view, while significant changes can be introduced, at least in prolonged occupation, these cannot include permanent changes to the institutional structure of the territory, unless it contradicts basic moral principles. This is an explicitly naturalist reading of article 43 Hague. Indeed, support for the idea that natural law overrides the conservationist principle could be found in some writings on the WWII occupation of Germany. Jennings, for instance, argued that even if article 43 Hague applied to the allied occupation—which, as we see below, he denied—the Allies were not only competent to modify Nazi law but *obligated* to do so, because German law was contrary to "the most elementary principles of natural law and justice."[81]

However, it is doubtful that natural law can be an effective benchmark for the legal assessment of transformation, not least because its application in concrete situations is contested, and can be readily abused.[82] Moreover, if the occupant invokes natural law to justify far-reaching reforms, it is unclear why it should not consider the will of the local population, as self-rule too is part of any credible conception of morality.

4.2.3 Transformation through the Application of IHRL

Considering the above, it is unsurprising that positive IHRL has been invoked—perhaps as a substitute for natural law—to justify changes in occupied territories. Recall, that article 64 GCIV establishes the supremacy of GCIV over the local law. Does this imply that IHRL *also* trumps the local law, when these norms clash?[83] If this is the case, there is, at least theoretically, a wide space for transformation—ranging from the suspension of specific laws to a complete institutional overhaul.

If a local law violates IHRL, and the occupant maintains it, it could be responsible for failing to ensure the rights of individuals in the territory.[84] For this reason, the Danish *Military Manual* states that in such cases the occupant is obliged by IHRL—and authorized by GCIV—to change the

[81] R.Y. Jennings, *Government in Commission*, 23 Brit. Y.B. Int'l L. 112, 132 (1946).

[82] *Compare* Scott J. Shapiro, Legality 275 (2011).

[83] Of course, some states argue that IHRL does not apply extraterritorially and during occupation. Yet, as previously discussed, this is the minority view. *See* Section 1.1.3.

[84] *See, e.g.*, Al-Skeini v. Sec'y of State for Def. [2007] UKHL 26, [2008] 1 AC 153 (HL) ¶ 129. Unless the occupant makes a lawful derogation from the relevant IHRL provisions. *See* Marco Sassòli, *Legislation and Maintenance of Public Order and Civil Life by Occupying Powers*, 16 Eur. J. Int'l L. 661, 676 (2005).

local law.[85] Notably, however, the argument here is not that IHRL overrides local law directly, but that IHRL obligations can be read into articles 43 Hague and 64 GCIV.[86] Thus, the necessity of "maintaining public order" or maintaining "orderly government," as provided respectively by the articles could be interpreted to encompass ensuring basic rights.[87] Similarly, the supremacy of GCIV, established by article 64, can also be read to impose an obligation to ensure and respect basic rights, such as those enshrined in article 27 GCIV.[88] According to the rules of treaty interpretation, these provisions of the law of occupation should be interpreted in light of other international obligations, such as IHRL.[89]

An interesting construction can be found in the CPA's order on the freedom of assembly. There, the CPA suspended Iraqi penal laws which it deemed unreasonably restrictive of the rights to freedom of expression and peaceful assembly.[90] Like most CPA orders, it was based both on UNSC resolutions and "the laws and usages of war," and specifically the obligation to restore and maintain order. Acting within these powers, the CPA claimed that the restrictions in Iraqi law are "inconsistent with Iraq's human rights obligations."[91] Rather than admitting the CPA was bound by IHRL and therefore obligated to suspend these provisions, the CPA relied on *Iraq's* own obligations as the basis for its actions.

Be that as it may, IHRL—if indeed superior to local law or read into the law of occupation—could be understood as permitting or requiring two types of changes.[92] The first are *local changes*, which alter or suspend specific provisions only. One common example could be mitigating criminal

[85] Danish Ministry of Def., Military Manual on International Law Relevant to Danish Armed Forces in International Operations 437 (2016([hereinafter Danish Manual]; *see also* Sassòli, *supra* note 84, at 676.

[86] Danish Manual, *supra* note 85, at 437.

[87] *See* Siobhán Wills, *Occupation Law and Multi-National Operations: Problems and Perspectives*, 77 Brit. Y.B. Int'l L. 256, 267–68 (2006); Yutaka Arai-Takahashi, *Law-Making and the Judicial Guarantees in Occupied Territories*, *in* The 1949 Geneva Conventions: A Commentary 1421, 1427 (Andrew Clapham, Paola Gaeta & Marco Sassòli eds., 2015).

[88] *See* Arai-Takahashi, *supra* note 87, at 1427.

[89] Vienna Convention on the Law of Treaties of 1969 art. 31(2)(c), May 23 1969, 1155 U.N.T.S. 331. The dilemma concerning the relations between IHRL and local law is largely avoided if the occupied state itself is party to IHRL treaties. *See* Section 6.1.5.

[90] CPA Order No. 19, Freedom of Assembly, CPA/ORD/9 July 2003/19 (July 10, 2003), *reprinted in* 2 Stefan Talmon, The Occupation of Iraq: The Official Documents of the Coalition Provisional Authority and the Iraqi Governing Council 141 (2013).

[91] CPA Order No. 19, *supra* note 90, ¶ 1.

[92] *But see* Aeyal M. Gross, *Human Proportions: Are Human Rights the Emperor's New Clothes of the International Law of Occupation?*, 18 Eur. J. Int'l L. 1 (2007).

punishments or ensuring due process.[93] Other examples are the prohibition of child labor,[94] or the abolishment of the death penalty.[95] The second type comprises *structural* changes, relating to foundational norms. While it is easy to imagine situations in which changing structurally discriminating norms would be normatively compelling, if IHRL were to be read to authorize such structural changes, the distinction between occupation and sovereignty might collapse altogether. For this reason, the predominant view is careful to read such an authority into IHRL.[96]

Admittedly, the difference between local and structural changes is not always clear, and oftentimes, what the occupant perceives as a mere local change would seem to the occupied like an intrusive cultural intervention. Furthermore, even a local change, allegedly for human rights purposes, can be used by the occupant to promote its own interests.[97] For these reasons, it has been argued that occupants must grant a "margin of appreciation," so to speak, to the local interpretation of IHRL standards, and to restrict changes only to cases in which they are absolutely necessary in order to comply with IHRL.[98] Subject to the latter caveat, there is considerable support for the occupant's obligation and authority to enact local changes.[99]

A related complexity arises from the fact that the right to self-determination is also entrenched in IHRL. Sometimes, norms in force in the occupied territory would violate the right to self-determination, as

[93] *See, e.g.*, Norman Bentwich, *The Legal Administration of Palestine Under the British Military Occupation*, 1 Brit. Y.B. Int'l L. 139, 142–43 (1920); Meir Shamgar, *The Observance of International Law in the Administered Territories*, 1 Isr. Y.B. Hum. Rts. 262, 269 (1971); CPA Order No. 7, Penal Code, CPA/ORD/9 June 2003/07 (June 10, 2003).

[94] Sassòli, *supra* note 84, at 676.

[95] *See* Roberts, *supra* note 5, at 99. *See also* Section 5.3.1.

[96] ICRC, Expert Meeting, *supra* note 22, at 90–91; *see generally* Fox, *supra* note 71, at 242–49.

[97] For example, under the local West Bank law, land can be sold only to Jordanians, Palestinians, or foreigners of Arab descent. In 2019, Israel considered changing this rule to remove these ethnic distinctions. In practice, this would facilitate purchasing land for Israeli settlements. *See* IDF, Legal Advisor in Judea and Samaria, Letter to Deputy Attorney General, Review of the Limitations on Transactions in Private Land in Judea and Samaria—Consideration of the Need to Amend the Law (Apr. 9, 2019), https://www.haaretz.co.il/embeds/pdf_upload/2019/20190915-135450.pdf.

[98] Sassòli, *supra* note 84, at 677; ICRC, Expert Meeting, *supra* note 22, at 59.

[99] ICRC, Expert Meeting, *supra* note 22, at 58–59; Robert Kolb, *Occupation in Iraq Since 2003 and the Powers of the UN Security Council*, 90 Int'l Rev. Red Cross 29, 48–49 n.58 (2008).

enshrined in IHRL treaties.[100] This would particularly be the case where the ousted sovereign is an unequivocally oppressive regime. In such cases, the occupant is in a significant bind: self-determination under IHRL compels it to change the local foundational norms, while simultaneously, the conservationist principle—supposedly meant to entrench the same right—constrains it. Without exhausting the debate on this question, the solution might be found in self-determination itself: it requires, at least, that the occupant consult with and involve the local population if it seeks to make such change.[101] In Iraq, notably, the drafting and adoption of the new, post-occupation constitution in 2005 involved the convening of a constitutional assembly and ratification by referendum.[102] Moreover, this process took place under the auspices of UNSC resolutions. It seems logical that an occupant who does *not* enjoy the backing of the UNSC would not possess wider powers to exclude the local public from such decisions.

4.2.4 Transformation through Disapplication of Article 43 Hague

Another manner in which states sought to legitimate transformation was to argue that although a territory is occupied, and remains separate from the occupying state, the law of occupation in general—and the conservationist principle specifically—does not apply. The paradigmatic examples for such an argument are found in the post–WWII occupations of Germany and Japan.

After gaining control over Germany, the Allies made two seemingly conflicting moves. On the one hand, they explicitly asserted that Germany has not been annexed;[103] but, on the other, they proceeded with a transformative policy of de-Nazification, which clearly went beyond what the

[100] International Covenant on Civil and Political Rights art. 1(2), Dec. 16, 1966, 999 U.N.T.S. 171.

[101] *Compare* Sassòli, *supra* note 84, at 677–78; Benvenisti, *supra* note 4, at 271–73.

[102] For a survey of the process *see Note: Democracy in Iraq: Representation Through Ratification*, 119 Harv. L. Rev. 1201, 1201–06 (2006).

[103] *See* Declaration Regarding the Defeat of Germany and the Assumption of Supreme Authority with Respect to Germany by the Governments of the United States of America, the Union of Soviet Socialist Republics, the United Kingdom and the Provisional Government of the French Republic, June 5, 1945, *reprinted in* 3 Charles I Bevans, Treaties and Agreements of the United States of America, 1776–1949 1140 (1969).

conservationist principle allowed.[104] In the ensuing debate, several possible legal explanations were given. One view was that "where a political system constitutes a permanent threat to the maintenance and safety of the military forces of the occupant" it can be abolished.[105] This view, essentially, inserts the defensive logic under *jus ad bellum* into the occupant's considerations under *jus in bello*. It requires accepting that the level of threat posed by the occupied state affects the occupant's powers under IHL. This necessitates a conflation between *jus ad bellum* and *jus in bello*, which is usually shunned by international law.

Other arguments revolved around the legal implications of Germany's total defeat. Kelsen, notably, argued that Germany ceased to exist as a *state* ("*debellatio*"), and therefore the conservationist principle was quashed.[106] This view, however, was subject to intense critique by German scholars.[107] Indeed, it is in tension with the idea that states and governments are legally distinct, and in any case contradicts the principle of self-determination.

Jennings argued, conversely, that Germany remained a state, since the Allies *chose* not to annex it.[108] Yet, he still claimed that its occupation was not subject to Hague IV: first, the conservationist principle was made irrelevant because of Germany's complete subjugation, even if Germany continued to exist legally; and, second, because of the aggressive policies of Nazi Germany, it would be "an anachronism of the most damaging kind" to limit the Allies to the "ordinary law of occupation."[109] Today, this argument, too, would be strained. This is either because of the advent in 1949 of Common Article 2 to the Geneva Conventions, which applies "to all cases

[104] Jennings, *supra* note 81, at 125, 132–33; Pitman B. Potter, *Legal Bases and Character of Military Occupation in Germany and Japan*, 43 Am. J. Int'l L. 323, 324 (1994).

[105] Schwenk, *supra* note 22, at 403, *cited in* Sassòli, *supra* note 84, at 671.

[106] Hans Kelsen, *The Legal Status of Germany According to the Declaration of Berlin*, 39 Am. J. Int'l L. 518 (1945).

[107] *See generally* Josef L. Kunz, *The Status of Occupied Germany Under International Law: A Legal Dilemma*, 3 Western Pol. Q. 538 (1950). for a comparatively recent discussion, see Alexandra Kemmerer, *Atempausen des Rechts: Wenn die Ordnung verstummt, ist die Völkerrechtstheorie gefragt*, 5 Internationale Politik 52 (2005).

[108] Jennings, *supra* note 81, at 135–37. At the time, annexation following complete subjugation was still acceptable by some.

[109] *Id.* at 139–40; *see also* United States v. Altstoetter (the Justice Case), *in* 3 Trials of War Criminals Before the Nuremberg Military Tribunals Under Control Council Law No. 10 1063–81 (1951); *cited in* Yoram Dinstein, The International Law of Belligerent Occupation 36 (2d ed. 2019).

of partial *or total* occupation";[110] or because of the demise of the doctrines of subjugation and *debellatio*, as discussed above and in Chapter 1.[111]

In Japan, the argument for transformative powers could not be based on *debellatio*—since the local structure of government was largely retained. The occupant's enhanced powers—over and above the conventional law of occupation—were based on the Instrument of Surrender to which Japan and the Allies agreed.[112] This construction would also be highly problematic today, considering the heightened scrutiny required when consent is granted in situations of control.[113]

4.2.5 Transformation through International Mandates

In some transformative cases, the occupant might invoke a special international authorization. The League of Nations' mandate system is an early example of this mechanism, and emphasizes its relations to empire. The mandate system, rooted in article 22 of the Covenant of the League of Nations, entrusted to victor states territories they occupied in WWI and "inhabited by peoples not yet able to stand by themselves under the strenuous conditions of the modern world," to promote "the well-being and development" of such peoples as a "trust of civilization."[114] The explicitly transformative powers of such mandates prevailed "over the strait confines of the powers of a temporary military occupant."[115] In Palestine, for example, the transformative element of the mandate was invoked to facilitate the "re-establishment of Jewish nationality" in the territory, as well as to discard what the British viewed as a "*damnosa hereditas*" from the Ottoman Empire.[116]

The most well-known instance of transformation in recent decades, allegedly based on international authorization, is the occupation of Iraq in

[110] Dinstein, *supra* note 109, at 37; Roberts, *supra* note 70, at 603 (emphasis added).
[111] Section 1.4.4.
[112] Kunz, *supra* note 107, at 539; Benvenisti, *supra* note 4, at 160–61; for a comparable dynamic in the post–WWI occupation of the Rhineland, see *id.* at 30.
[113] *See* Section 2.5.3.
[114] League of Nations Covenant art. 22; *see generally* Susan Pedersen, The Guardians: The League of Nations and the Crisis of Empire (2015).
[115] Norman Bentwich, *Mandated Territories: Palestine and Mesopotamia (Iraq)*, 2 Brit. Y.B. Int'l L. 48, 50 (1921–22).
[116] Bentwich, *supra* note 115, at 52–53.

2003–04. Already during the invasion in March 2003, the U.S.-led coalition was concerned that the law of occupation would restrict far-reaching structural changes in Iraq. It was advised, therefore, that a UNSC resolution would be necessary to authorize such reforms.[117] UNSC Resolution 1483 was accordingly adopted under Chapter VII in May 22, 2003, several weeks after the occupation of Iraq.[118] The resolution called upon the coalition to comply with the law of occupation.[119] Simultaneously, however, it called upon the occupants to create "conditions in which the Iraqi people can freely determine their own political future."[120] It further called for the appointment of a UN Special Representative for Iraq, to report and assist the occupants in their actions in accordance with the resolution.[121] The occupants were also mandated to assist the Iraqis in forming a transitional administration until a recognized, representative government was established.[122]

Some doubted whether Resolution 1483, owing to its vague language, could be read to provide powers beyond the conventional law of occupation, and whether the UNSC is at all empowered to alter the application of the law of occupation.[123] This controversy of general international law is beyond the scope of this book. What is clear is that the occupants in Iraq indeed viewed themselves as enhanced occupants: possessing the powers and obligations of "regular" occupants, supplemented by wider transformative powers under Resolution 1483. For this reason, the CPA, established officially a week before the resolution's adoption,[124] referred to two sources of powers: "U.N. Security Council resolutions, including Resolution 1483," and "the laws and usages of war."[125] This formula was repeated in virtually all of the CPA's documents. This makes it problematic, from the perspective of the development of international law, to deduce universally applicable

[117] Minute from Lord Goldsmith to the PM, Iraq Authorisation for an Interim Administration (Mar. 26, 2003), *reproduced in* The National Archives: The Iraq Inquiry Declassified Documents, http://www.iraqinquiry.org.uk/media/46487/Goldsmith-advice-re-occupying-powers-26March2003.pdf; Roberts, *supra* note 70, at 609.

[118] S.C. Res. 1483, *supra* note 65.

[119] *Id.* ¶ 5.

[120] *Id.*

[121] *Id.* ¶ 8.

[122] *Id.* ¶ 9.

[123] *See notably* Fox, *supra* note 71, at 267–70; Kolb, *supra* note 99, at 47–49; *also* Sassòli, *supra* note 84, at 681–82; David J. Scheffer, *Beyond Occupation Law*, 97 Am. J. Int'l L. 842 (2003); Gregory H. Fox, *The Occupation of Iraq*, 36 Geo. J. Int'l L. 195 (2005). *but see* Dinstein, *supra* note 109, at 14–15; U.S. Dep't Def., Law of War Manual, 732 (2016).

[124] Roberts, *supra* note 70, at 612; Benvenisti, *supra* note 4, at 254–55.

[125] CPA Regulation No. 1, Coalition Provisional Authority, CPA/REG/16 May 2003/1 (May 16, 2003).

state practice from the CPA's actions. This is because it is exceedingly difficult to disentangle the powers which emanated, in the view of the CPA, from "conventional" law of occupation, and those stemming from special powers that it might have received under UNSC resolutions. This remains true although many of the CPA's transformative objectives were already laid down in the "Freedom Message to the Iraqi People," distributed by the Commander of the Coalition Forces on April 16, 2003, over a month before Resolution 1483.[126] The legal status of this message, before its confirmation in official CPA Orders, remains unclear.[127]

Under its alleged enhanced powers, the CPA transformed Iraq radically, politically and economically.[128] Some of the most criticized of these moves—both in terms of their intrusiveness and results—were Order No. 1 on the De-Ba'athification of Iraqi Society, which dismantled Iraq's ruling Ba'ath Party;[129] Order No. 2 on the Dissolution of Entities, which abolished many Iraqi institutions including the military;[130] Order No. 12 on Trade Liberalization Policy, which suspended customs duties;[131] and Order No. 39 on Foreign Investment, which drastically liberalized Iraq's foreign investment regime.[132] In terms of substantive justifications, Orders 1 and 2, for instance, referred to "human rights abuses" by these institutions. Order No. 39 made reference to the CPA's consultation and coordination on this issue with the Governing Council of Iraq, to a report by the UN Secretary General on the need to liberalize Iraqi economy, and to the coordination with international financial institutions.[133] Importantly, at least concerning Iraq's economic transformation and its relations with international financial institutions, the CPA was careful to make frequent references to the involvement of the Governing Council of Iraq.[134] Presumably, this emphasis was made because the interaction with such institutions results in

[126] General Tommy R. Franks, Freedom Message to the Iraqi People (Apr. 16, 2003) (on file with authors).

[127] For instance, see CPA Order No. 2, Dissolution of Entities, Preamble, CPA/ORD/23 May 2003/02 (May 23, 2003).

[128] *See* Benvenisti, *supra* note 4, 257–67.

[129] CPA Order No. 1, De-Ba'athification of Iraqi Society, CPA/ORD/16 May 2003/01 (May 16, 2003).

[130] CPA Order No. 2.

[131] CPA Order No. 12, Trade Liberalization Policy, CPA/PRD/7 June 2003/12 (Feb. 26, 2004).

[132] CPA Order No. 38, Reconstruction Levy, CPA/ORD/19 September 2003/38 (Sept. 19, 2003). For a detailed critique of these orders, see Rittich, *supra* note 74, at 491–96.

[133] CPA Order No. 38.

[134] *See, e.g.*, CPA Regulation No. 7, International Donor Assistance, CPA/REG/5 December 2003/07 (Dec. 5, 2003).

significant intervention in domestic economic choices, and has been widely criticized precisely on such grounds.[135] The period of this enhanced occupation formally ended in June 2004 with the adoption of UNSC Resolution 1546.[136]

In sum, for better or for worse, it is impossible to discuss the transformation of Iraq divorced from the involvement of the UNSC. To the extent that Resolution 1483 indeed authorized at least some of the CPA's more intrusive changes, it is highly doubtful that this implies that occupants possess such powers *absent* UNSC authorization.[137] Arguably, the mere fact that the occupants sought such a resolution indicates that they thought that the "conventional" law of occupation itself *does not* provide for such powers.[138]

4.2.6 Transforming Boundaries, Demography, Settlements, and Education

Recall, that even if we accept that some instances of transformative occupation can be lawful—on any of the bases mentioned above—transformative measures must still conform with the interests recognized by the law of occupation: namely, promoting the welfare of the local population. As mentioned above, it is extremely difficult in practice to disentangle "good" transformations—genuinely concerned with the local population—and "bad" transformations, catering mainly to the occupant's own interests. Yet, there are transformative measures that would be clearly unlawful. Common examples are attempts to change the boundaries or demographic composition of the territory.

Sometimes the occupant seeks to do so by reference to historic grievances. One example is Germany's attempt to separate the Flemings and Walloons during its occupation of Belgium in WWI, as part of its policy to empower the Flemish population to counter the French-leaning Walloons.[139] Since its establishment in 1831, Belgium saw tensions between

[135] *See, e.g.*, Rittich, *supra* note 74.

[136] S.C. Res. 1546 (June 8, 2004); *see also* Section 2.5.

[137] *See* Fox, *supra* note 71, at 270; *compare with* Benvenisti, *supra* note 4, at 270–71.

[138] For a discussion whether the UNSC is at all authorized to modify obligations under *jus in bello*, see Kolb, *supra* note 99, at 38; Sassòli, *supra* note 84, at 680–81; Yutaka Arai-Takahashi, The Law of Occupation: Continuity and Change of International Humanitarian Law, and Its Interaction with International Human Rights Law 72–85 (2009).

[139] Benvenisti, *supra* note 4, at 116–17.

the two communities, centered, at that time, mainly over language.[140] Germany undertook several measures to bolster the use of the Flemish language in education and public administration, in contravention of the law in force. Germany argued that this was necessary to alleviate historical injustices suffered by the Flemish, and was therefore lawful under the law of occupation.[141] The culmination of these actions was the creation of separate administrations for Flanders and Wallonia in 1917.[142] When local courts attempted to curtail these moves, they were suspended and replaced by new courts.[143]

Some of the contemporaneous critiques of Germany's measures might have been considered nowadays as adopting a too narrow view of the occupant's powers.[144] Perhaps some of Germany's actions would even be phrased today in the language of self-determination. Yet, it is clear that if the conservationist principle is to have any meaning, addressing historical grievances through partition is precisely the type of structural transformation that must be reserved for the local population, acting through its own political apparatus.[145] This is particularly true since exploiting historical grievances might serve the occupant's strategic interests, which makes such measures especially suspect.

A contemporary example of this problem is Turkey's "resettlement" program in areas it occupies in north Syria, both in Afrin and in northeast Syria.[146] In October 2019, Turkey commenced operation "Peace Spring" in the de facto autonomous Kurdish region of Rojava, allegedly in self-defense against Kurdish-led armed groups. One of its aims for the operation was facilitating the return of Syrian (non-Kurdish) refugees to the area—even if these are from other regions in Syria. For that purpose, it promised to build new villages and towns.[147] Clearly, such moves would serve Turkey's strategic interest to diminish Kurdish dominance in the area, which it views as a national security threat. However, Turkey based its reasoning on the

140 *Id.* at 117.

141 For instance, Germany decreed that Ghent University would become a Flemish-speaking university. Order of March 15, 1916, 7 Pasinomie 21 (1916).

142 Benvenisti, *supra* note 4, at 118.

143 *Id.*

144 *See, e.g.*, James Wilford Garner, International Law and the World War 88–89 (1920); *see also* Benvenisti, *supra* note 4, at 120–22.

145 For other attempts to divide occupied territories, see Benvenisti, *supra* note 4, at 121.

146 *See* Eyal Benvenisti & Eliav Lieblich, *Assessing Turkey's "Resettlement" Plans in Syria Under the Law of Occupation*, Just Security (Oct. 23, 2019), https://www.justsecurity.org/66679/assessing-turkeys-resettlement-plans-in-syria-under-the-law-of-occupation/.

147 *Id.*

welfare of the local population: by facilitating the return of (non-Kurdish) refugees to the area, it would restore its "demographic richness,"[148] after Kurdish elements had previously displaced people belonging to other ethnic groups. Turkey's argument was therefore restorative: its resettlement project would remedy historical wrongdoing.[149] This type of demographic engineering highlights the dangers of allegedly restorative actions based on historical grievances, when undertaken by an occupant with clear interests in the area.

Allegations of demographic engineering have been frequently leveled against Israel, for example, concerning its "separation policy" between Gaza and the West Bank. According to the Oslo Accords, and as accepted by the international community, the two areas comprise a single territorial unit, notwithstanding its non-contiguity.[150] Yet, since Israel's disengagement from Gaza, and increasingly after the Hamas takeover in 2007, Israel has implemented a "separation policy," manifested mainly in restrictions on movement of Palestinians and goods from Gaza to the West Bank.[151] This policy has been justified by Israel both on security grounds—to prevent the transfer of "terrorist infrastructure" from Hamas-held Gaza to the West Bank—and by political rationales, which were never officially elaborated.[152] Since the policy generally allows the movement of West Bank Palestinians to Gaza, but not vice versa,[153] it was claimed that it was concerned primarily with the demography of the West Bank. In light of the occasional Israeli statements on possible annexation of parts of the West Bank—most intensively in 2020—the separation policy and its undergirding demographic implications can be criticized as measures meant to facilitate de jure or de facto annexation.[154]

Some transformations of demography in occupied territories are prohibited under specific provisions of the law of occupation. Article 49(1) GCIV prohibits all "deportations of protected persons" from the territory,

[148] Turkish Presidency (@trpresidency), TWITTER (Oct. 10, 2019, 2:21 PM), https://twitter.com/trpresidency/status/1182254900748656640.

[149] Lara Seligman, *Turkey Begins Resettling Refugees in Northeastern Syria*, FOREIGN POLICY (Dec. 9, 2019), https://foreignpolicy.com/2019/12/09/turkey-resettling-refugees-northeastern-syria/.

[150] The Israeli–Palestinian Interim Agreement on the West Bank and the Gaza Strip (Oslo II), Isr.–PLO., art. XI(1), Sept. 28, 1995.

[151] *See* GISHA, AREA G: FROM SEPARATION TO ANNEXATION: ISRAEL'S ISOLATION OF THE GAZA STRIP AND HOW IT SERVES ANNEXATIONIST GOALS IN THE WEST BANK 6–7 (2020).

[152] *Id.* at 4–5.

[153] *Id.* at 9

[154] *Id.* at 10–11.

regardless of their motives, inter alia to prevent the occupant from altering the local demography.[155] On the same logic, article 49(6) establishes the prohibition on settlements, providing that "[t]he Occupying Power shall not deport or transfer parts of its own civilian population into the territory it occupies."[156] Importantly, by juxtaposing "deportation" against "transfer," article 49(6) clarifies that it extends not only to forcible movement of the occupant's civilians to the territory, but to any situation in which a government actively induces such movement.[157] Established in response to policies in WWII,[158] article 49(6) can be said to serve three objectives. The first is to prevent demographic transformation; the second is to limit the intermingling of the occupant's interests in the territory, leading to de facto annexation; and the third is the prevention of the establishment of a discriminatory regime.[159] It is in light of article 49(6) that the Israeli settlements in the West Bank, as well as measures meant to facilitate them, are routinely condemned.[160] Beyond this, the literature on article 49(6) is vast, and the entire spectrum of its complexities is beyond the scope of this book.[161]

Last, another type of transformation is especially suspect: when the occupant interferes with the local educational programs, and particularly when it forces local institutions to adopt its own curriculum. This has notably been the case in Russia's occupation of areas in Ukraine in 2022, as

[155] On deportations, see Section 5.4.3.

[156] GCIV, *supra* note 2, art. 49(6). For criminal liability, see art. 85(4)(a) of Protocol Additional to the Geneva Conventions of 12 August 1949, and relating to the Protection of Victims of International Armed Conflicts (Protocol I) art. 69, June 8, 1977, 1125 U.N.T.S. 3; Rome Statute of the International Criminal Court, July 17, 1998, 2187 U.N.T.S. 3, art. 8(2)(b)(viii).

[157] Legal Consequences of the Construction of a Wall in the Occupied Palestinian Territory, Advisory Opinion, 2004 I.C.J. Rep. 136 ¶ 20 (July 9) [hereinafter Wall Opinion]; Christian Tomuschat, *The Prohibition of Settlements*, *in* Clapham et al., *supra* note 87, 1551, 1562–63; *see also* ICC, Office of the Prosecutor, Report on Preliminary Examination Activities ¶ 269 (2018); *see also* Arai-Takahashi, *supra* note 138, at 347–50.

[158] Tomuschat, *supra* note 157, at 1553–55.

[159] *Compare with id.* at 1559–60.

[160] *See, e.g.*, Wall Opinion; S.C. Res. 2334 (Dec. 23, 2016); ICC, Office of the Prosecutor, Prosecution Request Pursuant to Article 19(3) for a Ruling on the Court's Territorial Jurisdiction in Palestine (Dec. 20, 2019); Omar M. Dajani, *Israel's Creeping Annexation*, 111 Am. J. Int'l L. Unbound 51 (2017); *but see* Eugene Kontorovich, *Unsettled: A Global Study of Settlements in Occupied Territories*, 9 J. Leg. Analysis 285 (2017).

[161] *See* the various contributions in the *Symposium on Revisiting Israel's Settlements*, 117 Am. J. Int'l L. (2017).

part of its attempts to "Russify" the area.[162] Altering education programs in such manner clearly runs counter to the conservationist principle, and is also a prime example of measures that may amount to de facto annexation. This conclusion is strengthened when considering the explicit requirement, under the law of occupation, that the occupant cooperate with local authorities on issues relating to education.[163]

[162] Lauren Said-Moorhouse and Oleksandra Ochman, *This Is What the "Russification" of Ukraine's Education System Looks Like in Occupied Areas* CNN (May 16, 2022), https://edition.cnn.com/2022/05/16/europe/russia-ukraine-education-intl-cmd/index.html.
[163] *See* Section 3.6.2.

5
Security Measures and Military Necessity

Powers and Limitations

5.1 The Occupant's Security Powers and Their Limits: General Overview

As discussed in previous chapters, the interests addressed by the law of occupation include those of the ousted sovereign; the rights and interests of the local population (including self-determination); and the security of the occupant. In this chapter, we address the scope of the occupant's security powers.

The law of occupation's approach toward security is reminiscent of its framework concerning the occupant's powers to maintain public order. Security interests are broadly recognized as relevant considerations under articles 43 Hague and 64 GCIV. Recall that the occupant's powers to maintain public order and safety under article 43 are understood to include its own security interests. This is complemented by article 64 GCIV, which explicitly empowers the occupant to take security measures. Additionally, regarding measures that impinge on individual rights, article 27(4) GCIV recognizes the general power to take "measures of control and security" against protected persons. Like much of IHL, the law of occupation's approach to security is simultaneously constraining and enabling. The constraining aspects are implicit in the requirement under article 64 GCIV that the measures be *essential* to the occupant's security. Likewise, article 27(4) requires that security measures against protected persons be "*necessary* as a result of the war" (emphasis added).

These general provisions are supplemented by specific norms, which are also simultaneously empowering and limiting. Some of them provide explicit security powers, such as detaining protected persons or assigning residence for "imperative reasons of security."[1] Others are phrased as

[1] Convention (IV) relative to the Protection of Civilian Persons in Time of War art. 78, Aug. 12, 1949, 6 U.S.T. 3516, 75 U.N.T.S. 287 [hereinafter GCIV].

exceptions to prohibitions. The prohibition on requisitions of private property, for instance, includes an exception for requisitions "for the needs of the army of occupation."[2]

While this chapter deals with security powers in relation to protected persons, the occupant possesses similar powers over non-protected persons, emanating from its general powers under article 43.[3] In this context, the reference to protected persons in GCIV is meant, if at all, to ensure them *additional* protections. Arguably, however, the parallel application of IHRL, in addition to the fundamental guarantees enshrined under article 75 API, equalize the rights of protected and non-protected persons, at least in relation to security measures undertaken by the occupant.

5.2 The Scope of Relevant Security Considerations and Security Means

Two immediate questions arise concerning the occupant's security powers. The first relates to the scope of valid security considerations: Which of the occupant's interests can be understood as valid security interests? Which may be lawfully pursued? The second question concerns the permissible means to secure these interests.

5.2.1 Scope of Relevant Security Considerations: Between Operational and National Security Needs

The scope of the occupant's valid security considerations is far from clear. Are they limited to operational military advantages?[4] Or, rather, do they encompass broader, even strategic, security interests? Do they include only

[2] Convention (IV) respecting the Laws and Customs of War on Land and its annex: Regulations concerning the Laws and Customs of War on Land art. 52, Oct. 18, 1907, 187 C.T.S.227 [hereinafter Hague IV]. On security powers and property, see Chapter 6.

[3] *See, e.g.*, HCJ 4101/10 HaCohen v. IDF Commander of Judea and Samaria, Nevo Legal Database ¶¶ 18–19 (July 7, 2010) (Isr.); R. v. Sec'y of State for Def., [2006] EWCA (Civ) 327 [2007] QB 621.

[4] *Compare* Protocol Additional to the Geneva Conventions of 12 August 1949, and relating to the Protection of Victims of International Armed Conflicts (Protocol I) art. 51(5)(b), June 8, 1977, 1125 U.N.T.S. 3 [hereinafter API]; *see* ICRC, International Expert Meeting; The Principle of Proportionality in the Rules Governing the Conduct of Hostilities Under International Humanitarian Law, Part I (Laurent Gisel ed. 2016).

the security of the occupant's forces, as such, or also the security of the occupying state and its citizens? Do they encompass strictly the occupant's security needs vis-à-vis the local population, or also those relating to external threats to the territory?

The term "security considerations" is grossly indeterminant. In the *Jam'iyat Iscan* case, the HCJ held that in terms of valid security considerations, "[M]ilitary necessities are his [the military commander's] military needs and not the needs of national security in the broader sense."[5] Yet, this does not provide much guidance, since many broad national security needs can be rephrased in operational military terms, and many military needs can be discussed in terms of national security.

An important question is whether valid security considerations are only those relating to the occupant's forces *within* the territory. If this is so, security considerations cannot include the security of the occupying state as such, or its citizens *outside* the territory.[6] Military manuals are inconclusive on this issue. The Danish *Manual* refers—without elaboration—to the occupying power's "own security" as a relevant consideration, but proceeds to discuss security powers in the strict confines of "law enforcement" in the territory.[7] The U.S. *DoD Manual*, conversely, recognizes that the occupant's objectives may extend beyond maintaining the security of its forces, but also "to further the purpose of the war."[8] Likewise, the UK *Manual* refers to the occupant's power to construct defensive positions in the occupied territory, to protect it against external attacks.[9]

Article 64 GCIV lends some support to the wider view. Recall that article 64 recognizes the validity of measures *essential* "to ensure the security of the Occupying Power," and "of the members and property of the occupying forces."[10] The distinction between the occupying power and the occupying forces suggests that valid security interests may extend to threats to the

[5] HCJ 393/82 Jam'iat Iscan Al-Ma'almoun v. IDF Commander of Judea and Samaria, 37(4) PD 785, ¶13 (1983) (Isr.).

[6] Ardi Imseis, *Critical Reflections on the International Humanitarian Law Aspects of the ICJ Wall Advisory Opinion*, 99 Am. J. Int'l L. 102, 111–12 (2005).

[7] Danish Ministry of Def., Military Manual on International Law Relevant to Danish Armed Forces in International Operations 436–39 (2016([hereinafter Danish Manual].

[8] *Id.* at 728.

[9] U.K. Ministry of Def., The Joint Service Manual of the Law of Armed Conflict §11.78 (2004) [hereinafter UK Manual] *cited in* David Kretzmer, *The Advisory Opinion: The Light Treatment of International Law*, 99 Am. J. Int'l L. 88, 97 n.101 (2005).

[10] GCIV, *supra* note 1, art. 64.

occupying state itself.[11] Furthermore, the ICJ, in its *Wall Advisory Opinion*, indirectly recognized that the occupant has a right to protect its own citizens from threats emanating from occupied territories.[12] Nonetheless, the phrase *essential* clarifies that security considerations cannot extend to exploitation of the territory for interests only indirectly related to the security of the occupant.[13]

Arguably, if security measures are more broadly construed to encompass not only operational imperatives in the territory, but also the security of the occupant state or its citizens, they should accordingly be subjected to stricter scrutiny. This is because as security needs are given a broader understanding, so is the potential that they be used to conceal irrelevant considerations.[14] Ultimately, the danger is that the security of the occupant state, broadly construed, would be utilized to circumvent the prohibition on furthering the state's broader interests in the territory—whether political, demographic, or economic.[15]

5.2.2 Security Considerations and Context: The Wall Cases

These concerns are best reflected in the legal debate surrounding the Wall built by Israel in the West Bank in the early 2000s.[16] The building of the Wall commenced during the height of the Al-Aqsa intifada when frequent

[11] *See* ICRC, Commentary on IV Geneva Convention 337 (Jean S. Pictet ed. 1958) [hereinafter ICRC, Commentary 1958]; *see* Kretzmer, *supra* note 9, at 100–01; Yutaka Arai-Takahashi, The Law of Occupation: Continuity and Change of International Humanitarian Law, and Its Interaction with International Human Rights Law 124 (2009).

[12] Legal Consequences of the Construction of a Wall in the Occupied Palestinian Territory, Advisory Opinion, 2004 I.C.J. Rep. 136 ¶141 (July 9) [hereinafter Wall Opinion]. *Compare* Iain Scobbie, *Words My Mother Never Taught Me—"In Defense of the International Court,"* 99 Am. J. Int'l L. 76, 81–85 (2005).

[13] *See* Eliav Lieblich, *Wrong to the Core: The Supreme Court of Israel's Ruling on Masafer Yatta*, Verfassungsblog (May 8, 2022), https://verfassungsblog.de/wrong-to-the-core/ (criticizing the use of occupied territory as a firing zone for military training).

[14] *See id. See also*, Yael Berda, Living Emergency: Israel's Permit Regime in the Occupied West Bank (2017).

[15] For instance, in the *Jami'at Iscan* case, the HCJ opined, in *dicta*, that security considerations can encompass building a road system in the occupied territory, to facilitate troop movements. HCJ 393/82 Jam'iat Iscan, 37(4) PD 785, ¶ 15. Yet, as we have seen in Chapter 4, this road system significantly benefited Israeli civilian needs.

[16] *See, e.g.*, the contributions in Lori Fisler Damrosch & Bernard H. Oxman, *Agora: ICJ Advisory Opinion on Construction of a Wall in the Occupied Palestinian Territory*, 99 Am. J. Int'l L. 1 (2005).

suicide bombings took place in Israel.[17] However, it was not built on the Green Line, which separates Israel from the West Bank. Rather, it encroaches into the West Bank in a manner which ensures contiguity between Israel and 80% of its settlements, while creating Palestinian enclaves.[18] The land trapped between the Wall and Israel is designated as a special "seam zone," to which Palestinian access is extremely limited.[19]

The HCJ made its first principled ruling on the Wall in the *Beit Sourik* case of 2004.[20] The petitioners, representatives of Palestinian communities, argued that the Wall *as a whole* violated the law of occupation because it created de facto borders; that its specific route served the interests of the occupant *outside* the occupied area; and that the decision to build it exploited the language of security to conceal annexationist policies.[21] The state countered that the Wall was necessary to prevent the infiltration of terrorists into Israel and into its settlements in the area; and that its specific route was chosen strictly in light of military considerations.[22] More generally, it argued that Israel's right to defend itself against external threats justified the Wall.[23]

The Court conceded that security considerations cannot be used as pretext for "political" reasons, such as a desire to annex territory.[24] Yet, it accepted, without challenge, the state's position that the route was strictly motivated by security considerations, even if these related to Israel proper or its settlements.[25] As it ruled, the law of occupation recognizes both the powers of the military commander to "maintain security in the area," but also "to protect the security of his country and her citizens."[26] Counterintuitively, the fact that the Wall encroached into the West Bank rather than following the Green Line was viewed by the Court not as an indication of annexationist aspirations, but of the genuineness of the state's security considerations: this is because the Court considered the Green

[17] HCJ 2056/04 Beit Sourik Village Council v. The Government of Israel, 58(5) PD 807 ¶¶ 3–7 (2004) (Isr.).

[18] *See* Wall Opinion ¶¶ 80–85; *Beit Sourik*, 58(5) PD.

[19] *See* Orna Ben-Naftali, Michael Sfard & Hedi Viterbo, The ABC of the OPT: A Legal Lexicon of the Israeli Control over the Occupied Palestinian Territory 335–37 (2018).

[20] *Beit Sourik*, 58(5) PD.

[21] *Id.* ¶10.

[22] *Id.* ¶¶ 12, 20.

[23] *Id.* ¶ 15.

[24] *Id.* ¶ 27.

[25] *Id.* ¶ 29.

[26] *Id.* ¶ 33.

Line itself as a political line.[27] After ruling that building the Wall was generally within the state's power, the Court moved to assess segments of the Wall in light of the proportionality standard, as discussed in Section 5.2.4.

The perception that security considerations, for the purpose of the Wall's route, encompass not only those of the occupant's forces, but also the country and its citizens, was soon expanded to explicitly include Israeli citizens *in* the settlements. In the *Mara'abe* case,[28] at hand was a section of the Wall that encroached into the West Bank in order to encompass an Israeli settlement, while isolating five Palestinian villages from the West Bank.[29] The petitioners argued that this part of the Wall was illegal, since it aimed to encompass an unlawful settlement.[30] The Court rejected this argument, relying on article 43 Hague. As it ruled, the duty to "ensure public order and safety" included the protection of lives of *all* persons in the territory, even if they were not protected persons under GCIV.[31] The Court held that this duty extended also to persons *unlawfully* present in the territory. Without opining on the lawfulness of the settlements, it invoked individual rights, ruling that "[e]ven if a person is located in the area illegally, he is not outlawed" and that the legality of the Israeli settlement activity in the area is irrelevant in this context.[32] While the logic that no one is an outlaw, even if unlawfully found in the territory, is compelling, the Court's view that the *means* chosen to protect such persons can be assessed separately from any unlawfulness, was rightly criticized. In this case, these means did not only protect them physically from concrete threats, but also served to *entrench* their presence, a key political objective of the occupant.[33]

The HCJ's approach demonstrates that security considerations cannot be disconnected from the "bigger picture" of the occupant's policy. The ICJ, in the *Wall Advisory Opinion*, went the opposite way.[34] Rather than focusing on specific parts of the Wall, it analyzed it as a whole, and drew—from the bigger picture—the conclusion that the Wall's route was

[27] *Id.* ¶ 30.
[28] HCJ 7957/04 Mara'abe v. Prime Minister of Israel, 60(2) PD 477 (2005) (Isr.).
[29] *Id.* ¶¶ 8–9.
[30] The petitioners relied on the ICJ's reasoning in the Wall Opinion on this issue. Wall Opinion.
[31] *Mara'abe*, 60(2) PD, ¶ 18.
[32] *Id.* ¶ 19.
[33] *See, e.g.*, Aeyal Gross, The Writing on the Wall: Rethinking the Law of Occupation 292–96 (2017).
[34] *See generally* Wall Opinion.

not based on security considerations.[35] Crucial to this determination was the route's incorporation of approximately 80% of the settlers in the West Bank within the area created between the Green Line and the Wall. This, the ICJ held, created a fait accompli that could amount to de facto annexation; entrenches illegal settlements; and ultimately impedes the right to self-determination.[36]

The HCJ, in *Mara'abe*, criticized the ICJ's sweeping approach, arguing that security considerations must always be assessed in detail in light of specific facts. This required analyzing each segment of the Wall, "to clarify whether it impinges upon the rights of the Palestinian residents, and whether the impingement is proportional."[37] This allowed the HCJ to present the diverging views between the courts as emanating from different factual bases, rather than from legal disagreements.[38] Similarly, Kretzmer criticized the ICJ for its "light treatment of international humanitarian law," by failing to engage in the detailed analysis of specific relevant provisions, and by being opaque in the grounding of its sweeping conclusions.[39]

Ultimately, the difficulties in distinguishing between valid security considerations and concealed irrelevant ones are similar to those—discussed in Chapters 3 and 4—in distinguishing between actions for the benefit of the local population and those predominantly based on self-interest. As the Wall cases demonstrate, the key problem is the intermingling between security considerations and broader political interests. As much as valid security considerations are understood more broadly, this problem is exacerbated. Three tests can somewhat alleviate this problem. First, security considerations must be stated in concrete operational terms, and cannot be vague and speculative. Second, determining whether a measure is based on genuine security considerations requires both a factually intensive analysis of the measure, *and* a contextual analysis of the bigger picture. Third, when the measure serves both valid security considerations and *other* considerations, the occupant would have to show that the security considerations are the dominant objective of its actions.

[35] *See* Gross, *supra* note 33, at 271–77; Ben-Naftali et al., *supra* note 19, at 333–35.

[36] Wall Opinion ¶¶ 120–22, 137.

[37] *Mara'abe*, 60(2) PD 477.

[38] *Id.* ¶¶ 57, 59–60.

[39] Kretzmer, *supra* note 9, at 88–94; *see also* Wall Opinion ¶ 24 (Separate Opinion by Judge Higgins); *compare* Imseis, *supra* note 6, at 109–14; Martti Koskenniemi, *Occupied Zone—"A Zone of Reasonableness"?*, 41 Isr. L. Rev. 13, 25 (2008).

5.2.3 The Scope of Administrative Security Means

Assuming that the scope of valid security considerations is settled, what are the means available to achieve them? On its face, and in contrast to domestic law in liberal democracies, the occupant does not need to invoke a specific provision as a source for each security means it chooses, *as long as such means are not expressly prohibited or excluded by the general caps on security measures*, which we discuss later.[40] Crucially, however, this does not preclude limitations that might stem from *other* bodies of law. For example, while the law of occupation does not explicitly protect the freedom of expression, security measures that infringe on this right might be limited by IHRL. Importantly, the interpretive space provided by the law of occupation regarding security means cannot be read nowadays without reference to neighboring legal frameworks.

Within the law of occupation, the normative framework concerning security means is structured as follows. Regarding administrative security measures—that is, those that do not involve criminal proceedings—article 27 GCIV provides that occupants "may take such measures of control and security in regard to protected persons as may be necessary as a result of the war."[41] Article 78 GCIV, in turn, provides that if an occupant considers it necessary "for imperative reasons of security, to take safety measures concerning protected persons, it may, *at the most*, subject them to assigned residence or to internment."[42] It follows that the upper cap for permitted security measures, in terms of restriction of individual rights, is assigned residence or internment.[43] Less stringent means are therefore permitted, provided that they are not otherwise prohibited by other applicable rules and standards. Of course, there is ample space for disagreement on whether measures are indeed less or more stringent than internment or assigned residence.

On this basis, it is accepted that occupants can use, for instance, checkpoints, curfews, and other "restrictions on civilians," although these are not mentioned explicitly in the relevant conventions.[44] Similarly, the *Tallinn*

[40] ICRC, COMMENTARY 1958, *supra* note 11, at 207.
[41] GCIV, *supra* note 1, art. 27.
[42] *Id.* art. 78 (emphasis added).
[43] ICRC, COMMENTARY 1958, *supra* note 11, at 207.
[44] *See* UK Manual, *supra* note 9, at 287; ARAI-TAKAHASHI, *supra* note 11, at 125–26.

Manual interpreted the general security provisions under the law of occupation as permitting security measures in cyberspace, as well as measures to ensure the integrity of the occupant's own cyber-systems.[45] Of course, the lack of specification of means can lead to controversies when occupants introduce means not previously envisioned, such as mass surveillance.[46]

In light of the relatively open framework of security means, it is unsurprising that the HCJ has shifted the analysis from the mere permissibility of a certain security means to ad hoc proportionality, resulting in significant leeway for the state.[47] For example, both in the *Beit Sourik* and *Mara'abe* cases, the HCJ held that while there was no sweeping prohibition on building walls as security means, specific sections of the Wall could be disproportionate. Accordingly, it occasionally ordered the state to reroute the Wall.[48]

5.2.4 Proportionality (and Its Critique)

Even when security means are otherwise lawful, they must be proportionate in the specific context. During active hostilities, proportionality requires that an attack not cause incidental civilian harm which is excessive in relation to a concrete and direct military advantage.[49] When active hostilities take place in occupied territories, this standard would be relevant to attacks.[50] However, there are not always hostilities under occupation, and not all security measures are attacks. Since the occupant is not strictly a belligerent in occupied territories, but is also, if not primarily, an administrator, a wider proportionality test has been developed in the context of occupation, drawing from domestic constitutional law.[51]

Notably, this type of proportionality was frequently applied by the HCJ—in tandem, however, with a wide understanding of the occupant's powers.

[45] TALLINN MANUAL 2.0 ON THE INTERNATIONAL LAW APPLICABLE TO CYBER OPERATIONS 546–49 (Michael N. Schmitt ed., 2d ed. 2017).

[46] Benjamin G. Waters, *An International Right to Privacy: Israeli Intelligence Collection in the Occupied Palestinian Territories*, 50 GEO. J. INT'L L. 573 (2019); Elizabeth Dwoskin, *Israel Escalates Surveillance of Palestinians with Facial Recognition in West Bank*, WASH. POST (Nov. 8, 2021).

[47] *See* for instance HCJ 2056/04 Beit Sourik Village Council v. The Government of Israel, 58(5) PD 807 ¶¶ 33–36 (2004) (Isr.); BEN-NAFTALI ET AL., *supra* note 19, at 330, 333.

[48] *Beit Sourik*, 58(5) PD, ¶ 44, ¶¶ 48–85; HCJ 7957/04 Mara'abe, 60(2) PD ¶¶ 30, 102–116.

[49] API, *supra* note 4.

[50] *See* Section 5.5.

[51] *See* BEN-NAFTALI ET AL., *supra* note 19, at 329.

As discussed above, in the *Beit Sourik* case, the Court held that an occupant was permitted to build a security wall in occupied territories. However, it subjected segments of the Wall to a three-pronged proportionality analysis, drawn from Canadian, German, and Israeli public law.[52] This test requires first, that there is a rational connection between the means and the realization of the security objective; second, that the measure is the "least injurious means" to achieve the objective; and, third, that the damage caused to individuals by the measures "must be of proper proportion" to the security advantage it brings about (harm–benefit analysis).[53]

An important question is whether this particular proportionality emanates from international law, or, rather, was it applied extraterritorially by the HCJ as part of domestic Israeli law? In *Beit Sourik*, the Court implied both. It held that basic principles of Israeli administrative law apply to the military commander, among them proportionality.[54] It also ruled that since the "problem of balancing between security and liberty" is a general legal problem, its solution is universal,[55] and that, accordingly, proportionality is a general principle of international law.[56] However, the Court did not elaborate on the source of this *specific* three-tiered test as a general principle of international law.

Nevertheless, the first two sub-tests of proportionality—those of rational connection and least harmful means—seem to be integral to the requirement under the law of occupation that measures must be necessary, or *essential* to ensure security needs.[57] That a measure is essential means both that it can actually bring about the realization of the objective, *and* that it does not go beyond what is necessary to do so. The third sub-test of harm–benefit can be derived from *jus in bello* proportionality. If such an analysis is required vis-à-vis civilians during active hostilities, then similar requirements should a fortiori apply in occupation, when trusteeship relations exist. Appeal can also be made to the Martens clause to argue that "the laws of humanity and the requirements of the public conscience" call for this

[52] *Beit Sourik*, 58(5) PD, ¶ 40.
[53] *Id.* ¶ 41.
[54] *Id.* ¶¶ 24, 38–39.
[55] *Id.* ¶ 36.
[56] *Id.* ¶ 37. *See* Anne Peters, *Proportionality as a Global Constitutional Principle*, *in* Handbook on Global Constitutionalism 248, 268 (Anthony F. Lang & Antje Wiener eds., 2017).
[57] GCIV, *supra* note 1, art. 64.

type of analysis, in order to prevent gross human rights infringements.[58] Last, parallel notions of proportionality can apply through IHRL.[59]

However, one should not ignore the shortcomings of proportionality, and specifically its harm–benefit test. Proportionality is especially susceptible to the critique against "balancing" in rights discourse: namely, that balancing is used to conceal political choices[60] or that it is too indeterminate to guide behavior.[61] Such critiques were specifically levelled against proportionality under occupation. Gross argues that proportionality under occupation allows the debate to shift from larger questions of justice to a "managerial calculus" that ignores the general context.[62] Moreover, he claims that transplanting the principle from domestic public law into the law of occupation is deeply flawed. This is because in contrast to domestic settings, where rights of individuals are infringed in favor of the collective good of their own community, under occupation the good pursued is likely that of others. In the West Bank, for instance, the HCJ balances infringement of Palestinian rights in relation to the security of Israeli citizens and settlers.[63] To Gross, applying proportionality in occupation—and *at least when the occupant's citizens are involved*—"flattens" the relations between protected persons and others, diluting the special protections guaranteed to the former.[64]

Koskenniemi makes a comparable argument. Proportionality, like other standards of "reasonableness," presupposes "the presence of a minimal community about objectives and preferences that is denied by the occupation."[65] To him, applying proportionality under occupation wipes away the distinction between sovereignty and occupation, settlers and protected persons.[66] Additionally, proportionality grants occupation the vestige of a "mundane government," contributing to its normalization.[67] It furthermore allows occupants to make value judgments which lack the legitimacy

58 *See generally* Theodor Meron, *The Martens Clause, Principles of Humanity, and Dictates of Public Conscience*, 94 AM. J. INT'L L. 78 (2000).

59 *See, e.g.*, Kai Möller, *Proportionality: Challenging the Critics*, 10 INT. J. CONS. L. 709 (2012).

60 *See, e.g.*, Duncan Kennedy, *The Critique of Rights in Critical Legal Studies*, *in* LEFT LEGALISM/LEFT CRITIQUE 178, 197 (Wendy Brown & Janet Halley eds., 2002).

61 Koskenniemi, *supra* note 39, at 21–23; BEN-NAFTALI ET AL., *supra* note 19, at 337.

62 GROSS, *supra* note 33, at 266.

63 *Id.* at 283.

64 *Id.* at 343–49; *see also* Aeyal M. Gross, *Human Proportions: Are Human Rights the Emperor's New Clothes of the International Law of Occupation?*, 18 EUR. J. INT'L L. 1 (2007).

65 Koskenniemi, *supra* note 39, at 17.

66 *Id.* at 37–38.

67 *Id.* at 35, 38.

they might have in domestic settings, further depriving the occupied population of self-rule.[68]

An especially pertinent critical claim is that the availability of proportionality as a means to reduce harm might be utilized to confer legitimacy on otherwise unlawful actions.[69] Deploying proportionality might dilute the lack of authority to act in the first place, all while utilizing the language of human rights.[70] This claim is frequently leveled against the HCJ. For example, by using proportionality to analyze home demolitions, the HCJ has sidestepped the principled problem of the measure's legality.[71]

Yet, these critiques themselves face many challenges. For instance, is it possible to decouple them from the specific context of the Israeli occupation? Are they relevant in all possible occupations—for example, even where the occupant has not transferred its own citizens to the territory? Furthermore, without proportionality, what would serve to limit military necessity when security measures are undertaken? By excluding proportionality altogether, would military necessity not become an overriding consideration? Resolving these questions, however, is beyond our scope here.

5.3 Specifically Permitted Security Means

In this section, we discuss some of the security means specifically permitted under the law of occupation. Recall, however, that since the occupant's control at best confers a weak form of authority,[72] it cannot be said that its security measures—essentially intended to entrench its control—are "permitted" in the full, legitimating sense. We use the term "permission" here in the technical sense only.

5.3.1 Military Courts, Security Offenses, and Punishments

The most institutionalized form of security means explicitly recognized under the law of occupation, are military courts. As discussed in Chapter 3,

[68] *Id.* at 38–40.

[69] Gross, *supra* note 33, at 285; Eliav Lieblich, *The Facilitative Function of* Jus in Bello, 30 Eur. J. Int'l L. 321, 330 (2019).

[70] *See* Ben-Naftali et al., *supra* note 19, at 340–42.

[71] *See, e.g.*, HCJ 4853/20 Abu Baker v. IDF Commander in the West Bank, Nevo Legal Database ¶¶ 5–9 (Aug. 10, 2020) (Isr.); *see also* Ben-Naftali et al., *supra* note 19, at 330.

[72] *See* Section 1.4.1.

such courts constitute the second tier of judiciary in occupied territories, operating in parallel to the domestic courts. While domestic courts operate in accordance with the local law, military courts are specifically empowered to try new penal offenses enacted by the occupant ("security offenses").

The practice of establishing military courts is vast.[73] In contemporary law, the power to enact penal offenses "essential" for security purposes is found in article 64 GCIV, while article 66 permits the occupant to establish military courts in the occupied territories to trial such offenses.[74] Subsequent articles enshrine due process requirements, provisions on penalties, and highly detailed regulations on the treatment of detainees and internees.[75] A detailed discussion of these guarantees is beyond the scope of this work.[76] Importantly, article 67 GCIV provides that military courts must apply provisions which are "in accordance with general principles of law."[77] This provides ample space for complementing the law of occupation with IHRL norms, both in terms of due process and substance.

Military courts must be "properly constituted," "non-political," and located in the occupied territory.[78] Beyond these provisions, GCIV does not provide specific guidance on their structure. Importantly, article 73 enshrines convicts' "right of appeal." However, it is unclear whether this in itself requires establishing a separate *court* of appeal, or, rather, a right of petition to another authority suffices.[79] Although article 66 mentions "courts of appeals," it does not explicitly mandate their establishment, but only

[73] *See* Gerhard von Glahn, The Occupation of Enemy Territory: A Commentary on the Law and Practice of Belligerent Occupation 112–113 (1957); Yaël Ronen, *Blind in Their Own Cause: The Military Courts in the West Bank*, 2 Cambridge J. Int'l & Comp. L. 738, 740–41 (2013).

[74] Von Glahn, *supra* note 73, at 116.

[75] GCIV, *supra* note 1, arts. 65, 67–77, 79–131. Additional guarantees are found in API, *supra* note 4, art. 75(4). The term "internees" under GCIV refers to protected persons held under preventive or administrative detention, and accordingly their holding is classified as "internment." ICRC, Commentary 1958, *supra* note 11, at 343. The term "detainees" means protected persons held pending trial or convicted in military courts. GCIV, *supra* note 1, art. 76. By default, their holding is classified as "imprisonment." ICRC, Commentary 1958, *supra* note 11, at 343–44. Some confusion is understandable, since GCIV refers to the occupant as the "Detaining Power" even when it holds internees. GCIV, *supra* note 1, art. 82.

[76] *See* Payam Akhavan, *Judicial Guarantees*, *in* The 1949 Geneva Conventions: A Commentary 1215 (Andrew Clapham, Paola Gaeta & Marco Sassòli eds., 2015); Jelena Pejic, *Procedural Principles and Safeguards for Internment/Administrative Detention in Armed Conflict and Other Situations of Violence*, 87 Int'l Rev. Red Cross 375 (2005).

[77] GCIV, *supra* note 1, art. 67.

[78] *Id.* art. 66.

[79] *See* ICRC, Commentary 1958, *supra* note 11, at 359; Eric Stein, *Application of the Law of the Absent Sovereign in Territory Under Belligerent Occupation: The Schio Massacre*, 46 Mich. L. Rev. 341, 341 (1948).

provides that, preferably, if they are established, they will be located in the occupied territory.[80] In the West Bank, in the initial years of occupation, no court of appeals existed, and convicts could only petition the military commander.[81] The HCJ eventually ruled that while international law does not require establishing such courts,[82] a court of appeal should be established as a matter of policy, especially in prolonged occupations.[83] Following this recommendation, the Military Court of Appeals was established in the West Bank in 1989.[84] Be that as it may, the parallel application of IHRL can have special purchase in this context, considering IHRL's protection of judicial guarantees and the right of appeal.[85]

In terms of jurisdiction *ratione materiae*, GCIV does not elaborate on the specific breaches of security that can be met by a criminal offense. Based on article 64's language, these offenses must be essential to maintain the interests generally recognized as valid under the law of occupation: that is, to maintain orderly government and to ensure the security of the occupant. *Ratione temporis*, such offenses can only apply to acts committed post-occupation, since the occupant has no inter-temporal authority.[86] A related consequence is that regardless of the offense and the duration of punishment, convicts must be handed over to the local authorities once the occupation ends.[87]

Additionally, GCIV imposes limits on punishments. Two general limits are explicit. First, punishment must be proportionate to the specific offense. Second, punishment decisions must consider the fact that the accused is not a national of the occupant.[88] The first limitation stems from general principles of law; the second is a specific manifestation of the limited substantive authority of the occupant. It represents the lack of legitimate expectation on the part of the occupant, that the occupied population accept its laws from an internal point of view.[89]

80 GCIV, *supra* note 1, art. 66; VON GLAHN, *supra* note73, at 117.

81 HCJ 87/85 Arjub v. IDF Commander of Judea and Samaria, 42(1) PD 353, ¶ 2 (1988) (Isr.).

82 *Id.* ¶ 10.

83 *Id.* ¶¶ 13, 15. On prolonged occupation, see Section 4.1.

84 Security Provisions Order (Amendment No. 58) (Judea and Samaria) (No. 1265), 5749–1989, KMZM 77 134.

85 *See* Akhavan, *supra* note 76, at 1217–19, 1234–35; 1 JEAN-MARIE HENCKAERTS & LOUISE DOSWALD-BECK, ICRC, CUSTOMARY INTERNATIONAL HUMANITARIAN LAW, Rule 100 (2005).

86 GCIV, *supra* note 1, art. 70.

87 *Id.* art. 77.

88 *Id.* art. 67.

89 H.L.A. HART, THE CONCEPT OF LAW 88–91 (3d ed. 2012).

Article 68 GCIV introduces further principles of punishment, mainly by distinguishing between less serious and more serious offenses. If an act is "solely intended to harm the Occupying Power"—that is, it is *political* by nature—*and* does not attempt to or harm persons or seriously damage property relating to the occupant, the punishment can at most consist of proportionate "internment or simple imprisonment."[90]

Lamentably, regarding serious offenses listed in the article—namely, espionage, serious sabotage against military installations, and "intentional offences which have caused the death of one or more persons"—the occupant may, according to GCIV, impose the death penalty.[91] This, however, is subject to several qualifications. First, such offenses must be punishable by death under the local law prior to the occupation, presumably, when aimed internally against one's own state. This condition was heavily debated in the drafting of GCIV, and several states made reservations concerning this issue.[92] Second, here, too, courts must consider that the accused "is not bound to it by any duty of allegiance."[93] This reflects, again, the defective authority of the occupant. Third, the death penalty cannot be imposed on minors under the age of 18 at the time of the offense.[94] Fourth, article 76(3) API further limits, if not prohibits altogether, imposition of the death penalty on pregnant women and mothers of dependent children.[95]

Importantly, these provisions under IHL cannot be considered apart from the treatment of the death penalty under IHRL. First, under IHRL, the death penalty cannot be reintroduced in states that have abolished it.[96] Arguably, this binds occupants that have abolished the death penalty even

[90] GCIV, *supra* note 1, art. 68(1); ICRC, COMMENTARY 1958, *supra* note 11, at 343–44. Article 68 mentions "interment" as a possible punishment, although internment is in general administrative detention, because GCIV regulates the treatment of internees in detail (GCIV, *supra* note 1, arts. 79–135). The drafters sought to make these protections applicable also to convicts. ICRC, COMMENTARY 1958, *supra* note 11, at 343–44. As for the conditions for holding detainees (pre- and post-conviction), GCIV is more laconic, recognizing several minimum obligations. GCIV, *supra* note 1, art. 76. Conditions of imprisonment may be supplemented by relevant provisions of IHRL. *See generally* NIGEL RODLEY & MATT POLLARD, THE TREATMENT OF PRISONERS UNDER INTERNATIONAL LAW (3d ed. 2009).

[91] GCIV, *supra* note 1, art. 68(2).

[92] ICRC, COMMENTARY 1958, *supra* note 11, at 345–46.

[93] GCIV, *supra* note 1, art. 68(3).

[94] *Id.* art. 68(4).

[95] API, *supra* note 4, art. 76(3); YORAM DINSTEIN, THE INTERNATIONAL LAW OF BELLIGERENT OCCUPATION 157–58 (2d ed. 2019).

[96] International Covenant on Civil and Political Rights art. 6(2), Dec. 16, 1966, 999 U.N.T.S. 171 [hereinafter ICCPR]. Human Rights Committee, General Comment No. 36 on article 6

when it is available under the laws in the occupied territory.[97] Furthermore, the death penalty must not be imposed except "for the most serious crimes,"[98] and even in relation to such crimes, "only in the most exceptional cases and under the strictest limits."[99] Without exhausting the debate on this issue, the interpretation of the phrase "most serious crimes" may very well complement GCIV, and restrict the understanding of the offenses that may give rise to the death penalty under article 68(2) GCIV.[100] Likewise, the restriction of the death penalty, under IHRL, to the most exceptional cases, adds further limitations and considerations, beyond the requirement under article 68(3) to consider that the accused owes no allegiance to the occupant.[101]

Presumably, when serious offenses are involved, military courts can impose punishments beneath the death penalty, but that go beyond "internment or simple imprisonment."[102] However, since GCIV is silent on the nature of such punishments, they must be limited by general provisions on fundamental guarantees[103] and by IHRL.[104] Ultimately, it seems implausible that such punishments can indeed go beyond regular imprisonment.

Although, as mentioned above, the primary function of military courts is to try criminal cases based on security legislation, there have been instances in which military courts exercised jurisdiction over civil and criminal cases based on the local law.[105] Until today, for instance, Israel's military courts in the West Bank are empowered not only to try "security offenses," but also criminal offenses enshrined in the local Jordanian law.[106] Owing to the conservationist principle, this should not be the preferred route, and should be resorted to only as a short-term measure where local governance collapses.[107]

of the International Covenant on Civil and Political Rights, on the Right to Life, U.N. Doc. CCPR/C/GC/36, ¶34 (Oct. 30, 2018) [hereinafter GC 36].

[97] *Compare* Dinstein, *supra* note 95, at 158–59.
[98] ICCPR, *supra* note 96, art. 6(2); *see also* arts. 6(3)–6(6).
[99] GC 36, *supra* note 96, para. 5.
[100] *See id.* para. 35.
[101] *See id.* para. 37.
[102] ICRC, Commentary 1958, *supra* note 11, at 345–46.
[103] GCIV, *supra* note 1, art. 27, 32; API, *supra* note 4, art. 75(2).
[104] ICCPR, *supra* note 96, art. 7.
[105] *See* von Glahn, *supra* note 73, at 113–14.
[106] § 10a, Security Provisions Order (Amendment No. 58) (Judea and Samaria) (No. 1265), 5749–1989, KMZM 77 134; *see also* Ronen, *supra* note 73, at 744; for another example, see Stein, *supra* note 79, at 341.
[107] *Compare* von Glahn, *supra* note 73, at 115.

Additionally, military courts have been occasionally granted powers to hear various claims *against* the occupant.[108] In the West Bank, for example, in addition to criminal jurisdiction,[109] the military courts may exercise judicial review over administrative security measures;[110] and an "Appeal Committee" with recommendatory power may review various administrative decisions of the military commander.[111] Yet, whether to entrust this function to military courts or to other mechanisms is ultimately subject to the decision of the occupant.

5.3.2 Assigned Residence and Internment (Administrative Detention)

Article 78 GCIV provides for preventive "safety measures" that can be taken against protected persons, in an administrative manner. As mentioned above, article 78 recognizes the occupant's power to order, in this context, "assigned residence or internment." Yet, since there is great danger that occupants would resort to arbitrary administrative measures, article 78 and related provisions—as well as their subsequent interpretations—impose several limitations on such measures.

From a humanitarian perspective, it is clear that criminal indictment should be preferred over administrative measures.[112] The usual rationale given by occupants for preferring administrative measures over criminal indictment is the need to protect intelligence resources, which would have to be disclosed to the accused should they be indicted.[113] Yet, this interest stands against grave infringements of individual rights: administrative measures are imposed without prior conviction, and typically have no definite date of termination. They are almost universally based on secret

[108] *Id.* at 113.

[109] For critical views, see Lisa Hajjar, Courting Conflict: The Israeli Military Court System in the West Bank and Gaza (2005); Neta Ziv, *Navigating the Judicial Terrain Under Israeli Occupation: Palestinian and Israeli Lawyers in the Military Courts*, 42 Ford. Int'l L. J. 729 (2018); Nery Ramati, *The Rulings of the Israeli Military Courts and International Law*, 25 J. Confl. & Sec. L. 149 (2020).

[110] Security Provisions Order (Consolidated Version) (Judea and Samaria) (No. 1651), 5770–2009.

[111] Administrative Committees Order (Order No. 172) (Judea and Samaria), 5728–1968 KMZM 9 350. On its recommendatory power, see *id.* at 6.

[112] HCJ 7015/02 Ajuri v. IDF Commander in the West Bank, 56(2) PD 352 ¶ 26 (2002) (Isr.).

[113] *See* Dinstein, *supra* note 95, at 187.

evidence, which makes them nearly impossible to challenge.[114] This requires that administrative measures be undertaken only when confronted with exceptional danger. Article 78(2) seeks to ensure this, by requiring procedural safeguards: namely, that administrative measures be subject to a "regular procedure" which includes the right of appeal, and a periodical review "if possible" every six months.[115] These procedures can be supplemented by requirements from IHRL, as the ECtHR ruled in the *Hassan* case.[116]

A key limitation on administrative measures under article 78 is that they may be undertaken only for "imperative reasons of security." This requirement is more stringent than the "regular" security interests that can be pursued by the occupant, and implies the existence of an exceptional threat.[117] As phrased by the U.S. Supreme Court, this is "the narrowest available test."[118] It is clear that the threat should emanate from the individuals themselves, and that persons cannot be interned based on a collectivized notion of threat.[119] Accordingly, the HCJ ruled that a person cannot be subject to administrative measures merely to deter others.[120] Importantly, the rationale for administrative measures is strictly preventive against a defined threat, rather than punitive or retributive.[121] This entails that measures can extend only as long as the person remains a threat.[122] For the same reasons, a person cannot be detained merely for intelligence exploitation, absent a specific threat.[123]

Nonetheless, the notion of "imperative reasons of security" suffers from wide margins of indeterminacy. Unfortunately, there is no explicit requirement in black-letter law that imperative reasons of security be limited, for instance, to imminent threats to life and limb. Thus, in a related context, Pictet suggested that what would constitute a sufficient threat is "left very largely to Governments to decide."[124] He mentioned, as examples,

[114] *See* Shiri Krebs, *Lifting the Veil of Secrecy: Judicial Review of Administrative Detentions in the Israeli Supreme Court*, 45 VAND. J. TRANSNAT'L L. 639 (2012).
[115] On procedural guarantees, see DINSTEIN, *supra* note 95, at 188–90; Al-Waheed v. Ministry of Def., [2017] AC 821 (SC) [104–110] (appeal taken from Eng.).
[116] Hassan v. UK, 2014-VI Eur. Ct. H.R. 1 ¶¶ 102–107.
[117] ICRC, COMMENTARY 1958, *supra* note 11, at 368. *But see Al-Waheed*, [2017] AC [58].
[118] *Al-Waheed*, [2017] AC [17].
[119] ICRC, COMMENTARY 1958, *supra* note 11, at 78.
[120] HCJ 7015/02 Ajuri v. IDF Commander in the West Bank, 56(2) PD 352 ¶ 24 (2002) (Isr.).
[121] *Id.*
[122] GCIV, *supra* note 1, art. 132.
[123] *Al-Waheed*, [2017] AC [80].
[124] ICRC, COMMENTARY 1958, *supra* note 11, at 258.

"subversive activity," actions which "are of direct assistance to an enemy Power"; membership in an organization "whose object is to cause disturbances," or other serious threats to security such as sabotage or espionage.[125] Leaving the term "security reasons" to wide governmental discretion is lamentable, since it might deprive this limitation from much of its constraining potential.[126]

The HCJ, referring to Pictet's examples, required the existence of "administrative evidence" which show "clearly and convincingly that if the measure ... is not adopted, there is a reasonable possibility that he [the individual] will present a real danger of harm to the security of the territory."[127] Yet, it stressed that the security reasons, in this context, are broader than mere "military reasons," and that within these confines, the military commander enjoys broad discretion, subject only to a "zone of reasonableness."[128] Loyal to its practice of shifting the discussion from authority to proportionality, the Court required proportionality between the "forbidden act" and the security measure, both in terms of severity and in terms of harm–benefit; an "appropriate relationship" between the measure and the prevention of the danger; and that the measure is the least harmful one available.[129] It could be inferred that the logic of least harmful requires that internment would only be undertaken when assigned residence would not suffice to alleviate the danger.[130] Nonetheless, in practice, Israel's use of administrative detention has been routinely criticized as "promiscuous."[131] In sum, the combination of the fact that the basis for administrative measures is usually classified, and the open texture of the notion of "security," greatly reduces the constraining power of article 78.

[125] *Id.*

[126] For the UK in Afghanistan, the valid test seems to have been "whether, on the balance of probabilities ... [the person] has done something which makes him a threat to self-defence, force protection, or wider mission accomplishment." *Al-Waheed*, [2017] AC [87]. While the two first reasons are highly concrete, the latter allows for much discretion.

[127] HCJ 7015/02 Ajuri v. IDF Commander in the West Bank, 56(2) PD 352 ¶ 25 (2002) (Isr.).

[128] *Id.* ¶ 29; *see also Al-Waheed*, [2017] AC [58].

[129] *Ajuri*, 56(2) PD ¶ 26; *compare* Al-Jedda v. UK, 2011-IV Eur. Ct. H.R. 305 ¶ 107.

[130] However, the HCJ ruled that once there is a valid cause for administrative measures against an individual, the occupant can decide to intern that person rather than to assign residence, in order to deter others. *Ajuri*, 56(2) PD ¶ 27. This position is by no means unproblematic.

[131] *See, e.g.*, United Nations, Press Release, Special Rapporteur on the Situation of Human Rights in the OPT Calls for Israel to End Practice of Administrative Detention and Immediately Release Maher Al-Akhras (Oct. 23, 2020), https://www.un.org/unispal/document/special-rapporteur-on-the-situation-of-human-rights-in-the-opt-calls-for-israel-to-end-practice-of-administrative-detention-and-immediately-release-maher-al-akhras-press-release/.

A last point of importance concerns the relations between security measures under article 78 and IHRL, namely the right to liberty. In general, IHRL does not permit assigned residence or administrative detention, *at least* absent a lawful derogation by the state party.[132] However, the Grand Chamber of the ECtHR ruled, in the *Hassan* case, that the subsequent practice of states is *not* to derogate from their obligations under the ECHR, or under the ICCPR, in order to detain persons on the basis of GCIV.[133] It proceeded to interpret article 5 of the ECHR, enshrining the right to liberty, to include the power to take security measures explicitly provided under article 78 GCIV.[134] In *Georgia v. Russia (II)*, the Court repeated this approach.[135]

5.4 Protection of Individuals: Specifically Prohibited Measures

As discussed above, all security measures in occupied territories must be rationally connected to valid security considerations. Furthermore, some measures are specifically provided for under the law of occupation, and include their own limitations. However, over and above these requirements, all security measures are capped by several general limitations. This means, in practice, that security necessity cannot be an overriding consideration. While this might seem obvious today, this was not always the case.[136]

5.4.1 Humane Treatment, Fundamental Guarantees, and Nondiscrimination

The first overarching limitation on security powers is found in article 27(1) GCIV:

[132] *See* Convention for the Protection of Human Rights and Fundamental Freedoms arts. 5, 15, Nov. 4, 1950, 213 U.N.T.S. 222 [hereinafter ECHR].

[133] Hassan v. UK, 2014-VI Eur. Ct. H.R. 1 ¶ 101; *but see* José Alvarez, *Limits of Change by Way of Subsequent Agreements in* Treaties and Subsequent Practice 123, 126 (Georg Nolte ed., 2013).

[134] *Hassan*, 2014-VI Eur. Ct. H.R., ¶¶ 102–107.

[135] Georgia v. Russia (II), App. No. 38263/08 ¶¶ 234–237, 253 (Jan. 21, 2021).

[136] For German practice in WWI, see Isabel V. Hull, A Scrap of Paper: Breaking and Making International Law During the Great War 95–140 (2014).

> Protected persons are entitled, in all circumstances, to respect for their persons, their honour, their family rights, their religious convictions and practices, and their manners and customs. They shall at all times be humanely treated, and shall be protected especially against all acts of violence or threats thereof and against insults and public curiosity.

For the law of occupation, article 27(1) GCIV plays a quasi-constitutional role, much like article 43 Hague. As phrased in the Commentary on GCIV, article 27 "is the basis of the Convention, proclaiming ... the principles on which the whole of 'Geneva Law' is founded."[137]

As always, the key issue is to determine the content of the rights enshrined in article 27(1). Article 32 GCIV clarifies, for example, that humane treatment includes inter alia the prohibition on murder, torture, and "any other measures of brutality."[138] These requirements should be read alongside article 75 API, which enshrines fundamental guarantees applicable to all those affected by international armed conflict.[139] The importance of article 75 goes beyond its more detailed enumeration of fundamental guarantees. In contrast to article 27(1), which applies to protected persons as they are defined in GCIV,[140] article 75 API applies to *all* persons in the power of a belligerent.[141]

The catalog of guarantees enshrined in these provisions limits all security measures available to the occupant, irrespective of their real or perceived contributions to the occupant's security interests. Of course, an additional cap on security powers can be found in IHRL, *at least* concerning rights not *explicitly* enshrined in these provisions, such as the freedom of speech, the freedom of movement, and the right to privacy[142]—to the extent that the occupant has not lawfully derogated from these rights.[143]

[137] ICRC, COMMENTARY 1958, *supra* note 11, at 199–200.

[138] GCIV, *supra* note 1, art. 32.

[139] API, *supra* note 4, art. 75.

[140] *See* Section 3.1.2.

[141] API, *supra* note 4, art. 75(1).

[142] This is especially pertinent nowadays regarding mass surveillance. *See, e.g.*, Waters, *supra* note 46; *but see* Asaf Lubin, *"We Only Spy on Foreigners": The Myth of a Universal Right to Privacy and the Practice of Foreign Mass Surveillance*, 18 CHI. J. INT'L L. 502 (2018). It should be noted that privacy rights can be read into the general terms of art. 27 GCIV.

[143] *See* Marko Milanovic, *Extraterritorial Derogations from Human Rights Treaties in Armed Conflict*, *in* THE FRONTIERS OF HUMAN RIGHTS: EXTRATERRITORIALITY AND ITS CHALLENGES 55 (Nehal Bhuta ed., 2016).

Additionally, even security measures that are otherwise not prohibited cannot be discriminatory. Article 27(3) GCIV provides that "all protected persons shall be treated with the same consideration ... without any adverse distinction based, in particular, on race, religion or political opinion."[144] This clearly means, for instance, that the occupant cannot discriminate in its security policies between protected persons belonging to different ethnic groups. Crucially, however, article 27(3) does not explicitly address discrimination between protected persons and *others* in the occupied territory. In particular, it overlooks the most acute potential for discrimination—that between protected persons and citizens of the occupant. For example, Israel is frequently criticized for applying severe security measures against Palestinians, while refraining from such measures against Israeli settlers.[145] One possible reason for this omission is that GCIV does not envision extensive presence of the occupant's citizens in the territory, owing to the prohibition enshrined in article 49(6) GCIV.[146]

Yet, to the extent that the occupant's citizens are in fact in the occupied territory, whether lawfully or unlawfully, this omission cannot be read as a license to discriminate.[147] Importantly, article 75(1) API applies to all persons "who do not benefit from more favourable treatment under the Conventions or under this Protocol." It adds prohibited grounds of discrimination not found in article 27(3) GCIV, including national origin. This provision can be understood as broadening the protection of protected persons, in instances in which they do not benefit from more favorable treatment under other provisions—namely, concerning their discrimination in relation to non-protected persons.[148] This is the better interpretation, since the raison d'être of the status of protected persons is to provide enhanced protection, and accordingly it cannot be read in manner justifying the preferential treatment of non-protected persons. Additionally,

[144] GCIV, *supra* note 1, art. 27(3).

[145] *See* Eliav Lieblich, *House Demolitions 2.0*, JUST SECURITY (Dec. 18, 2015), https://www.justsecurity.org/28415/house-demolitions-2-0/; *see* HCJ 8091/14 Hamoked v. Minister of Def., Nevo Legal Database (Dec. 31, 2014) (Isr.) *and* HCJ 2189/20 Hamid v. IDF Commander in the West Bank, Nevo Legal Database (Sept. 1, 2021) (Isr.).

[146] *See* Section 4.2.6.

[147] *See* HCJ 168/91 Murcus v. Minister of Def., 45(1) PD 467, 470–71 (1991) (Isr.).

[148] *See* ICRC, COMMENTARY ON ADDITIONAL PROTOCOLS OF 8 JUNE 1977 TO THE GENEVA CONVENTIONS OF 12 AUGUST 1949, 868 ¶ 3016 (1987) [hereinafter API 1987 COMMENTARY].

nondiscrimination obligations between protected and non-protected persons can be inferred from various IHRL treaties.[149]

5.4.2 The Principle of Individual Responsibility: Collective Punishment, Intimidation, Reprisals, and Hostage Taking

Even when measures are not discriminatory, or do not per se contravene fundamental guarantees, they must conform to the basic principle of individual responsibility.[150] Simply put, security measures against an individual must relate to a specific threat posed or offense committed by that person. Accordingly, article 33 GCIV prohibits measures that breach this principle, and amount to collective punishment, intimidation or terrorism, or reprisals.[151] Actions which violate this principle are wrongful because they violate basic principles of justice (just deserts), or because they use individuals merely as means to an end. This dual wrongfulness should undergird the understanding of the actions prohibited by article 33.

The most obvious contravention of the principle of individual responsibility is collective punishment. While the basic meaning and wrongfulness of collective punishment is quite intuitive, some complexities arise when attempting to give substance to the prohibition. This is especially true in occupation, since there is a potential of conflation between security measures with broad incidental effects and collective punishment.

The "collective" element of the prohibition refers, quite simply, to the infliction of "penalties on persons who have themselves not committed the acts complained of."[152] Unsurprisingly, occupants might attempt to assign some culpability to persons affected by the measure, and then argue that for this reason, the measure is not really "collective" punishment. For example,

[149] For instance, the Committee on the Elimination of Racial Discrimination (CERD) called on Israel to ensure that security measures it takes "[d]o not discriminate in purpose or in effect against . . . Palestinians." CERD, Concluding observations on the combined seventeenth to nineteenth reports of Israel, U.N. Doc. CERD/C/ISR/CO/17-19 (Jan. 27, 2020); *see also* Noam Lubell, *Human Rights Obligations in Military Occupation*, 94 Int'l Rev. Red Cross 317, 333–34 (2012).

[150] *See* Shane Darcy, *The Prohibition of Collective Punishment*, *in* Clapham et al., *supra* note 76, 1155, 1155–57.

[151] GCIV, *supra* note 1, art. 33. Collective punishments are also prohibited in all circumstances as a fundamental guarantee. API, *supra* note 4, art. 75(2)(d). *See* Darcy, *supra* note 150, at 1156–60.

[152] ICRC, Commentary 1958, *supra* note 11, at 225.

in a pre–WWI semiofficial German military publication, it was suggested that "failure to report criminal plans or to stop them" establishes guilt for the purpose of levying collective fines.[153] Israel, for example, argues in some cases of home demolitions of Palestinians militants that their family members *knew* about their actions in advance.[154] Yet, it seems that to preclude the *collective* nature of an act, it is not sufficient to demonstrate *any level* of culpability by the third person; rather, their responsibility must be reasonably comparable to that of the culprit, or one that would alone justify the specific measure (if it is not prohibited in any case).

An important question is what type of actions constitute "punishment." Clearly, punishments are responsive to a certain act, and must infringe on a certain right, interest, or otherwise adversely affect their addressees. While some cases would be obvious, law does not define precisely which adverse effects amount to punishment.[155] The question is whether the term includes only measures that resemble criminal penalties, or—on the other side of the spectrum—any measure that causes inconvenience. The Pictet commentary states that collective punishment is not limited to criminal sentences against non-responsible individuals, but extends to "penalties of any kind."[156] Yet, this begs the question, since the term "penalties" remains unclear. The API *Commentary* is more helpful, as it defines the term more functionally, suggesting that the concept "must be understood in the broadest sense: sanctions and harassment of any sort, administrative, by police action or otherwise."[157] Still, does any infringement of interests, or adverse effect on life quality, suffice to constitute such sanction or harassment? Or, rather, is it required that the act infringe the *rights* of the affected person?[158] This cannot be exhausted here. It suffices to say that the occupant's trusteeship duties militate toward a broader understanding of the prohibition. It seems contradictory that the law of occupation simultaneously obligates the occupant to further the interests of the local

[153] HULL, *supra* note 136, at 81.

[154] According to the HCJ, such advance knowledge is not a precondition for home demolitions, but only a factor to be taken into account when considering proportionality. *See, e.g.*, HCJ 480/21 Rabha v. Military Commander in the West Bank, Nevo Legal Database ¶ 12 (Feb. 3, 2021) (Isr.). For opposing views, see *infra* note 161.

[155] *Compare* Darcy, *supra* note 150, at 1161–62.

[156] ICRC, COMMENTARY 1958, *supra* note 11, at 225.

[157] API 1987 COMMENTARY, *supra* note 148, § 3055; *see also* HENCKAERTS & DOSWALD-BECK, ICRC, *supra* note 85, Rule 103.

[158] *See* Amichai Cohen, *Economic Sanctions in IHL: Suggested Principles*, 42 ISR. L. REV. 117, 128–32 (2009).

population, while tolerating the assignment of collective guilt or the use of persons merely as means to an end, even if the measure itself does not impinge on *rights* strictly construed.

This raises a further issue. Does "punishment" refer only to purely retributive, backward-looking measures? And, on the flipside, are preventive—or forward-looking—measures excluded from the definition? This question has arisen concerning the Israeli practice of demolishing homes of Palestinian militants in the West Bank.[159] Frequently, petitioners argued that the practice amounted to the collective punishment of families living in these homes. Typically, in such cases, the state retorts either that the families were not "innocent"—because they knew of the assailant's plans—or that since "the specific terrorist lived" in the house, there was no collective punishment but an act meant for "deterrence only."[160] In other words, since the act was meant to deter future assailants, it was not a retributive act of punishment. Throughout the years, the majority of the HCJ acquiesced in this interpretation.[161] This interpretation of collective punishment, however, has been widely criticized.[162] Since every act of retribution can be rephrased as an act of deterrence, this understanding allows sidestepping the prohibition on collective punishment entirely, simply by adjusting the terms of the language.[163]

Ultimately, the determinative factor in the definition of collective punishment seems to be the intent of the occupant concerning the affected individuals. If the measures are purely retributive against innocents, or intended to *opportunistically* use them as means—for instance, to deter others—they constitute collective punishment.[164] However, if the suffering of non-responsible individuals is only *incidental to an otherwise lawful measure* aimed at achieving a genuine security aim—consider, for instance, the suffering of the family of a lawfully detained person—then the measures would *not* amount to collective punishment.[165]

[159] See Section 6.1.1.

[160] *See, e.g.*, HCJ 8091/14 *Hamoked*, Nevo Legal Database.

[161] For minority views, see HCJ 7220/15 Aliwa v. IDF Commander in the West Bank, Nevo Legal Database (Dec. 1, 2015) (Isr.) (Opinion of Justice Mazuz); David Kretzmer & Yaël Ronen, The Occupation of Justice: The Supreme Court of Israel and the Occupied Territories 386–88 (2d ed. 2021).

[162] *See id.* at 388–91; Dinstein, *supra* note 95, at 171–72.

[163] *See* Lieblich, *supra* note 145.

[164] On opportunistic harm, see Adil Ahmad Haque, Law and Morality at War 11 (2017).

[165] However, such incidental adverse effects would still have to be proportionate.

The same distinction is valid concerning the prohibition of intimidation. While punishments are necessarily reactive, intimidation can be proactive, and is intended to prevent future action.[166] Here, too, isolating opportunistic uses of intimidation, as opposed to measures that cause incidental fear, is key. Arguably, prohibited measures of intimidation are acts that opportunistically use the fear of individuals in order to achieve a certain aim. This is as opposed to fear that can be incidentally caused by lawful actions. Of course, the difficulty is found in the fact that opportunistic intimidation can always be portrayed as merely "incidental" fear which accompanies legitimate goals (and vice versa). An example is Israel's deliberate use of sonic booms over Gaza in 2005–06.[167] Petitioners invoked article 33 GCIV, arguing that the sole objective of the sonic booms was to opportunistically cause fear and anxiety among civilians in Gaza in order to mount pressure on Palestinian armed groups. The state responded that in fact, the measure was not *intended* to cause fear among civilians. Rather, their fear was *incidental* to the objective of spreading confusion among members of armed groups.[168] The case was never decided since Israel ceased the practice.

The fact that the distinction between prohibited collective punishment and intimidation on the one hand—and incidental effects of lawful security measures on the other—revolves on intent makes it difficult for an external observer to differentiate between these cases. Arguably, a presumption is in order in such cases: when a measure is disproportionate in terms of its effects on third persons it is possible to surmise that these are not merely side effects, but the real intent of the action.[169]

Article 33 GCIV also prohibits reprisals against protected persons and their property.[170] API broadened this prohibition to include *all* civilians, beyond protected persons.[171] In traditional international law, belligerent reprisals were defined as proportionate measures undertaken by a belligerent in response to a previous violation of the laws of war, intended to induce

[166] *See* ICRC, Commentary 1958, *supra* note 11, at 225–26.

[167] *See* Eliav Lieblich, *Beyond Life and Limb: Exploring Incidental Mental Harm Under International Humanitarian Law*, *in* Applying International Humanitarian Law in Judicial and Quasi-Judicial Bodies: International and National Aspects 185, 198 (Derek Jinks, Jackson N. Maogoto & Solon Solomon eds., 2014).

[168] *Id.*

[169] *See* OSCE, Report on Violations of International Humanitarian and Human Rights Law, War Crimes and Crimes Against Humanity Committed in Ukraine Since 24 February 2022 25 (Apr. 13, 2022) (deriving intent from patterns).

[170] Françoise J. Hampson, *Belligerent Reprisals and the 1977 Protocols to the Geneva Conventions of 1977*, 37 Int'l & Comp. L.Q. 818, 825–26 (1988).

[171] API, *supra* note 4, arts. 51(6), 52(1); Hampson, *supra* note 170, at 828–29.

the violator to end the violation.[172] In the past, such actions were viewed as acceptable means of decentralized enforcement, and were permitted even if they would harm individuals.[173] However, belligerent reprisals against individuals are clearly contrary to the idea of individual responsibility, since they use persons merely as means to compel belligerents to comply with international law.

Last, article 34 GCIV prohibits taking hostages, which also amounts to a grave breach of the Convention.[174] Taking hostages is an opportunistic use of an individual par excellence. It is therefore prohibited even if the occupant invokes security considerations—such as the need to release its own captive soldiers.[175] IHL, however, does not define the term "hostages." A comprehensive definition can be found in the International Convention Against the Taking of Hostages.[176] This definition can inform the interpretation of hostage-taking as prohibited in article 34 GCIV and other provisions of IHL.[177]

5.4.3 Forcible Transfer and Deportation

A significant limitation on security powers is found in article 49(1) GCIV, prohibiting "[i]ndividual or mass forcible transfers, as well as deportations of protected persons from occupied territory ... regardless of their motive."[178] This prohibition has its roots in the transfers and deportations of WWII, and its objectives are double: obviously, it reflects a humanitarian imperative; yet it also supports the prohibition on altering the demographic composition of the occupied territories, as part of the conservationist principle.[179] The prohibition in article 49(1) encompasses two separate actions: forcible transfer and deportation. Forcible transfers are coerced

[172] *See* ICRC, COMMENTARY 1958, *supra* note 11, at 227; Hampson, *supra* note 170, at 821–24; *see also* FRITS KALSHOVEN, BELLIGERENT REPRISALS (1971).

[173] *See, e.g.*, FRANCIS LIEBER, INSTRUCTIONS FOR THE GOVERNMENT OF ARMIES OF THE UNITED STATES IN THE FIELD ¶¶ 27–28 (1863); Hampson, *supra* note 170, at 824–25.

[174] GCIV, *supra* note 1, art. 147. *See also* DINSTEIN, *supra* note 95, at 165–68.

[175] *See* ICRC, COMMENTARY 1958, *supra* note 11, at 229–31; CrimFH 7048/97 Anonymous v. Minister of Def., 54(1) PD 721 ¶ 20 (2000) (Isr.).

[176] International Convention Against the Taking of Hostages art. 1, Dec. 17, 1979, 1316 U.N.T.S. 205.

[177] *Compare* HENCKAERTS & DOSWALD-BECK, ICRC, *supra* note 85, Rule 96.

[178] GCIV, *supra* note 1, art. 49(1); it is also recognized as a grave breach in art. 147.

[179] *See* Section 4.2.6.

movements of protected persons *within* the occupied territory,[180] while deportation means their removal from the territory.[181]

The language of article 49(1) clarifies that the prohibition applies both to individual and mass actions, and that the prohibition is not subject to security or necessity exceptions. Granted, the majority of the HCJ ruled, in the 1980s, that the prohibition's object and purpose is to prevent mass deportations comparable to those undertaken by Nazi Germany, and therefore it does not apply to deportations of specific individuals for security reasons. On that basis, Israel carried out deportations of Palestinians from the occupied territories until the early 1990s.[182] Yet, this view was widely criticized, inter alia in light of the plain reading of the text.[183]

The prohibition on deportation is augmented and clarified by several other specific provisions. For instance, it is emphasized that in cases where, and to the extent that, compulsory labor is permitted, such work can only take place within the occupied territory.[184] Moreover, protected persons accused of offenses or convicted must be detained and serve their sentence in the territory.[185] As opposed to article 76(1) GCIV which addresses the accused or convicted, article 78—which deals with administrative detention ("internment")—does not mention explicitly that internees must also be held in the occupied territory. Nevertheless, this omission cannot be read as a permission to do what is prohibited by the general provision in article 49(1).[186]

[180] Internment, assigned residence, or imprisonment in accordance with the relevant provisions of GCIV do not constitute forcible transfer. GCIV, *supra* note 1, arts. 68, 78.

[181] *See* ICC, Decision on the Prosecution's Request for a Ruling on Jurisdiction under Article 19(3) of the Statute, ICC-RoC46(3)-01/18. ¶¶ 52–59 (Sept. 6, 2018).

[182] *See, e.g.*, HCJ 97/79 Awwad v. IDF Commander of Judea and Samaria, 33(3) PD 309, 316 (1979) (Isr.); HCJ 785/87 Afo v. IDF Commander in the West Bank, 42(2) PD 4 (1988) (Isr.) (opinion of President Shamgar).

[183] *See* Kretzmer & Ronen, *supra* note 161, at 74–75, 165–71, 184–86.

[184] GCIV, *supra* note 1, art. 51(3).

[185] *Id.* art. 76(1).

[186] ICRC, Commentary 1958, *supra* note 11, at 368. Since 1967, Israel holds Palestinian internees and prisoners both in facilities in the West Bank and in Israel. This was challenged twice in the HCJ, in cases two decades apart. In both cases, the Court ruled that Israeli domestic law on this issue trumped international law, and that in any case this practice was lawful under GCIV. In HCJ 253/88 Sajediya v. Minister of Def., 42(3) PD 801 (1988) (Isr.), petitioners were internees. The majority simply held that since articles 78 and 79 do not explicitly mention internees, they can be held in Israel notwithstanding article 49(1). *Id.* 812. The minority objected to this reading, holding inter alia that if convicted persons must be held in the territory, a fortiori that this applies to administrative internees. *Id.* at 828–29. For a critique of this majority ruling, see Kretzmer & Ronen, *supra* note 161, at 76–78. In HCJ 2690/09 Yesh Din v. IDF Commander in the West Bank, Nevo Legal Database (Mar. 28, 2010) (Isr.), petitioners requested the Court to reconsider its position both considering internees and prisoners. They emphasized that the reasoning of the ruling in *Sajediya* did not apply to the holding of *convicts* in Israel, which is expressly precluded by art. 76 GCIV. *Id.* ¶ 4. The Court in effect extended its

Spatially, the prohibition of deportation should be straightforward: it refers to the removal of a protected person from the occupied area. However, the issue becomes more complex when the occupant is in control of non-contiguous areas that belong to the same state or territorial unit. Here, the question arises whether the boundaries of the territory, for the sake of the prohibition, are determined *formally* or *functionally*. In the *Ajuri* case of 2002, the HCJ grappled with this question. The military commander issued orders of "assigned residence" to the petitioners, residents of the West Bank, ordering them to relocate to the Gaza Strip for two years. The orders were predicated on "decisive security reasons."[187] The state argued that the measure was lawful, since article 78 GCIV permits subjecting individuals to "assigned residence" within the occupied territory for imperative reasons of security.[188] The petitioners, however, argued that this was deportation, because the West Bank and Gaza are two different territories for the sake of article 49(1) GCIV. As they argued, the West Bank was taken from Jordan, while Gaza was taken from Egypt. Therefore, at hand are two different occupations, administered by two different military commanders.[189]

The Court rejected this argument, based on both formal and functional reasoning. Formally, it relied on the Oslo Accords, which defined the West Bank and Gaza as a single territorial unit. Functionally, it held that "from a social and political viewpoint" the territories are conceived as one territorial unit. It added that the purpose of the restriction of assigned residence only to the occupied territory "lies in the societal, linguistic, cultural, social and political unity of the territory, out of a desire to restrict the harm caused by assigning residence to a foreign place."[190] The application of this reasoning to the West Bank and Gaza is far from straightforward, considering that movement between the territories was heavily controlled at the time of the ruling. It would certainly not apply today, when Israel applies a "separation policy" between Gaza and the West Bank,[191] and argues that Gaza is no longer occupied.[192]

previous ruling, holding inter alia that the prolongation of occupation, the geographic proximity between the West Bank and Israel, the better conditions in facilities in Israel, and the need to refrain from expropriating land for prisons in the West Bank justify deviating from a strict textual reading of GCIV. *Id.* ¶¶ 7, 13–14.

[187] HCJ 7015/02 Ajuri v. IDF Commander in the West Bank, 56(2) PD 352 ¶ 7 (2002) (Isr.).
[188] *Id.* ¶ 9.
[189] *Id.* ¶¶ 19–21.
[190] *Id.* ¶ 22.
[191] *See* Section 4.2.6.
[192] *See* Section 2.6.2. Indeed, in later rulings, post-disengagement and Hamas's takeover of Gaza, when petitioners from Gaza requested permits to move to the West Bank, the Court held

It should be noted that basing boundaries—for the sake of distinguishing between assigned residence and deportation—on functional reasoning might in certain cases lead to the result that assigned residence within a single formal territory might amount to de facto deportation, if the person is ordered to move to a vastly different part of the occupied territory. Furthermore, even if such measure would not constitute deportation under article 49(1) GCIV, it might be considered a disproportionate application of article 78, because of the harm it causes to the individual.

Common to both forcible transfer and deportation is their coercive element. The term "coercion," however, is notoriously difficult to define. Particularly difficult are situations in which the occupant does not directly, or with physical force, expel persons from the territory or transfers them to another location, but rather creates conditions which induce such movement (whether by action or omissions). Such forms of "bureaucratic" coercion are difficult to identify. For instance, it has been argued that forcible transfer can be induced not only by physical coercion, but also by maintaining "coercive environments."[193]

Without exhausting this issue, some understanding of coercion, in this context, can be drawn from international criminal law. The ICC's Elements of Crime provide that the crime of "deportation or forcible transfer" requires "expulsion or other coercive acts."[194] On that basis, the ICC held that the crime is an "open-conduct crime," which may include various types of conducts such as "deprivation of fundamental rights, killing, sexual violence, torture, enforced disappearance, destruction and looting."[195] This contextual understanding of coercion follows previous jurisprudence in international tribunals.[196] In sum, both forcible transfers and deportation are based on an element of coercion that extends beyond physical expulsion.

A possible complication might arise concerning the conflation between forcible transfers and the occupant's powers to enforce the public order.[197]

that although the territories are formally one unit, "in reality" that is not the case. HCJ 11120/05 Hamdan v. Commander of Southern Front, Nevo Legal Database ¶ 14 (Aug. 7, 2007) (Isr.).

[193] *See, e.g.*, Simon Reynolds, Badil, Resource Center for Palestinian Residency and Refugee Rights, Coercive Environments: Israel's Forcible Transfer of Palestinians in the Occupied Territory (Nidal Al-Azza ed., 2017).

[194] ICC, Elements of Crimes, art. 7(1)(d) (2011) [hereinafter Elements of Crimes].

[195] ICC, *supra* note 181, at ¶ 62.

[196] *See* Ken Roberts & James G. Stewart, *Delimiting Deportation, Unlawful Transfer, Forcible Transfer and Forcible Displacement in International Criminal Law: A Jurisprudential History*, African J. Int'l Crim. Justice 56 (2019); Simon Reynolds, Badil, *supra* note 193, at 7–8.

[197] *Compare* CPA Order No. 6, Eviction of Persons Illegally Occupying Public Buildings, CPA/ORD/8 June 2003/06 (June 28, 2004), *reprinted in* 2 Stefan Talmon, The Occupation

For example, an occupant might seek to remove protected persons from a certain property or area, and claim that this removal was premised on their unlawful presence.[198] A clear-cut case would be where a person unlawfully enters private property, or builds in violation of local planning and zoning laws.[199] In such cases, removing these persons could be viewed as legitimate enforcement of public order. Yet, this cannot be the case when these laws are applied in a discriminatory manner to further the occupant's own interests in the territory, rather than the welfare of the local population.[200] It follows that the distinction between legitimate law enforcement and forcible transfer cannot be analyzed separately from the broader context in which it takes place.

An exception to the prohibition entrenched in article 49(1) is found in article 49(2), which addresses temporary evacuations of areas "if the security of the population or imperative military reasons so demand." The former consideration, pertaining to the security of the population, obviously refers to situations in which the population is at risk because of the proximity of hostilities. The other exception, that of "imperative military reasons," poses a significant risk of abuse. Interpreted too broadly, it might be used to circumvent the prohibition and render it ineffective. For this reason, it is suggested that this exception be narrowly construed, to include situations in which due to ongoing hostilities, and for clear operative reasons, the presence of civilians is an obstacle to military operations and it is essential to evacuate them.[201] This narrow construction is supported by the language of the article, which requires that evacuated persons shall be returned "as soon as hostilities in the area" end.[202] This phrasing suggests that in the absence of active hostilities, there are no ground for evacuations to begin with. In any case, evacuations should take place within the

of Iraq: The Official Documents of the Coalition Provisional Authority and the Iraqi Governing Council 20 (2013).

[198] *See* HCJ 6288/09 Ara'ara v. Head of Civil Administration in Judea and Samaria, Nevo Legal Database (Mar. 2, 2010) (Isr.); the ICC Elements of Crime, for example, require that the person was present *lawfully* in the Area. *See* Elements of Crimes, *supra* note 194, 7(1)(d).
[199] *Compare* Simon Reynolds, Badil, *supra* note 193, at 27.
[200] *Compare* European Parliament Resolution of 13 September 2018 on the Threat of Demolition of Khan al-Ahmar and Other Bedouin Villages, 2019 O.J. (C 433) 134; *Statement of ICC Prosecutor, Fatou Bensouda, Respecting an Investigation of the Situation in Palestine*, Int'l Crim. Ct. (Mar. 3, 2021), https://www.icc-cpi.int/Pages/item.aspx?name=210303-prosecutor-statement-investigation-palestine; Lieblich, *supra* note 13.
[201] *Compare* Dinstein, *supra* note 95, at 184–85 *with* Arai-Takahashi, *supra* note 11, at 342–43; *see* ICRC, Commentary 1958, *supra* note 11, at 280.
[202] GCIV, *supra* note 1, art. 49(2).

occupied territory, unless "material reasons" require evacuations outside the territory.[203]

5.4.4 Starvation, Siege, and Blockade

Several military tactics raise significant questions, when undertaken under occupation or by the occupant against the occupied territory as a whole. Common to these tactics is that in theory, while some of them might pursue legitimate security or military objectives, they simultaneously deprive the population of goods that the occupant is otherwise required to provide. To begin with, it is clear that intentional starvation of a population in occupied territories is prohibited, both as a general method of warfare and as a security measure under occupation.[204] The difficult question concerns situations of closures, sieges, and blockades, which even if not *intended* to cause starvation, cause significant deprivation to the protected population.[205] Note that we are not referring here to sieges as a limited operational measure in a specific instance,[206] but to long-term blockade and closures of a significant part of the occupied territory.

The most pertinent contemporary case concerns Israel's maritime and land measures against the Gaza Strip.[207] Israel consistently argues that these are lawful under international law, but as discussed at length earlier on, this is under Israel's assumption that Gaza is not occupied.[208] Assuming a territory is occupied, it should be conceded that there is no explicit prohibition, under the law of occupation, on blockades against the occupied territory[209]

[203] *Id.* art. 49(2); Dinstein, *supra* note 95, at 184. Furthermore, the occupant is obligated, in article 49(3) GCIV, *supra*, to ensure "to the greatest practicable extent" that evacuees are provided with basic living conditions. *See* ICRC, Commentary 1958, *supra* note 11, at 281. Arguably, this duty is complemented by IHRL. Comm. on Economic, Social and Cultural Rights (CESCR), General Comment No. 3: The nature of States Parties' Obligations (art. 2, para. 1, of the Covenant) Doc. No. E/1991/23 ¶ 10 (Dec. 14, 1990).

[204] API, *supra* note 4, art. 54(1); Dinstein, *supra* note 95, at 162–63.

[205] *See generally* Tom Dannenbaum, *Encirclement, Deprivation, and Humanity: Revising the San Remo Manual Provisions on Blockade*, 97 Int'l L. Stud. 307, 335–36 (2021).

[206] For instance, the 2002 siege by Israel of the Church of Nativity in Bethlehem. Dinstein, *supra* note 95, at 163–64.

[207] Eyal Benvenisti, *The International Law of Prolonged Sieged and Blockades: Gaza as a Case Study*, 97 Int'l L. Stud. 969 (2021).

[208] *See, e.g.*, 1 The Public Commission to Examine the Maritime Incident of 31 May 2010: The Turkel Commission Rep. (2010).

[209] Yet these must conform to the law of blockade, including the requirement of proportionality. *See* Int'l Inst. of Humanitarian L., San Remo Manual on International Law Applicable to Armed Conflicts at Sea arts. 102–103 (Louise Doswald-Beck ed., 1995).

or on establishing restrictions of movement of persons and goods to and from the occupied territory, to the extent that these can be justified as valid security measures. The question is whether it is possible to square an instance of blockade and closure with the occupant's duties in a specific case. In most cases, it would be difficult to reconcile a blockade with the duties toward the local population. For example, in the case of Gaza—and under the assumption that it is indeed occupied—an argument has been made that the measures undertaken by Israel in their entirety violate its duties to act in favor of the local population under article 43 Hague, as well as the occupant's positive duties to provide essential needs and not to interfere with relief consignments.[210]

Arguably, prolonged sieges or blockades create their own form of control over the life of the besieged population, even if they do not create an occupation in the legal sense. This form of control can result in wider obligations, which must consider not only the basic survival of the besieged population, but also their human dignity. These wider obligations might stem from the proportionality rule, and specifically the least harmful means test. Since prolonged sieges and blockades cause significant harm to the local besieged population, proportionality requires *at least* protecting the freedom of movement of civilians into and out of the blockaded area.[211] Further obligations might stem from IHRL, to the extent that sieges or blockades trigger state control or jurisdiction.[212]

5.5 Issues Concerning the Resort to Force in Occupied Territories

Within its provisions addressing security measures, the law of occupation does not explicitly refer to the use of lethal force by occupation authorities.[213] This has led to some controversy. Is such force subjected to rules applicable in law enforcement operations ("the law enforcement paradigm"), or those regulating the conduct of hostilities ("the hostilities paradigm")?

[210] *See, e.g.*, Marco Longobardo, *The Legality of Closure on Land and Safe Passage Between the Gaza Strip and the West Bank*, 11 Asian J. Int'l L. 50 (2020); *see also* Section 3.6.

[211] Benvenisti, *supra* note 207, at 981–82.

[212] *See id.* at 986–89.

[213] *See* Marco Longobardo, The Use of Armed Force in Occupied Territory 169–71 (2018).

The question is important since the hostilities paradigm is generally understood as less restrictive compared to the law enforcement paradigm.[214]

The use of force in law enforcement is subjected to the right to life under IHRL. Under this paradigm, resort to potentially lethal force may be permitted only at last resort, when strictly necessary to protect life or prevent serious injury from an imminent threat.[215] A common reference point for use of force in this context are the UN Basic Principles on the Use of Force and Firearms by Law Enforcement Officials.[216]

The hostilities paradigm kicks in whenever an *armed conflict* exists. It allows the status-based targeting of combatants,[217] as well as the targeting of civilians that directly participate in hostilities (DPH).[218] Even under the most restrictive understanding of DPH, this category allows targeting individuals in wider circumstances than would be permitted under the law enforcement paradigm.[219] According to some, during hostilities, it is also permitted to target individuals based on their membership in an organized armed group. While there are less and more restrictive positions on the conditions for such membership, all tolerate force beyond what is acceptable under the law enforcement paradigm.[220] Furthermore, under the hostilities paradigm, incidental civilian harm is tolerated as long as it is not excessive in relation to a concrete and direct military advantage.[221] According to the

[214] *See* ICRC, Expert Meeting: The Use of Force in Armed Conflicts, Interplay Between the Conduct of Hostilities and Law Enforcement Paradigms 4–13 (Gloria Gaggioli ed., 2013) [hereinafter Expert Meeting, The Use of Force].

[215] *See, e.g.*, Human Rights Council, Rep. of the Detailed Findings of the Independent International Commission of Inquiry on the Protests in the Occupied Palestinian Territory, U.N. Doc. A/HRC/40/CRP.2 ¶¶ 87–93 (Mar. 18, 2019) [hereinafter Rep. on Protests]; GC 36, *supra* note 96, ¶ 12.

[216] U.N. Secretariat, Eighth UN Congress on the Prevention of Crime and the Treatment of Offenders: Basic Principles on the Use of Force and Firearms by Law Enforcement Officials, at 110, U.N. Doc. A/CONF.144/28/Rev.1, U.N. Sales No. E.91.IV.2 (1990).

[217] *See* Gabriella Blum, *The Dispensable Lives of Soldiers*, 2 J. Leg. Analysis 115 (2010).

[218] API, *supra* note 4, art. 51(3).

[219] *See generally* Nils Melzer, ICRC, Interpretive Guidance on the Notion of Direct Participation in Hostilities Under International Humanitarian Law (2009) [hereinafter ICRC DPH Guidance].

[220] The ICRC requires that an individual perform a "continuous combat function" within the organization. *Id.* at 33–36; *see also* Human Rights Council, Report of the Independent Commission of Inquire on the 2014 Gaza Conflict, U.N. Doc. A/HRC/29/52 ¶ 37, ¶¶ 219–20 (June 22, 2015); Israel and the United States, conversely, argue for a much more permissive criterion of "formal" membership. Israel Ministry of Foreign Affairs, The 2014 Gaza Conflict: Factual and Legal Aspects ¶¶ 263–70 (2015); U.S. Dep't Def., Law of War Manual, 222 (2016) [hereinafter DoD Manual].

[221] API, *supra* note 4, art. 51(5)(b).

still orthodox view, during armed conflict, deprivations of life that conform to the hostilities paradigm would generally not be considered violations of the right to life.[222]

In this context, a misconception must first be set aside. Sometimes, it is implied that since the law of occupation is a branch of the law of IAC—as prescribed by Common Article 2 of the Geneva Conventions—this means that occupation *ipso facto* entails an armed conflict *within* the occupied territory.[223] This might lead to the conclusion that resort to force in occupied territories is by default governed by the hostilities paradigm. However, this view is imprecise. Occupation can indeed exist without any organized armed opposition within the territory. In such cases, there is no rationale that can justify applying the more permissive hostilities paradigm. For this reason, the better view is that the default framework regulating the resort to force in occupied territories is the law enforcement paradigm.[224]

There is some disagreement about the source of the law enforcement paradigm during occupation and its content.[225] Unsurprisingly, states that reject the application of IHRL in occupied territories, have sought to derive law enforcement standards from IHL itself.[226] In terms of content, they might argue that military necessity requires that in occupation the law enforcement paradigm admits "greater latitude" for resort to force than is permitted under IHRL.[227] Whether a law enforcement paradigm "exists" under IHL—and, if so, whether it is possible to argue that it differs in its content from IHRL—is doubtful. The concern is that such an understanding would lead to overly permissive interpretations that would dilute the protection of

[222] *But see* Eliav Lieblich, *The Humanization of* Jus ad Bellum, 32 Eur. J. Int'l L. 579 (2021); GC 36, *supra* note 96, ¶¶ 64, 70; Haque, *supra* note 164, at 35–38.

[223] *See* Tristan Ferraro, ICRC, Expert Meeting, Occupation and Other Forms of Administration of Foreign Territory 111 (2012) [hereinafter Expert Meeting, Occupation].

[224] *Id.* at 116; Longobardo, *supra* note 213, at 186–93. In fact, historically, their commitment to apply standards of policing was one of the key reasons why occupants thought they could demand "obedience" from occupied populations "in exchange" for such leniency. *See* Eyal Benvenisti, The International Law of Occupation 16 (2d ed. 2012).

[225] *See* Expert Meeting, Occupation, *supra* note 223, at 110–12.

[226] *See* Yahli Shereshevsky, HCJ 3003/18 Yesh Din—Volunteers for Human Rights v. Chief of General Staff, Israel Defense Forces (IDF), 113 Am. J. Int'l L. 361 (2019); Expert Meeting, Occupation, *supra* note 223, at 119–20; Expert Meeting, The Use of Force, *supra* note 214, at 11.

[227] Expert Meeting, Occupation, *supra* note 223, at 120. Compare the state's argument in HCJ 3003/18 Yesh Din v. IDF Chief of Staff, Nevo Legal Database (May 24, 2018) (Isr.); for a critique, see Shelly Aviv Yeini, *The Law Enforcement Paradigm Under the Laws of Armed Conflict: Conceptualizing* Yesh Din v. IDF Chief of Staff, 10 Harv. Nat'l Sec. J. 461 (2019).

civilians. For example, Israel has been criticized for deriving from a putative IHL-based law enforcement paradigm, a permission to use force against "key inciters or key rioters" during demonstrations and riots near the Gaza fence.[228] Nonetheless, given the more accepted view that IHRL applies in occupied territories,[229] the straightforward route is to apply, in such situations, the standards on resort to force found in IHRL.[230] This conclusion should not be controversial. Since the resort to force in law enforcement operations is not explicitly addressed by IHL, there is no conflict between these two frameworks, and consequently no grounds to argue that IHL norms displace IHRL.

While the law enforcement paradigm is the default, there could certainly be situations in which the hostilities paradigm would apply in occupied territories. Hostilities can erupt in a certain occupied area, without necessarily implying that the occupation is terminated on the whole.[231] The preferable model to identify such situations—which is in harmony with IHL at large—is that the hostilities paradigm applies whenever an armed conflict takes place in the relevant area within the territory.[232] Since such conflicts typically involve the occupying state and armed groups within the territory—the criteria to determine the existence of such armed conflict should follow those of NIAC: that is, that there is "protracted armed violence between governmental authorities and organized armed groups."[233] While some reach this conclusion by analogy, Longobardo argues that the application of this standard is a consequence of the fact that the occupant is subject to the same limitations on resort to force that would apply to the ousted sovereign.[234]

When armed conflict occurs in occupied territory, hostilities might take place in parallel with other forms of resistance, such as demonstrations

[228] Rep. on Protests, *supra* note 215, at 84–88; Eliav Lieblich, *Between the Paradigms: Israel's Rules of Engagement Around the Gaza Border in Light of Recent Supreme Court Jurisprudence*, 43 Tau L. Rev. 73 (2020).

[229] *See* Chapter 1.

[230] *Compare* Expert Meeting, Occupation, *supra* note 223, at 116–19;

[231] For a detailed discussion, see Longobardo, *supra* note 213, at 197–205.

[232] *Compare* Expert Meeting, Occupation, *supra* note 223, at 113–16.

[233] Prosecutor v. Tadić, Case No. IT-94-1-I, Decision on Def. Motion for Interlocutory Appeal on Jurisdiction, ¶ 70 (Int'l Crim. for the Former Yugoslavia Oct. 2, 1995). This does not prejudice the potential *status* of such conflicts as IACs, to the extent that the relevant state is bound by article 1(4) of API, *supra* note 4.

[234] *Compare* Expert Meeting, Occupation, *supra* note 223, at 115, *with* Longobardo, *supra* note 213, at 234–38. For an analysis of classification of conflicts between the occupant and NSAs, see *id.* at 214–29.

or riots. In such scenarios, the hostilities and law enforcement paradigm might apply in parallel, each regulating the relevant situation. The precise interaction between the paradigms in such mixed scenarios is beyond the scope of this book.[235]

Some confusion exists concerning the relevance of article 51 of the UN Charter, which enshrines states' right to self-defense, to occupied territories. Can states invoke article 51 to justify resort to force within occupied territories? In justification of its Wall within the West Bank, Israel argued that its construction was consistent with article 51 of the Charter, as a measure of self-defense.[236] In the *Wall Advisory Opinion*, the ICJ held that article 51 was irrelevant here, both because there was no threat by a foreign state, and since the threat emanated from within an occupied territory.[237] The first reason concerns the general controversy regarding self-defense against NSAs, which we do not discuss here.[238] The second conclusion—despite its laconic reasoning—is ultimately sound. To the extent that article 51 is relevant in situations of occupation, it is for the purpose of assessing the necessity or proportionality of *continuing* an occupation.[239] However, threats from within occupied territory are to be addressed through the application of article 43 Hague and other relevant security provisions of the law of occupation.[240]

Last, a recurring question concerns the existence of the occupied population's "right to resist" by armed force. This question is of course of much political and legal importance, and accordingly was a longstanding, unresolved issue during the negotiations of the treaties comprising the law of occupation. As discussed in Chapter 1,[241] these negotiations resulted in an uneasy compromise: resistance is not explicitly *prohibited*

[235] *See* Expert Meeting, Occupation, *supra* note 223, at 113; Expert Meeting, The Use of Force, *supra* note 214, at 24–29.

[236] Legal Consequences of the Construction of a Wall in the Occupied Palestinian Territory, Advisory Opinion, 2004 I.C.J. Rep. 136 ¶ 138 (July 9).

[237] *Id.* ¶ 139; but *see* Declaration of Judge Buergenthal, ¶¶ 4–5.

[238] *See, e.g.*, Monica Hakimi, *Defensive Force Against Non-State Actors: The State of Play*, 91 Int'l L. Stud. 1 (2015); 1 Mary Ellen O'Connell, Christian J. Tams & Dire Tladi, Self-Defense Against Non-State Actors (2019).

[239] A related question concerns the *jus ad bellum* legality of defensive action to recover occupied territories. *Compare* Tom Ruys & Felipe Rodríguez Silvestre, *Military Action to Recover Occupied Land: Lawful Self-Defense or Prohibited Use of Force? The 2020 Nagorno-Karabakh Conflict Revisited*, 97 Int'l L. Stud. 665 (2021) *with* Dapo Akande & Antonios Tzanakopoulos, *Legal: Use of Force in Self-Defence to Recover Occupied Territory: When Is It Permissible?*, 32 Eur. J. Int'l L. 1299 (2022).

[240] *See* Scobbie, *supra* note 12, at 81–86; *compare* Longobardo, *supra* note 213, at 88–133.

[241] *See* Section 1.4.1.

by international law, or per se considered a war crime; however—at least when article 1(4) API does not apply—the occupant may subject resistance fighters to penal law, as long as it accords them basic rights.[242]

Ultimately, the question of the right to resist is not exhausted by the law of occupation, as part of *jus in bello*. At the end of the day, this question is a corollary of the legal effects of the right to self-determination, and the extent to which it provides a right of armed resistance if a certain occupation violates it. Like other questions which mainly involve legal frameworks neighboring to the law of occupation, we cannot exhaust it here.[243]

[242] BENVENISTI, *supra* note 224, at 16. API, *supra* note 4, art. 1(4). Article 1(4) defines self-determination struggles against "alien occupation" as IACs, which might entail POW status for persons fighting in such conflicts, if they abide by conditions outlined in articles 43–44 API.

[243] *See* LONGOBARDO, *supra* note 213, at 134–64.

6
Private and Public Property and Natural Resources

6.1 Protection of Private Property

The right to private property, along with the right to life and "family honour and rights," is one of the few individual rights explicitly protected under Hague IV,[1] a clear testament to the laissez-faire approach predominant in the law of occupation's formative years.[2] This protection of private property has negative and positive aspects. Negatively, the occupant must *respect* the right to private property, by not violating it itself.[3] Positively, the occupant must protect private property against violations by others, as part of its general public order duties.[4] Importantly, the protection of private property does not only encompass prohibitions on unlawful transfers of title, or arbitrary destruction, but also interference in the exercise of the right such as limiting use or access.[5] Furthermore, the protection of property under the law of occupation does not refer only to property belonging to protected persons, but also to foreign-owned property .[6]

The modern protection of property replaced older customary norms which permitted belligerents to take all private property in enemy territory.[7] Granted, during the 18th century, the wholesale pillage of enemy

[1] Convention (IV) respecting the Laws and Customs of War on Land and its annex: Regulations concerning the Laws and Customs of War on Land art. 46, Oct. 18, 1907, 187 C.T.S.227 [hereinafter Hague IV].

[2] *See* Section 3.1.3.

[3] Hague IV, *supra* note 1, art. 46.

[4] *Id.* art. 43.

[5] Yoram Dinstein, The international Law of Belligerent Occupation 243 (2d ed. 2019).

[6] *See* Ernst H. Feilchenfeld, The International Economic Law of Belligerent Occupation 139 (1942).

[7] Gerhard von Glahn, The Occupation of Enemy Territory: A Commentary on the Law and Practice of Belligerent Occupation 185 (1957).

private property was renounced;[8] however, it was replaced by "systemic and organized plunder" through widespread requisitions and contributions paid to the occupying state, justified by the maxim that *war pays for war*. Enriching the state by despoiling the enemy's subjects was viewed, at the time, as a legitimate end of war.[9] As Bentwich pointed out, the ideas of the French Revolution, and Rousseau's perception of war as a relationship between sovereigns only, led to the gradual acceptance of the idea that individual property, like civilians in general, should be distinguished from the "enemy" qua political entity.[10] The treatment of private property in Hague IV reflects this perception.

Of course, a different, materialistic account can explain this protection of property. If the conservationist impulse of the law of occupation was, to an extent, a pact between ruling elites, it is unsurprising that it would seek to ensure to elites their property in case of foreign occupation. While there is certainly truth in this account, the humanitarian imperatives of the protection of property under occupation cannot be disregarded, given the relationship between property and basic livelihood in contemporary political economy.

Arguably, by protecting property, the law of occupation disregards non-western, customary forms of ownership, mostly attributed to indigenous peoples.[11] This is unsurprising, considering that in its formative years, the law of occupation did not apply beyond Europe to begin with.[12] If property would be understood strictly in the formal, western manner, the door would be open to vast deprivation in occupied territories where different forms of ownership are practiced. Therefore, the protection of property must be constructed flexibly, taking into account the particular customs and practices of the specific territory.[13]

[8] Norman Bentwich, Law of Private Property in War, with a Chapter on Conquest 10 (1907).

[9] *Id.* at 10.

[10] *Id.* at 11; Feilchenfeld, *supra* note 6, at 12.

[11] *See generally* David Lea, Property Rights, Indigenous People and the Developing World: Issues from Aboriginal Entitlement to Intellectual Ownership Rights (2008).

[12] *See* Section 1.2.

[13] *See* Shlomit Stein, *Reflections on Indigenous Peoples' Rights vis-à-vis the Law of Occupation*, 23 Int'l J. Hum. Rights 297 (2019); G.A. Res. 61/295, U.N. Declaration on the Rights of Indigenous Peoples (Sept. 13, 2007); Eliav Lieblich, *Wrong to the Core: The Supreme Court of Israel's Ruling on Masafer Yatta*, Verfassungsblog (May 8, 2022), https://verfassungsblog.de/wrong-to-the-core/.

Unsurprisingly, although the law of occupation provides for basic protection of private property, it also permits certain interferences. These can be classified into two categories. The first comprises interferences phrased as security exceptions. Such is the case of *requisitions*, which can only be demanded "for the needs of the army of occupation";[14] of destruction of property, which is prohibited except when "rendered absolutely necessary by military operations";[15] and of levying money contributions "for the needs of the army."[16] Another interference in this category is the power to seize means of communications and transport, and all kinds of munitions of war—even if they are privately owned.[17] Last, a potential infringement of property is implicit in the occupant's power to subject protected persons to penal provisions, which includes the power to impose fines.[18]

The second category concerns infringements of property for public purposes. These include *expropriation* of property, in line with the occupant's trusteeship obligations under article 43 Hague, as well as collecting existing taxes for the administration of the territory, and levying money contributions for the same purpose.[19]

Although this section focuses in detail on the protections of private property and their exceptions, some of the issues here are also relevant to public property, as will be pointed out. Issues specific to public property only are discussed in subsequent sections.

6.1.1 Prohibitions on Confiscation, Pillage, and Destruction

The law of occupation explicitly prohibits three interrelating infringements of the right to property: confiscation,[20] pillage,[21] and destruction.[22] Common to all three is that they result in permanent deprivation.[23]

[14] Hague IV, *supra* note 1, art. 52.

[15] Convention (IV) relative to the Protection of Civilian Persons in Time of War art. 53, August 12, 1949, 6 U.S.T. 3516, 75 U.N.T.S. 287 [hereinafter GCIV].

[16] Hague IV, *supra* note 1, art. 49.

[17] *Id.* art. 53.

[18] *See* von Glahn, *supra* note 7, at 188; Dinstein, *supra* note 5, at 247.

[19] Hague IV, *supra* note 1, arts. 48–49. On taxation, see Section 7.1.

[20] Hague IV, *supra* note 1, art. 46.

[21] *Id.* art. 47; GCIV, *supra* note 15, art. 33.

[22] GCIV, *supra* note 15, art. 53.

[23] Furthermore, reprisals against property are also prohibited. *See* Section 5.3.2.

Confiscation is best viewed as a residual prohibition that applies to any infringement of property contrary to specific provisions.[24] The core wrong of confiscation is not only in deprivation of property, but also in its coercive nature. For this reason, offering compensation for the property does not legalize the taking, absent other valid justifications.[25]

The prohibition on *pillage* is phrased in absolute terms, and as such it applies to private and public property.[26] Dinstein suggests a further distinction between pillage and plunder (or spoliation). Plunder (or spoliation) refer to "widespread and systemic acts of dispossession" in occupied territories aiming to enrich the occupying *state* or to sustain its war.[27] Such actions do not fall under the prohibition on pillage, but under the prohibition on confiscation (in relation to private property), and under the norms protecting public property. It is also criminalized as a grave breach of GCIV.[28] Pillage, according to Dinstein's view, is distinguished from plunder (or spoliation) by applying to taking of any property by *individual soldiers* for private use.[29]

It is doubtful whether the prohibition on pillage applies or ought to apply only to acts by individual soldiers.[30] The modern prohibition on pillage was introduced not only to oblige occupants to prevent pillage by individual soldiers, but also to prohibit organized taking of property as payment for the occupant's soldiers, as was common in the past.[31] Accordingly, the definition of the crime of pillaging, under the Elements of Crimes of the ICC, does not exclude cases of organizational involvement. Rather, the core of the wrong of pillage is in the taking of property for private use, not that it is taken *by* an individual.[32]

[24] FEILCHENFELD, *supra* note 6, at 51.

[25] I.G. Farben Trial (Krauch et al.), X United Nations War Crimes Comm'n, Law Reports of Trials of War Criminals 1, 44 (U.S. Military Tribunal, Nuremberg) [hereinafter I.G. Farben case], *cited in* DINSTEIN, *supra* note 5, at 243.

[26] *See* FEILCHENFELD, *supra* note 6, at 31.

[27] DINSTEIN, *supra* note 5, at 224, referring inter alia to the I.G. Farben case, *supra* note 25, at 133–35.

[28] GCIV, *supra* note 15, art. 147.

[29] DINSTEIN, *supra* note 5, at 225; *see also* FEILCHENFELD, *supra* note 6, at 32.

[30] Although it could be that the prohibition on pillage was devised precisely as an instrument by states to rein in their *own* individual soldiers in the field. *Compare* Eyal Benvenisti & Amichai Cohen, *War Is Governance: Explaining the Logic of the Laws of War from a Principal–Agent Perspective*, 112 MICH. L. REV. 1363 (2014).

[31] *See* ICRC, COMMENTARY ON IV GENEVA CONVENTION 226–27 (Jean S. Pictet ed., 1958) [hereinafter ICRC, COMMENTARY 1958]; Prosecutor v. Delalić, Case No. IT-96-21-T, Judgment, ¶ 590 (Int'l Crim. Trib. for the Former Yugoslavia Nov. 16, 1998).

[32] ICC, ELEMENTS OF CRIMES 26 (2011). *See I.G. Farben* case, *supra* note 25.

Furthermore, the taking does not have to be for the taker's *own* use, but also for the benefit of a third party.[33] This distinction is pertinent in the context of occupation. In principle, the act of pillaging, understood in this manner, could extend to unjustified exploitation of resources by the occupant for the benefit of third parties; to granting concessions to third parties in a manner inconsistent with the occupant's trusteeship duties; as well as to transferring land to settlers and comparable acts.[34]

The prohibition on *destruction* of property is enshrined in article 53 GCIV, which prohibits the destruction of any property, private or public, except when it is "rendered absolutely necessary by military operations."[35] Of course, the key question here concerns the scope of this exception, which largely turns on the definition of the terms "absolutely necessary" and "military operations." Notably, the ICJ, in both the *Wall Advisory Opinion* and *Armed Activity* case found violations of article 53 without elaboration on the content of its exception.[36]

The perils of widening the exception under article 53 are reflected in the context of West Bank home demolitions. Petitioners frequently argued, in front of the HCJ, that Israel's demolitions of homes of Palestinian militants are not only collective punishments (as discussed in Chapter 5), but also unlawful destruction under article 53. As they claimed, *arguendo*, even if demolitions were meant to deter future attacks, the objective of deterrence is not "absolutely necessary for military operations."[37] The Court, however, ruled that article 53 must be adapted to the "war against terror," and consequently that it should accommodate measures of deterrence.[38] This is

[33] *Delalić*, Case No. IT-96-21-T, ¶ 585; FEILCHENFELD, *supra* note 6, at 30.

[34] Armed Activities on the Territory of the Congo (Dem. Rep. Congo v. Uganda), Judgment, 2005 I.C.J. Rep. 168 ¶ 245 (Dec. 19) [hereinafter *DRC v. Uganda*]; for a discussion, see Larissa van Der Herik & Daniëlla Dam-De Jong, *Revitalizing the Antique War Crime of Pillage: The Potential and Pitfalls of Using International Criminal Law to Address Illegal Resource Exploitation During Armed Conflict*, 22 CRIM. L. FORUM 237 (2011).

[35] GCIV, *supra* note 15, art. 53 is an explicit application to occupied territories of the prohibition found in article 23(g) Hague IV, *supra* note 1, "[t]o destroy or seize the enemy's property, unless such destruction or seizure be imperatively demanded by the necessities of war." In the Legal Consequences of the Construction of a Wall in the Occupied Palestinian Territory, Advisory Opinion, 2004 I.C.J. Rep. 136, ¶¶ 80–85 (July 9) [hereinafter Wall Opinion], the ICJ opined in dictum that article 23(g) Hague does not apply in occupied territories. Wall Opinion, at 185. However, this approach has been criticized. *See* DINSTEIN, *supra* note 5, at 210–11.

[36] Wall Opinion ¶¶ 126, 132, 135. *See* David Kretzmer, *The Advisory Opinion: The Light Treatment of International Law*, 99 Am. J. Int'l L. 88, 98–100 (2005); *DRC v. Uganda* ¶ 219.

[37] HCJ 8091/14 Hamoked v. Minister of Def., Nevo Legal Database ¶ 8 (Dec. 31, 2014) (Isr.).

[38] *Id.* ¶¶ 23–24.

highly problematic. First, if deterrence can be considered absolutely necessary for military operations, it is difficult to imagine a security interest that would be excluded. Second, the term "absolutely necessary" requires a level of certainty regarding the relation between the measure and the military aim, which deterrence simply does not possess. Third, the phrase "military operations" does not fit conveniently with quasi-law enforcement measures.[39]

Two understandings of the exception under article 53 GCIV are possible. Arguably, the essence of article 53 reflects the general principle of distinction. As such, it must be read in light of later codifications of the principle, as enshrined in API.[40] If this is true, it can be said that the absolute necessity required in article 53 GCIV materializes only when the object would qualify as a military objective under article 52(2) API.[41] Such necessity would also require that hostilities are taking place in the territory, since only then attacks against objects might be lawful.

Conversely, Dinstein argues that "[t]he phrase 'military operations' in occupied territories must be understood as spreading a wide net," which extends beyond active hostilities, also to actions to "quell violence" by armed groups and individuals.[42] Based, inter alia, on judgments of the HCJ, Dinstein claims that the occupant enjoys wide discretion to assess what is "absolutely necessary by military operations," limited by proportionality requirements.[43] Yet, the justification for powers to destroy property during occupation which are wider than those available in active hostilities is far from clear.

[39] *See generally* Philip C. Jessup, *A Belligerent Occupant's Power over Property*, 38 AM. J. INT'L L. 457, 458 (1944); Eliav Lieblich, *House Demolitions 2.0*, JUST SECURITY (Dec. 18, 2015), https://www.justsecurity.org/28415/house-demolitions-2-0/; Guy Harpaz, *When Does a Court Systematically Deviate from Its Own Principles: The Adjudication by the Israel Supreme Court of House Demolitions in the Occupied Palestinian Territories*, 28 LEID. J. INT'L L. 31, 34–35 (2015). *See also* YUTAKA ARAI-TAKAHASHI, THE LAW OF OCCUPATION: CONTINUITY AND CHANGE OF INTERNATIONAL HUMANITARIAN LAW, AND ITS INTERACTION WITH INTERNATIONAL HUMAN RIGHTS LAW 186–91 (2009).

[40] Protocol Additional to the Geneva Conventions of 12 August 1949, and relating to the Protection of Victims of International Armed Conflicts (Protocol I) art. 1(3), June 8, 1977, 1125 U.N.T.S. 3 [hereinafter API].

[41] *See also* U.S. Dep't Def., Law of War Manual, 780 (2016) [hereinafter DoD Manual].

[42] *But see* DINSTEIN, *supra* note 5, at 212. On force in occupied territories, see Section 5.5.

[43] *Id.* at 213–14, relying on ICRC, COMMENTARY 1958, *supra* note 31, at 302.

6.1.2 Requisitions

The occupant possesses significant power to interfere in private property, by demanding requisitions "for the needs of the army of occupation"—in accordance with the conditions of article 52 Hague. While the article explicitly refers to requisitions "in-kind and services," it is often interpreted to extend also to immovable property.[44] This is the better view, otherwise occupants might seize immovable property without the limiting aspects of article 52, citing general security considerations or military necessity.[45] Whether requisition amounts to transfer of title depends on the nature of the requisitioned item. Regarding consumable items, requisition naturally amounts to de facto transfer of title, since they cannot be returned. Regarding immovable property, the case is different because the property is only temporary held by the occupant and must be released once the military need is exhausted.[46] For this reason, the occupant cannot treat requisitioned immovables as if they are held permanently, or transfer title to third parties.[47]

Importantly, requisitions of services are also regulated by article 51 GCIV, which addresses compulsory labor. Article 51 contains limitations concerning the permitted aims of such work; a requirement of fair wage; and mandates the subjection of requisitioned services to the labor laws in force.[48]

Perhaps the key condition for requisitions is that they "shall not be demanded ... except for the needs of the army of occupation." Since explicit reference is made to the needs of the *army of occupation*, requisitions aiming to enrich the occupying state or to impoverish the occupied territory are clearly excluded. Likewise, requisitions cannot be employed to serve needs outside of the occupied territory, even if these are ultimately military.[49] Requisitions must therefore be needed for the *local operations* of the occupying army.

[44] *See* ARAI-TAKAHASHI, *supra* note 39, at 218–22; G. Schwarzenberger, *The Protection of Private Property in the Law of Belligerent Occupation*, 1 INDIAN J. INT'L L. 193 (1960); *compare* DINSTEIN, *supra* note 5, at 245–47; DoD Manual, *supra* note 41, at 787. Regarding computer data, see TALLINN MANUAL 2.0 ON THE INTERNATIONAL LAW APPLICABLE TO CYBER OPERATIONS 550 (Michael N. Schmitt ed., 2d ed. 2017) [hereinafter TALLINN MANUAL 2.0].

[45] *Compare* VON GLAHN, *supra* note 7, at 186.

[46] *See* FEILCHENFELD, *supra* note 6, at 38–39.

[47] *But see* HCJ 606/78 Ayub v. Minister of Def., 33(2) PD 113 (1979) (Isr.) where the HCJ ruled controversially that civilian settlement on private land can be viewed as a temporary measure.

[48] GCIV, *supra* note 15, art. 51.

[49] FEILCHENFELD, *supra* note 6, at 34; Krupp Trial (Krupp et al.), X United Nations War Crimes Comm'n, Law Reports of Trials of War Criminals 134 (U.S. Military Tribunal,

Nonetheless, the overarching problem of the law of occupation—the indeterminacy of security exceptions—persists also concerning requisitions. Article 52 Hague lacks a definition of the relevant *needs of the army*, as well as the circumstances under which requisitions can be demanded to serve them.[50]

The Israeli practice on requisitioning land in the West Bank is particularly telling.[51] The *Ayub* case concerned requisitions of private Palestinian land in the West Bank, ostensibly for military needs, but ultimately for Israeli settlements.[52] The landowners challenged the requisition, arguing that military needs and civilian settlements are a contradiction in terms. They claimed that military needs should be strictly construed, as relating to the operational and logistical needs of the occupying army—and not to broader security considerations. The HCJ rejected the latter argument, holding that military needs and preventive security are "in fact the same aspect,"[53] and that whatever is required for public order and safety "is required anyway for the needs of the occupying army in the sense of Article 52."[54] It furthermore held that settlements comprising citizens of the occupant do, in fact, contribute to the local security, by helping the military in its mission.[55] Clearly, the expansion of article 52 Hague to any security aspect, along with the view that security considerations can include the establishment of civilian settlements, deprive the article of its meaningful limiting potential, and demonstrate the need for a narrow construction.[56] In subsequent years, the HCJ limited requisitions of private property for settlements—albeit without changing its broad interpretation of article

Nuremberg), *cited in* DINSTEIN, *supra* note 5, at 248. Germany transferred requisitioned items outside of the occupied territory in WWI, and was widely condemned. *See* FEILCHENFELD, *supra* note 6, at 35.

50 *See* DINSTEIN, *supra* note 5, at 246–47; ARAI-TAKAHASHI, *supra* note 39, at 222–25. In the context of cyber operations, see TALLINN MANUAL 2.0, *supra* note 44, at 550.

51 *Ayub*, 33(2) PD 11.

52 *Id.*

53 *Id.* Opinion of Justice Vitkon.

54 *Id.* Opinion of Justice Landau.

55 *Id.* The Court refrained from applying article 49(6) GCIV, based on considerations discussed in Section 2.2.2.

56 *See* DAVID KRETZMER & YAËL RONEN, THE OCCUPATION OF JUSTICE: THE SUPREME COURT OF ISRAEL AND THE OCCUPIED TERRITORIES 193–205 (2d ed. 2021). *Compare* the case of Ralli Brothers v. German Gov't, 2 Ann. Dig. Pub. Int'l L. 446 (Anglo-German Mixed Arbitral Trib. 1924), *cited in* FEILCHENFELD, *supra* note 6, at 36 n.2.

52—by requiring that the dominant objective of the requisition must be security related and not "political."[57]

When military needs do in fact exist, it seems that under the principle of proportionality, the occupant must refrain from requisitions when less intrusive means are available. For example, if the occupant can reasonably provide the items itself, or purchase them on the open market in the territory,[58] resort to requisitions seems unjustified.[59] The discussion, in Chapter 4, on prolonged occupation is pertinent: it is reasonable that as occupation is prolonged and control is entrenched, there would be less justification for requisitions.

Article 52 Hague further provides that requisitions "shall be in proportion to the resources of the country." The traditional view was that since this limitation refers to the aggregate resources of the country, as opposed to the resources of individuals, the effect of the requisition over a specific owner is irrelevant. Feilchenfeld even argued that "an occupant may take a farmer's last cow and piece of bread as long as … he does not unduly exhaust the cattle and bread supply of the whole country."[60] This interpretation is impossible nowadays, considering the application of IHRL in occupied territories, and the subjection of security measures to the principle of proportionality.[61] A two-tier proportionality test is therefore necessary: first in relation to the resources of the country at large; and second in relation to the directly affected individuals.

Article 52 limits requisitions in three additional ways, which we mention here only in passing. First, requisitions cannot impose an obligation to take part in military operations against the individual's own country. This requirement, which is naturally more relevant to services rather than goods, is a specific reflection of the general principle that the occupant possesses limited authority over the occupied population.[62] Second, requisitions must only be demanded "on the authority of the commander in the locality occupied."[63] The article fails to specify the level of command required, but

[57] HCJ 390/79 Duweikat v. Government of Israel, 34(1) PD 1, 20 (1979) (Isr.). *See also* HCJ 1308/17 Silwad Municipality v. The Knesset, Nevo Legal Database ¶9 (June 9, 2020) (Isr.).

[58] *See* Jessup, *supra* note 39, at 460.

[59] *Compare* von Glahn, *supra* note 7, at 169–70.

[60] Feilchenfeld, *supra* note 6, at 37; *see also* Dinstein, *supra* note 5, at 248; von Glahn, *supra* note 7, at 168.

[61] *See* Section 5.2.5.

[62] *See, e.g.*, arts. 44–45.

[63] Hague IV, *supra* note 1, art. 52.

its rationale is clear: to ensure that requisitions are ordered only by those qualified to know that they are necessary and authorized to provide compensation.[64] Third, payment for requisitions should be "as far as possible" in cash, and, if not, a receipt must be given and payment must be made as soon as possible.[65] This is meant to clarify that compensation must be paid by the occupant and not by the de jure sovereign at the conclusion of the war, as some previously argued.[66] A major gap is found in the fact that article 52 does not specify the manner of valuation.[67] Article 55 GCIV supplements article 52 Hague with the requirement that "fair value" be paid for requisitions.[68] There is no reason to assume that fair value should not reflect the market value of the requisition.

Importantly, GCIV and API place special limitations on certain requisitions. As discussed in Chapter 3, GCIV imposes positive obligations to ensure necessary supplies for the population in the territory—foodstuffs, medical stores, and "other [necessary] articles."[69] It furthermore emphasizes that requisition of such supplies can only be demanded once the "requirements of the civilian population have been taken into account."[70] Similar requirements are found in GCIV concerning the requisition of civilian hospitals and their "material and stores." These can only be demanded in case of "urgent necessity," and where civilian needs have been ensured.[71] Similarly, API limits requisitions of buildings or material belonging to civil defense organizations, as well as shelters.[72] Taken together, these provisions clarify that the occupant's trusteeship obligations do not recede in the context of requisitions, and that ultimately military needs do not trump civilian needs.[73] Last, it is clear that requisitions cannot be used to circumvent specific prohibitions, such as against forcible transfer.[74]

[64] *Compare* Dinstein, *supra* note 5, at 248.
[65] Hague IV, *supra* note 1, art. 52.
[66] This is evident in the change in the language of article 52 between 1899 and 1907. On the former version, see Bentwich, *supra* note 8, at 34.
[67] *See* Dinstein, *supra* note 5, at 249.
[68] GCIV, *supra* note 15, art. 55; Dinstein, *supra* note 5, at 249.
[69] GCIV, *supra* note 15, art. 55(1).
[70] *Id.* art. 55(2).
[71] *Id.* art. 57.
[72] API, *supra* note 40, arts. 63(4)–64(6).
[73] *See also id.* art. 14.
[74] *See* Section 5.4.3.

6.1.3 Expropriation

While requisitions envision—at least concerning immovable property—temporary use for military needs, expropriation involves permanent transfer of title, undertaken when property is needed for the *public* good. As opposed to requisitions, the law of occupation does not mention expropriation explicitly. In practice, powers to expropriate have been read into the occupant's general powers under article 43 to act in favor of the local population.[75] In line with the overarching principles of the law of occupation, the power to expropriate may exist solely for this purpose.[76] Because questions of distribution are fundamental questions of the *body politic*, the obligation to respect the status quo ante on expropriations is especially stringent.[77] Granted, the especially restrictive approach toward expropriation can be criticized as another manifestation of laissez-faire logic, as it appears to protect property more robustly than other rights and interests. However, the restrictive approach is understandable since transfer of title is irreversible; the power to expropriate might be rampantly abused under occupation; and there is a close relationship between ownership and livelihood.

Expropriation in occupied territories was central in the HCJ's *Settlements Regularization Law* case.[78] The Court was called to rule on the constitutionality of Israeli domestic legislation which, in simplified terms, required the military commander in the West Bank to "regularize" ex post certain settlements that were built on private Palestinian land, by seizing the land and allocating it for the settlements' use.[79] In 2020, The HCJ struck down the law as unconstitutional. The significance for our purposes is that the Court viewed the allocation of usage rights to settlements as "*de facto* expropriation," although the regularization law did not explicitly provide for the transfer of title.[80] Furthermore, the Court analyzed the valid "public need" for expropriation in occupied territory in light of the status of the owners

[75] *See, e.g.*, 2 G. Schwar zenberger, International Law as Applied by International Courts and Tribunals: The Law of Armed Conflict 266 (1968); HCJ 393/82 Jam'iat Iscan Al-Ma'almoun v. IDF Commander of Judea and Samaria, 37(4) PD 785, ¶ 31 (1983) (Isr.).

[76] *See* von Glahn, *supra* note 7, at 186.

[77] *See id.*; Feilchenfeld, *supra* note 6, at 50–51; Arai-Takahashi, *supra* note 39, at 236–38.

[78] HCJ 1308/17 Silwad Municipality v. The Knesset, Nevo Legal Database ¶ 9.

[79] *See* Elena Chachko, *The Israeli Knesset Passes the Settlement Regularization Law*, Lawfare (Feb. 7, 2017), https://www.lawfareblog.com/israeli-knesset-passes-settlement-regularization-law.

[80] *Silwad Municipality*, ¶ 67 (President Hayut).

as protected persons.[81] It held that expropriation must primarily serve protected persons, and accordingly Israeli settlers cannot be considered as the valid "public" for the purpose of expropriation.[82] More generally, the HCJ held that expropriations cannot encompass transfers of property from one population group to another, since the logic of expropriation requires that the property owners, as part of the general public, will enjoy the public benefits of the taking.[83] The latter conclusion is pertinent mainly in the context of the West Bank, since Israel does not recognize the applicability of article 49(6) GCIV which prohibits settlements to begin with. Nevertheless, the notion of "*de facto* expropriation," and the special position of protected persons as the valid beneficiaries of expropriation, might be relevant in other situations as well.

6.1.4 Seizure

Article 53(2) Hague provides a list of items that can be seized by the occupant, even if they are privately owned, for the duration of the occupation. These include all appliances "adapted for the transmission of news"; means of transport; arms depots and "all kinds of munitions of war" (*munitions de guerre*).[84] Such items must be returned, or compensation made if necessary, only "when peace is made."[85] However, if *munitions de guerre* are seized during active use against the occupant, they can be confiscated without an obligation to return or compensate.[86]

On its face, the rationale for seizures is clear. They are meant to prevent armed resistance or the passing of intelligence to the occupied state. On this logic, it is reasonable that the occupant would seize private *munitions de guerre*. In the past, some argued that *munitions de guerre* included all items "for which a modern army can find any normal use."[87] This view, however, seems much too wide. Elihu Lauterpacht suggested the better approach, according to which the seized object must "be capable of playing a part in

[81] *Id.*
[82] *Id.* ¶¶ 69–70.
[83] *Id.* ¶ 79.
[84] Hague IV, *supra* note 1, art. 53(2).
[85] *Id.*
[86] Cession of Vessels and Tugs for Navigation on the Danube (Allied Powers v. Ger., Austria, Hung. & Bulg.), 1 R.I.A.A. 97, 105–06 (1921), *cited in* DINSTEIN, *supra* note 5, at 254.
[87] H.A. Smith, *Booty of War*, 23 BRIT. Y.B. INT'L L. 227, 228–29 (1946), *cited in* ARAI-TAKAHASHI, *supra* note 39, at 231.

battle, in the sense either of causing or preventing physical injury to persons or military objectives."[88]

A controversy concerns the question whether energy sources, such as private oil, can be seized as *munitions de guerre*. There is some agreement that pumped oil can be considered as such,[89] but the issue is far from clear concerning crude oil underground. In this context, the majority of the Singapore Court of Appeal held that underground oil is not *munitions de guerre*, mainly because a complex process is required before direct military use.[90] However, a minority opinion doubted this view, and, as Dinstein points out, the UK *Manual* states that "raw resources," including crude oil, qualify as munitions of war.[91] Possibly, the answer to this question revolves around the rationale behind seizures under article 53(2). If the rationale is to curtail security threats to the occupant, it is unclear how oil, crude or pumped—or any comparable resource—can be *ipso facto* viewed as contributing to such a threat, in a manner comparable to weapons or ammunition. If, however, the rationale is to prevent the materiel from falling into the hand of the enemy state should it retake the territory, the conclusion might change. Nonetheless, the latter approach raises significant concerns, since it might allow preventive seizure of wide categories of private property only because they might be used by the enemy state in the future.

While the term *munitions de guerre* was always imbued with some indeterminacy, its "fringe of vagueness"[92] has become wider with the advent of new technologies—such as the weaponization of cyberspace. Since every private computer can be used for hostile cyber operations, it is clear that the term cannot extend to the preventive seizure of all computers and servers in the territory.[93] Therefore, the view more consistent with the object and purpose of the law of occupation requires limiting the term *munitions de guerre* to kinetic weapons and ammunition.

For similar reasons, the power to seize "all appliances adapted for the transmissions of news" seems overbroad and anachronistic. First, every

[88] Elihu Lauterpacht, *The Hague Regulations and the Seizure of* Munitions de Guerre, 32 Brit. Y.B. Int'l L. 218, 218 (1955–56), *cited in id.*; *see also* In *Re Esau* 16 I.L.R. 482 (Special Ct. of Cassation 1949) (Netherlands), *cited in* Dinstein, *supra* note 5, at 251.

[89] *Id.* at 252–53.

[90] N.v. de Bataafsche Petroleum Maatschappij et al. v. The War Damage Commission (C.A., SG, 1956) 23 I.L.R. 810, 822–24, *cited in* Dinstein, *supra* note 5, at 252.

[91] U.K. Ministry of Def., Joint Service Manual of the Law of Armed Conflict 301 (2004) [hereinafter UK Manual]; *see also* Dinstein, *supra* note 5, at 253.

[92] H.L.A. Hart, The Concept of Law 123 (3d ed. 2012).

[93] *Compare* Tallinn Manual 2.0, *supra* note 44, at 551; DoD Manual, *supra* note 41, at 787.

cellphone can fall within this definition, and it would be absurd to argue that the occupant may seize them wholesale.[94] Second, the human dependence on such appliances, and the application of IHRL in occupied territories—including the right to freedom of expression and to seek, receive, and impart information—call for a narrower understanding.[95] The same applies to the power to seize means of transport, in light of the right to freedom of movement.[96] Because of their effects on the enjoyment of human rights, the occupant would be required to present a specific security justification for such seizures, and subject them to a proportionality analysis.[97] Additionally, like other sweeping powers under the law of occupation, with the passage of time the need for such powers would require a heavier burden of justification.

Furthermore, law enforcement provisions concerning the forfeiture of criminal property are not uncommon in domestic legislation,[98] and might be part of the law in force in the territory. As such, their activation by the occupant as part of the duty to maintain public order is not per se excluded by article 53(2) GCIV. However, such provisions cannot be applied to circumvent the object and purpose of the article by extending them to encompass any security interest of the occupant as such.

Last, the law of occupation's provisions on private property apply both to property owned by locals and foreigners. This is also true concerning seizure powers under article 53(2). However, specifically concerning foreign-owned means of transportation which happen to be in the territory at the time of occupation, customary international law provides for a special arrangement (known as "angary"), according to which their seizure requires *absolute necessity* and compensation must be paid immediately.[99]

[94] Compare DoD Manual, *supra* note 41, at 551.

[95] International Covenant on Civil and Political Rights art. 19, Dec. 16, 1966, 999 U.N.T.S. 171.

[96] *Id.*, art. 12.

[97] Section 5.2.4.

[98] Stefan D. Cassella, *Asset Forfeiture Law in the United States*, *in* The Palgrave Handbook of Criminal and Terrorism Financing Law 427 (Colin King, Clive Walker & Jimmy Gurulé eds., 2018).

[99] *See* Dinstein, *supra* note 5, at 255–56; Convention (V) respecting the Rights and Duties of Neutral Powers and Persons in Case of War on Land art. 19, Oct. 18, 1907, 36 Stat. 2310 [hereinafter Hague V].

6.1.5 Foreign Property and Investment Agreements (and the Treaties in Occupied Territories)

The powers of occupants regarding private property might clash with treaties protecting foreign investors, which have proliferated in recent decades. Since this question is likely to be of increasing importance, and is relatively underexplored, we examine it in some detail.

Investor rights and interests are often protected in bilateral investment treaties (BITs), which limit expropriation and other interferences in investor interests by the host state, and frequently provide for mandatory investor-state dispute settlement (ISDS) mechanisms.[100] In the intersection between occupation and foreign investment law, two main questions follow. First, is the occupant bound by the occupied state's investment agreements (*territorial application*)? Second, do the occupant's *own* investment agreements apply extraterritorially in the occupied territory (*extraterritorial application*)?[101] Under both options, the application of BITs in occupied territories might have three consequences. Substantively, they could narrow the occupant's powers in relation to foreign property. Procedurally, BITs could subject the occupant to ISDS mechanisms. Additionally, if the occupant violates BITs, it might incur state responsibility vis-à-vis the other state party.

The *territorial application* of BITs during occupation raises the general question whether the occupied state's treaties bind the occupant when it operates in the territory.[102] In this context, there has been support for the contention that *at least* international labor conventions, as well as human rights treaties in force in the territory, can bind the occupant as part of the local law.[103] Likewise, in 2009, the Venice Commission held that Russia was

[100] *See generally* Jonathan Bonnitcha, Lauge N. Skovgaard & Michael Waibel, The Political Economy of the Investment Treaty Regime in Context (2017); for a critique, see Gus Van Harten, The Trouble with Foreign Investment Protection (2020).

[101] *See* Tobias Ackerman, *Investments Under Occupation: The Application of Investment Treaties to Occupied Territory*, *in* International Investment Law and the Law of Armed Conflict 67 (Katia Fach Gómez, Anastasios Gourgourinis & Catharine Titi eds., 2019).

[102] *See* Eyal Benvenisti, *Water Conflicts During the Occupation of Iraq*, 97 Am. J. Int'l L. 860 (2003); Adam Roberts, *Transformative Military Occupation: Applying the Laws of War and Human Rights*, 100 Am. J. Int'l L. 580, 589 (2006).

[103] *See* Eyal Benvenisti, The International Law of Occupation 83 (2d ed. 2012); Ackerman, *supra* note 101, at 73–75; Ofilio J. Mayorga, *Occupants, Beware of BITS: Applicability of Investment Treaties to Occupied Territories*, Palestine Y.B. Int'l L. 136, 152–61 (2016); *DRC v. Uganda*.

expected to abide by the 1951 Geneva Convention on the Status of Refugees, to which Georgia was a party, in the Georgian territories it occupied.[104]

Meron has offered an explanatory framework for the legal effects of the occupied state's treaties. The simple case is when treaty provisions have been incorporated into the local law before the occupation, and therefore the occupant must respect them as the laws in force.[105] Furthermore, Meron argued, even when a treaty ratified by the occupied state was *not* incorporated into the local law, its mere ratification serves as strong evidence that it was considered suitable for the occupied territory.[106] Accordingly, the treaty should be respected by the occupant under its general trusteeship duties.[107] Importantly, the implication of Meron's reasoning is not that the occupant becomes *party* to these treaties, but rather that it is bound to respect them through the operation of the conservationist principle.

Following Meron's approach, Ackerman contends that the occupant must respect investment treaties in force in the territory, while emphasizing that it does not thereby become a *state party* to these treaties, but merely administers them temporarily.[108] This view has several upshots: first, like all laws in force, they can be set aside when the occupant is "absolutely prevented" to respect them, in light of the relevant interests recognized by the law of occupation.[109] Second, foreign investors would not be able to trigger ISDS proceedings against the occupant on the basis of a territorial investment treaty. This is because such a dispute would not concern a direct violation of the treaty, but the occupant's failure to respect it under the law of occupation.[110]

The extension of the occupant's *own* investment treaties to occupied territories, is part of the broader question of the extraterritorial application of treaties on the one hand, and the relations between such application and the duty to respect the status quo ante. The question of the extraterritorial

[104] European Commission for Democracy Through Law, *Opinion on the Law of Occupied Territories of Georgia*, CDL-AD (2009) 15 (Mar. 17, 2009), https://www.venice.coe.int/webforms/documents/default.aspx?pdffile=CDL-AD(2009)015-e.

[105] Theodore Meron, *Applicability of Multilateral Conventions to Occupied Territories*, 72 Am. J. Int'l L. 542, 550 (1978). The same reasoning must apply when the legal system in the occupied territory recognizes the direct application of treaties.

[106] *Id.* at 551.

[107] *See* Michael Bothe, *The Administration of Occupied Territory*, *in* The 1949 Geneva Conventions: A Commentary 1455, 1480 (Andrew Clapham, Paola Gaeta & Marco Sassòli eds., 2015).

[108] Ackerman, *supra* note 101, at 76.

[109] *Id.* at 77.

[110] *Id.* at 78–79. *But see* Mayorga, *supra* note 103.

application of BITs came up in the context of Russia's occupation of Crimea. Following Russia's 2014 annexation of Crimea, several ISDS complaints were lodged by Ukrainian investors regarding Russia's treatment of their investments. A Ukrainian fuel corporation argued that Russia's actions in Crimea violated the Ukraine–Russia BIT, by interfering with and expropriating its investments in petrol stations.[111] In 2017, an arbitral tribunal held that the term "territory"—as it appears in the BIT—encompassed also territories under the de facto control of the parties, and for this reason, the BIT applied to Russia's actions in Crimea.[112] The award was confirmed by the Swiss Federal Supreme Court, which added that the object and purpose of the BIT is to promote and protect investments, which pushes toward a wider interpretation of its provisions.[113]

These decisions demonstrate that ISDS arbitrators might decide to apply the occupant's BITs in occupied territories. However, the ability to generalize from them is limited. First, nothing prevents states from explicitly barring such application in future BITs. Second, ISDS rulings are notoriously inconsistent, and other tribunals may not follow this reasoning.[114] Third, and crucially, in this case, Russia *itself* did not—and could not—contest that the BIT applied territorially to Crimea, since Russia claims that Crimea is part of its own territory.[115] Fourth, interpretation of the term "territory" as including occupied territory was rejected in other contexts, where occupants sought to treat occupied territories as their own for the purpose of trade.[116] Fifth, from the point of view of the conservationist principle, it is highly doubtful that an occupant's decision to bind itself to certain obligations to foreign investors should extend to occupied territories—where

[111] Case No. 2015-35 Stabil v. R.F. (Perm. Ct. Arb. 2017), https://www.italaw.com/cases/4034.

[112] Tribunal fédérale [TF] Oct. 16, 2018, 4A_396/2017 (Switz.); *see* Simon Bianchi, *The Applicability of the Ukraine–Russia BIT to Investment Claims in Crimea: A Swiss Perspective*, Kluwer Arbitration Blog (Mar. 16, 2019), http://arbitrationblog.kluwerarbitration.com/2019/03/16/the-applicability-of-the-ukraine-russia-bit-to-investment-claims-in-crimea-a-swiss-perspective/.

[113] Tribunal fédérale [TF] Nov. 23, 2017, 4A_396/2017, ¶ 4.4.2 (Switz.), summarized in Bianchi, *supra* note 112.

[114] Malcolm Langford, Michele Potestà, Gabrielle Kaufmann-Kohler and Daniel Behn, *Special Issue: UNCITRAL and Investment Arbitration Reform: Matching Concerns and Solutions: An Introduction*, 21 J. World Investment & Trade 167 (2020).

[115] Rather, it argued that the BIT did not apply to investments made in Crimea prior to its incorporation into Russia. *See id.*

[116] Case C-104/16 P, Council of the E.U. v. Front Polisario, ECLI:EU:C:2016:973, ¶¶ 28–30 (Dec. 21, 2016); Organisation juive européenne & Vignoble Psagot Ltd v. Ministre de l'Économie et des Finances, ECLI:EU:C:2019:954 (Nov. 12, 2019); *but see* Ackerman, *supra* note 101, at 82–86.

the proper balance between private rights and public interests might be different.[117] In this context, the Crimean case is very particular, since the claims were made by investors that were nationals of the occupied state, on the basis of a BIT between their own state and the occupant. Therefore, applying the Ukraine–Russia BIT in Crimea qua occupied territory did not introduce a significant change to the territory.[118]

6.2 Protection of Public Property

The law of occupation's regime on public property is markedly different from that concerning private property, mainly because there is no explicit obligation to respect public property paralleling the same obligation concerning private property.[119] Yet, the general duty to respect and protect public property emanates from article 43 Hague, as part of the general obligation to maintain public order. Two rationales undergird this obligation. The first is the relation between public property and welfare, as such property forms the basis for essential public services. Second, and in more realist terms, the ousted government has an interest that its resources be protected not only from the occupant, but also from possible looting by its own population.

Nonetheless, the protection of public property is less stringent than that of private property, as part of the Rousseauian distinction between states and individuals.[120] Accordingly, it is unsurprising that occupants would try, where possible, to qualify property as public.[121]

Beyond the general obligation stemming from article 43, two different regimes apply to public property. Some movable public property can be taken by the occupant without any obligation of restoration or compensation. This generally applies to money, "and all movable property belonging to the State which may be used for military operations."[122] Regarding

[117] While similar critique can be leveled against the application of IHRL, it is difficult to ascribe to foreign investors' rights the same level of importance.

[118] *Compare* Ackerman, *supra* note 101, at 84.

[119] Hague IV, *supra* note 1, art. 46.

[120] *See* Cession of Vessels and Tugs for Navigation on the Danube (Allied Powers v. D.E., A.T, H.U. & Bulg.), 1 R.I.A.A. 97, 107 (1921), 97, 107, *cited in* Arai-Takahashi, *supra* note 39, at 195.

[121] *See, e.g.*, Isabel Kershner, *In West Bank, 99.7% of Public Land Grants by Israel Go to Settlers*, N.Y. Times (July 17, 2018), https://www.nytimes.com/2018/07/17/world/middleeast/west-bank-public-land-israel-palestinians.html.

[122] Hague IV, *supra* note 1, art. 53(1).

immovable public property—namely, real estate and natural resources—these must be administered by the occupant under a form of trusteeship known as *usufruct*.[123]

Nonetheless the public–private property distinction under the law of occupation is not absolute. Some protections apply equally to *all* property. Like private property, public property cannot be arbitrarily destroyed or pillaged.[124] Furthermore, some property enjoys the protection of private property, even if it is formally public owned. This is the case of property owned by municipalities, charities, religious institutions, institutions of arts, sciences, and education.[125] Importantly, for the purpose of requisitions, municipalities are treated as private entities to which requisition demands can be addressed, but on the same conditions that apply to private individuals.[126] Furthermore, some public property—namely cultural objects—enjoys special protection, which we will not discuss here.[127] A special provision concerns also "submarine cables" between the occupied territory and neutral states.[128]

6.2.1 Distinguishing between Private and Public Property

A persistent problem concerns the classification of property as private or public.[129] This problem is not specific to occupation, and might occur wherever privatization and public–private partnerships are common. According to Feilchenfeld, three tests could be relevant in such cases: formal ownership, function, and direction.[130] While the formal test is the most straightforward, functional tests have also been applied. For instance, there is some support for the claim that pensions and comparable assets that are held by the state for the future use of private individuals should be considered as

[123] *Id.*, art. 55.

[124] *See* Section 6.1.1.

[125] Hague IV, *supra* note 1, art. 56.

[126] *Id.*, art. 52. Notably, the property of higher levels of local government such as provinces, districts, etc. are not considered private property.

[127] *See* Section 3.3.2.

[128] Hague IV, *supra* note 1, art. 54. The rationale for the special regime toward such cables—which can be logically extended to comparable forms cross-border infrastructure—is that interference in them affects rights of third parties.

[129] Dinstein, *supra* note 5, at 229.

[130] Feilchenfeld, *supra* note 6, at 58.

private property; and conversely that funneling funds from the state to private entities with the advent of occupation should be disregarded.[131]

It has also been argued that private property can be considered public if it is directed or supervised by the state, whether by statute or contract.[132] Arguably, it is possible to draw an analogy from the rules of attribution under the law of state responsibility, to claim that public property can include any property used in exercise of privatized governmental authority, regardless of ownership, or that property controlled and directed by the state can be considered its own property.[133] Importantly, however, since the law of occupation provides private property with more stringent protection, there is risk in introducing ambiguity into this distinction, and a bright-line rule might be preferable.[134]

Some practice supports the view that in cases of doubt, property is considered public. As noted by Dinstein, this has been the approach of the HCJ,[135] and of the UK and DoD manuals.[136] Yet, this presumption has been criticized for broadening the powers of the occupant,[137] and it may indeed facilitate designating property as public for illegitimate reasons. Ultimately, and based on article 43 Hague, it seems reasonable to eschew presumptions in favor of an analysis according to the laws in force on property. If such laws exist in the territory, it is unclear why the law of occupation should establish its own presumptions.

In Iraq, the CPA treated the property of the Ba'ath Party as public property, to be seized and held "in trust" for Iraqis.[138] This was notwithstanding the fact that political parties as such are generally not governmental entities. The CPA justified this decision on the basis that Iraq has been a one-party state under the Ba'ath Party for decades.[139] It seems plausible that in cases

[131] *Id.* at 59.

[132] *Id.* at 60; von Glahn, *supra* note 7, at 179.

[133] Int'l Law Comm'n, Draft Articles on Responsibility of States for Internationally Wrongful Acts, *extract from* the Rep. of the International Law Commission on the work of Its Fifty-third Session, U.N. Doc. A/56/10, arts. 5, 8 (2001).

[134] For instance, a question has arisen whether property of central banks is public or private. *See* Krysztof Skubiszewski, *Currency in Occupied Territory and the Law of War*, 9 German Y.B. Int'l L. 161, 167 (1961).

[135] *See, e.g.*, HCJ 285/81 El Nazer v. IDF Commander of Judea and Samaria, 36(1) PD 701 (1982) (Isr.).

[136] UK Manual, *supra* note 91, at 303; DoD Manual, *supra* note 41, at 784.

[137] Antonio Cassese, *Powers and Duties of an Occupant in Relation to Land and Natural Resources*, *in* International Law and the Administration of Occupied Territories 419, 420 (Emma Playfair ed., 1992), *cited in* Dinstein, *supra* note 5, at 230.

[138] CPA Order No. 4, Management of Property and Assets of the Iraqi Ba'ath Party, CPA/ORD/25 May 2003/04, art. 3 (June 28, 2004).

[139] *Id.* Preamble.

where there is no effective separation between party and state, party property can be considered as state property.

6.2.2 State Funds and Movables

Article 53(1) Hague recognizes one of the most sweeping powers under the law of occupation, providing that the occupant "can only take possession of cash, funds, and realizable securities which are strictly the property of the State, depots of arms, means of transport, stores and supplies, and, generally, all movable property belonging to the State which may be used for military operations." The ostensibly limiting language of the provision ("can *only* take") clarifies that article 53(1) was historically intended to limit the ransacking of *all* state property as war booty, as was done in the past. As opposed to the parallel arrangement concerning seizure of private property, as discussed in Section 6.1.4, article 53(1) extends also to money, and does not mandate restoration or compensation.

Two types of state property can be seized by the occupant. The first concerns specific types of economic assets (cash, funds, realizable securities) owned by the *state alone*. These can be seized without regard for their intended use by the occupied state. This provision seems anomalous nowadays, and can be viewed as a remnant of the old idea of *war pays for war* or war booty.[140] One possible (and problematic) justification for such seizure is that such economic assets can be used by the state, in the future, to acquire more arms.[141]

The second type of seizable state property is all movable property "which may be used for military operations," the specifically mentioned objects—such as depots of arms—being only examples. The reference to the phrase "may be used for military operations" raises a problem that by now should be familiar to the reader. A broad interpretation would essentially allow taking almost all state-owned objects.[142] This interpretation, however, is undesirable. First, it renders article 53(1)'s limiting language ("only") meaningless. Second, considering the trusteeship obligations undergirding the law of occupation, and since the preservation of state property is required

[140] *Compare* FEILCHENFELD, *supra* note 6, at 52–53.

[141] *Compare*, in another context, Ryan Goodman, *Targeting "War-Sustaining" Objects in Non-International Armed Conflict*, 110 AM. J. INT'L L. 663, 663–68, 677–79 (2017).

[142] FEILCHENFELD, *supra* note 6, at 52. DINSTEIN, *supra* note 5, at 237–38.

for the welfare of the local population, there must be a reasonable nexus between the property and some use for hostile military operations. Perhaps, an analogy can be drawn from the rules of distinction. On this view, seizable state property includes objects which could make an effective contribution to military action, and their seizure would offer a definite military advantage at the time.[143]

A further problem concerns the property of organized armed groups, or of NSAs that control territory. Is it private property, subject to the more restrictive regime of article 53(2), or should it be viewed as functionally public, falling within the more permissive provisions of article 53(1)?[144] Essentially, the status of NSA property is part of the broader debate concerning the existence and desirability of a "third status" under IHL, which would apply to members of organized armed groups,[145] and perhaps—by extension—to property belonging to such groups. This general problem is beyond the scope of this book.[146]

Be that as it may, the HCJ seems to have adopted the third status approach regarding property.[147] The *Al-Ajouli* case concerned the seizure of funds held by a Palestinian money changer in the West Bank, allegedly for Hamas. He petitioned the HCJ, arguing inter alia that since the funds were private they could not be seized absent military necessity.[148] The Court held that since the petitioner tried to conceal the funds' origins, he incurred the burden to prove that they did not belong to Hamas.[149] Following previous case law, it ruled that armed conflicts against "terror organizations" challenge the clear-cut distinction between public and private property, as manifested in article 53 Hague.[150] Without elaboration, it proceeded to analyze the seizure under the assumption that article 53 does not exclude it.

[143] *See* API, *supra* note 40, art. 52(2).

[144] There might be cases in which an occupant would be under the duty to seize such property, pursuant to an UNSC resolution. *See, e.g.*, S.C. Res. 1373 (2001) (Sept. 28, 2001); Inger Österdahl, *Due Diligence in International Anti-Terrorism Law: Developments in the Resolutions of the UN Security Council*, *in* DUE DILIGENCE IN THE INTERNATIONAL LEGAL ORDER 234 (Heike Krieger, Anne Peters & Leonhard Kreuzer eds., 2020).

[145] *See* NILS MELZER, ICRC, INTERPRETIVE GUIDANCE ON THE NOTION OF DIRECT PARTICIPATION IN HOSTILITIES UNDER INTERNATIONAL HUMANITARIAN LAW (2009).

[146] *See, e.g.*, Frédéric Mégret, *From "Savages" to "Unlawful Combatants": A Postcolonial Look at International Humanitarian Law's "Other,"* *in* INTERNATIONAL LAW AND ITS OTHERS 265 (Anne Orford ed., 2006).

[147] HCJ 10244/06 Al-Ajouli v. Minister of Def., Nevo Legal Database (Feb. 9, 2011) (Isr.).

[148] *Id.* ¶ 21.

[149] *Id.* ¶ 22.

[150] *Id.* ¶ 23.

6.3 State Real Estate and Natural Resources

The previous section concerned public *movable* property. A separate regime exists regarding public owned real estate and natural resources. The exploitation of natural resources is one of the gravest dangers in occupation—in fact, it can motivate the occupation to begin with. Article 55 Hague attempts to address this problem, by defining the occupant "only as administrator" of such properties; by obliging it to safeguard their capital; and requiring it to administer them "in accordance with the rules of usufruct." None of these phrases are self-explanatory, especially the Roman law institution of usufruct at the core of article 55.

6.3.1 Administration and Usufruct

The clearest implication of the designation of the occupant as an administrator and usufructuary *only* is that it cannot acquire title over state real property and natural resources.[151] This undeniably reflects the temporariness of occupation, and the trusteeship role of the occupant. However, the concept of usufruct entails that the administrator may both use the property (*usus*) and profit from its products or "fruits" (*fructus*), as long as it does not change or destroy the property itself.[152] Traditional scholarship presents several examples for permitted uses such as quartering soldiers or using public buildings for administration, selling or consuming crops, leasing buildings, and collecting and using toll charges.[153]

The idea that the occupant cannot acquire title over natural resources also reflects the principle of permanent sovereignty over natural resources.[154] Some doubt whether this principle reflects a legally binding norm, although the ICJ held that it has achieved the status of customary international law.[155] In the same case, however, the ICJ ruled that the principle is not applicable to resource exploitation during armed conflict, which is governed by *jus in bello*.[156] However, Longobardo makes the compelling

[151] Von Glahn, *supra* note 7, at 176; HCJ 285/81 *El Nazer*, 36(1) PD 701, 704.
[152] Von Glahn, *supra* note 7, at 176–77; L.F.E. Goldie, *Title and Use (and Usufruct)—An Ancient Distinction Too Oft Forgot*, 79 Am. J. Int'l L. 689, 691–92 (1985).
[153] Von Glahn, *supra* note 7, at 177; Feilchenfeld, *supra* note 6, at 55.
[154] *See, e.g.*, G.A. Res. 1803 (Dec. 14, 1962); G.A. Res. 3201 (May 1, 1974); G.A. Res. 3281 (Dec. 12, 1974).
[155] *DRC v. Uganda* ¶ 244; *but see* sources cited in Dinstein, *supra* note 5, at 236.
[156] *See DRC v. Uganda* ¶ 245.

case that since the notion of permanent sovereignty stems from the right to self-determination—itself a cornerstone of the law of occupation—it must also be part of the latter.[157] Furthermore, it is unclear why the principle of permanent sovereignty should be displaced, as *lex generalis*, by the law of occupation, considering that it is in no obvious conflict with article 55 Hague.[158] To the extent that the principle of permanent sovereignty reflects customary international law, it should complement the interpretation of article 55.[159]

6.3.2 Safeguarding the Capital

The requirement that the occupant "safeguard the capital" restates the principle of usufruct that the property cannot be destroyed or changed. Sometimes, the content of this duty is clear. For example, concerning public buildings, they may be used or leased, but they must be properly kept and cannot be demolished. The issue becomes complicated, however, when it comes to natural resources.

On its face, it can be said that *any* extraction of nonrenewable resources fails to safeguard the capital. While renewables such as solar energy or crops can be used without damaging the capital, this is not so concerning oil and minerals. In the HCJ's *Quarries* case, the petitioners accordingly argued that mining per se damages the capital, and therefore all quarrying activities in the West Bank are unlawful.[160] Yet, this might lead to the problematic result that the occupant must *cease* preexisting mining or extraction operations in the territory, or refrain from operating existing infrastructure (which might lead to its degeneration). The more practicable position recognizes a

[157] Marco Longobardo, *State Responsibility for International Humanitarian Law Violations by Private Actors in Occupied Territories and the Exploitation of Natural Resources*, 63 NETH. INT'L L. REV. 251, 256–57 (2016).

[158] Oona A. Hathaway, Rebecca Crootof, Philip Levitz & Haley Nix, *Which Law Governs During Armed Conflict? The Relationship Between International Humanitarian Law and Human Rights Law*, 96 MINN. L. REV. 1883, 1903–06 (2012); *compare* Case C-266/16, Western Sahara Campaign UK v. Comm'r for Her Majesty's Revenue and Customs, ECLI:EU:C:2018:118, Opinion of Advocate General Wathelet ¶ 268 (Feb. 27, 2018).

[159] *See* Iain Scobbie, *Natural Resources and Belligerent Occupation: Mutation Through Permanent Sovereignty*, *in* HUMAN RIGHTS, SELF-DETERMINATION AND POLITICAL CHANGE IN THE OCCUPIED PALESTINIAN TERRITORIES 221, 281 (Stephen Bowen ed., 1997).

[160] HCJ 2164/09 Yesh Din v. IDF Commander in the West Bank, Nevo Legal Base ¶ 8 (Dec. 26, 2011) (Isr.); *see also* David Kretzmer, *The Law of Belligerent Occupation in the Supreme Court of Israel*, 94 INT'L REV. RED CROSS 207, 222 (2012).

"principle of continuity," allowing the occupant to operate existing resource facilities.[161] The notion of "safeguarding the capital" is understood here as requiring to refrain from diminishing the resource beyond what the owner itself would have done, as evidenced by the production levels *ante*. The principle of continuity can be reconciled with the duty to safeguard the capital if the latter is understood as including the resource minus the extraction that would have taken place by the absent sovereign.[162]

A different question is whether the occupant may embark on *new* resource exploitation. This question was raised in the 1970s when Israel sought to explore offshore oil in the Gulf of Suez, during its occupation of the Egyptian Sinai Peninsula.[163] Similar concerns underlie U.S.-supported oil exploration in northeastern Syria during the early 2020s, which Syria and Russia condemned as violations of the law of occupation.[164] In the case of Israel in Sinai, Egypt and the United States objected to Israel's activities. The United States—in support of a U.S. concession holder that sought to explore the same area—argued that an occupant cannot exploit resources beyond the status quo ante.[165] Israel claimed, however, that discovery of oil will enhance the value of the territory, which serves the interest of the sovereign—who will eventually enjoy the increased value when the territory is restored.[166] Similarly, Gerson claimed that while new *mining* operations might destroy and change the land itself—in violation of the duties of usufruct—this was not the case regarding offshore drilling, since it enhances the value of the waterway without destroying anything.[167] Critics

[161] *See* Dinstein, *supra* note 5, at 233; *see, e.g.*, DoD Manual, *supra* note 41, 785; *Yesh Din*, ¶ 8.

[162] *Compare* von Glahn, *supra* note 7, at 177; Dinstein, *supra* note 5, at 235. The DoD Manual suggests a more flexible reading, according to which "the Occupying Power should not exercise its rights in such a wasteful and negligent manner as seriously to impair the property's value." DoD Manual, *supra* note 41, at 785; *see also* Myres S. McDougal & Florentino P. Feliciano, Law and Minimum World Public Order: Or—The Legal Regulations of International Coercion 812–13 (1961).

[163] Allan Gerson, *Off-shore Oil Exploration by a Belligerent Occupant: The Gulf of Suez Dispute*, 71 Am. J. Int'l L. 725, 725 (1977). On maritime zones, see Section 2.3.1.

[164] Jack Detsch, *U.S. Troops Really Are in Syria to Protect the Oil—For the Kurds*, Foreign Policy (Aug. 5, 2020), https://foreignpolicy.com/2020/08/05/kurds-oil-syria-us-troops-trump/; MFA Russia, Press Release on Oil Resources of Northeastern Syria (Aug. 7, 2020), https://www.mid.ru/en/foreign_policy/legal_problems_of-international_cooperation/-/asset_publisher/HCN0yFLs7lFy/content/id/4280898; *but see* AFP, *US Forces Focus on IS, Not Protecting Syrian Oil Fields, Pentagon Says*, VOA (Feb. 9, 2021), https://www.voanews.com/middle-east/us-forces-focus-not-protecting-syrian-oil-fields-pentagon-says.

[165] Gerson, *supra* note 163, at 725.

[166] Government of Israel, *Memorandum of Law*, 17 I.L.M. 432, 434 (1978).

[167] Gerson, *supra* note 163, at 730–33.

responded that the duty to "safeguard the capital" is not qualified by the possible market value of the new resource.[168]

As discussed in Chapter 4, the HCJ held in the *Quarries* case that in prolonged occupation *new* quarries could be permitted if they benefit the local population and prevent economic stagnation.[169] As it ruled, as long as the effects on the "[a]rea's resources pool" are relatively limited, mining activity, even if new, "could be deemed as usage ... which does not constitute a depletion of the capital."[170]

The views permitting new resource exploration and exploitation in occupied territories are hard to reconcile with the language of article 55, since it cannot accommodate, as "safeguarding the capital," resource exploitation beyond the levels of production that the sovereign would have undertaken anyway. Such views also disregard the fact that the question of resource exploitation goes far beyond "pure" economic considerations, as it often comes at high environmental costs, and requires a balance of values that must be undertaken by the local society. The principle of "permanent sovereignty" too pushes for the more restrictive understanding of the rule concerning the extraction of new resources.[171]

6.3.3 Use of Resources: Permitted Purposes and Consequences of Prohibited Extraction or Use

Even assuming that a certain extraction of resources in fact "safeguards the capital," is their use permitted for *any* purpose? Article 55 is notably silent on the permitted purposes of use. For example, can an occupant simply take the oil it extracts, and transfer it to its territory for its own use? Can it sell the oil to others, and use the profit for any purpose? Or, if a contractor operates the oil field, can the occupant make use of the royalties as it sees fit?[172] Dinstein argues that the occupant can indeed use the fruit "at its discretion," whether in the territory or otherwise. He claims that this is implicit

[168] *See, e.g.*, Brice M. Clagett & O. Thomas Johnson Jr., *May Israel as a Belligerent Occupant Lawfully Exploit Previously Unexploited Oil Resources of the Gulf of Suez?* 72 AM. J. INT'L L. 558, 575–78 (1978).

[169] HCJ 2164/09 Yesh Din v. IDF Commander in the West Bank, Nevo Legal Base ¶ 13 (Dec. 26, 2011) (Isr.).

[170] *Id.* ¶ 11.

[171] Scobbie, *supra* note 159, at 281.

[172] *See* Rex J. Zedalis, *Iraqi Oil and Revenues from Its Sale: A Review of How Existing Security Council Resolutions Affected the Past and May Shape the Future*, 18 EUR. J. INT'L L. 499 (2007).

in article 55, since it only requires the occupant to safeguard the capital, and therefore presumably allows it to take full possession of the fruit.[173] This was also Israel's view concerning the use of oil off the coast of Sinai.[174] Admittedly, this interpretation conforms with the traditional concept of usufruct in domestic law, which recognizes full ownership of the fruit, once extracted.[175]

However, this view makes sense only if we read article 55 in isolation from the law of occupation as a whole. That article 55 does not enumerate the permitted uses of the fruit cannot be read to circumvent the general trusteeship obligations of the occupant.[176] According to the latter, the only valid purposes for action are the needs of the local population and the occupant's security interests, *not* economic exploitation.[177] If this is true, the fruits, or the proceeds from selling them, can ultimately be used only for these purposes.[178] The desirability of this interpretation is also reflected in the UNSC's approach concerning resources in Iraq, according to which they could be used only for the benefit of the Iraqi people.[179]

Indeed, one of the rationales of usufruct is to provide a mechanism through which a property owner can pay another person for administrating the property, by permitting them to enjoy the profits. Arguably, a similar structure applies in occupation: the law seeks to incentivize the occupant to administer public property properly by allowing it to enjoy the fruit. However, if this enjoyment constitutes a right to profit from the fruit, it can easily become a motivation to occupy to begin with. This concern supports the interpretation of article 55 as allowing the occupant to use the fruit *only* for the benefit of the local population and administration, or for the occupant's security, as required by article 43 Hague. This interpretation provides a sufficient incentive to properly administrate public property—since the occupant could fund its administration based on local resources—without rewarding occupation.

[173] DINSTEIN, *supra* note 5, at 233.

[174] Gerson, *supra* note 163.

[175] Goldie, *supra* note 152, at 692; Giovanni Pugliese, *On Roman Usufruct*, 40 TUL. L. REV. 523, 530 (1965–66).

[176] *See* BENVENISTI, *supra* note 103, at 82; KRETZMER & RONEN, *supra* note 56, at 213.

[177] HCJ 393/82 Jam'iat Iscan Al-Ma'almoun v. IDF Commander of Judea and Samaria, 37(4) PD 785, ¶ 13 (1983) (Isr.).

[178] *See also* Antonio Cassese, *supra* note 137, at 427–30.

[179] *See* S.C. Res. 1483, ¶ 20 (May 22, 2003); Eyal Benvenisti, *Water Conflicts During the Occupation of Iraq*, 97 AM. J. INT'L L. 860, 863–64 (2003).

It seems that even under this view, article 55 would not prohibit selling the fruit to third parties *outside* the occupied territories, as long as the proceeds are used for the legitimate purposes mentioned above. Nor does it *ipso facto* prohibit granting concessions to private entities if "in the interest" of the local population.[180] The problem is that occupants might funnel the fruits to their own territory, whether by direct sale at below-market prices, or by granting royalty-low concessions to their domestic corporations. Furthermore, it is very difficult to track whether the occupant actually uses the proceeds for legitimate purposes. In the HCJ's *Quarries* case, petitioners argued that quarrying activities in the West Bank ran counter to article 55, inter alia because most of the minerals were used by Israeli industries, and the profits from their sale were kept by the Israeli concession holders. As such, they argued, the quarrying did not serve the local population or the occupant's security needs.[181] The state responded that the quarrying did in fact serve local interests, since "some" of the products were used in the area and sold both to Palestinians and Israeli settlers, and the royalties were generally used for the administration of the territory.[182] On this basis, and noting the special features of "prolonged occupation," the Court was satisfied that it cannot be said that "the quarrying operations are in no way promoting the best interests of the Area."[183] As discussed in Chapter 4, the fact that the existence of *some* incidental benefit to the local economy was deemed sufficient is problematic.[184] In the context of article 55, this construction can be used to legitimate abusive resource exploitation, under the pretense that the state is fulfilling its trusteeship obligations.[185]

Without exhausting this problem, some tests can be envisioned to distinguish between legitimate sales and concessions and illegitimate exploitation. Concerning sale, are the products only offered to entities or corporations belonging to the occupying state? Are they offered at market price? Regarding concessions, is the occupant offering concessions only to its own citizens or corporations, or is it conducting an open tender? Do the royalties conform with accepted market practice? Does the occupant

[180] *See* VON GLAHN, *supra* note 7, at 209.

[181] HCJ 2164/09 Yesh Din v. IDF Commander in the West Bank, Nevo Legal Base ¶ 9 (Dec. 26, 2011) (Isr.).

[182] *Id.* ¶¶ 12–13.

[183] *Id.* ¶ 13.

[184] *See also* KRETZMER & RONEN, *supra* note 56, at 155.

[185] *See* Section 4.1.2. *See also* Al-Haq, *Business and Human Rights Resource Center Al-Haq Response to HeidelbergCement*, AL-HAQ (Oct. 10, 2017), https://media.business-humanrights.org/media/documents/files/documents/Al-Haq_Response_Heidelberg.pdf/.

grant concessions to protected persons?[186] In the latter context, especially suspect are situations in which the occupant seeks to expropriate an existing local concession in order to transfer it to a foreign-based entity.[187] Furthermore, is the occupant transparent about the profits and their use? These are merely examples.

Similar concerns apply not only to the use of extractable resources, but also to the allocation of land use. In the West Bank, all public land is administered by the military commander.[188] In 1979, Israel decided that new Jewish settlements in the occupied territories will be established on "state land," and a wide-scale project was undertaken to map public land in the territories, which nowadays comprise close to 40% the West Bank.[189] Over the years, Israel's method of designation of land as public has been heavily criticized, notably due to its reliance on dormant Ottoman law to declare uncultivated private land as public.[190] Moreover, the vast majority—virtually all—of public land use is allocated to Israeli settlements and their supporting infrastructure.[191] This policy obviously contravenes article 49(6) GCIV, but also article 55 Hague, properly understood as requiring that public land be administered for the benefit of the local population (or for security reasons), in accordance with article 43 Hague.[192] The HCJ, however, declined to rule on this question.[193]

Once resources are extracted, or used, in contravention of the law of occupation, this might entail consequences not only in terms of the occupant's own state responsibility, but also in relation to third parties which seek to import these resources. These may include, possibly, a prohibition on the import of such resources as part of the duty of nonrecognition; or as part of the obligation to ensure respect for IHL; or under the obligation not to

[186] *See* Kretzmer, *supra* note 160, at 222.

[187] *See* HCJ 351/80 Jerusalem District Electric Company Ltd. v. Minister of Energy and Infrastructure, 35(2) PD 673 ¶ 14 (1981) (Isr.).

[188] § 4, Order on Administrative and Legal Procedures (Order No. 2) (West Bank Area), 5728–1967, KMZM 1, 3; Order on Government Property (Order No. 59) (Judea and Samaria), 5728–1967, KMZM 5 162.

[189] *See* HCJ 1308/17 Silwad Municipality v. The Knesset, Nevo Legal Database ¶¶ 10–14 (June 9, 2020) (Isr.).

[190] *See, e.g.*, Ibrahim Matar, *Exploitation of Land and Water Resources for Jewish Colonies in the Occupied Territories*, *in* International Law and the Administration of Occupied Territories, *supra* note 137, at 443, 449; regarding water as natural resource, see also Scobbie, *supra* note 159.

[191] HCJ 9949/08 Hamed v. Minister of Def., Nevo Legal Database ¶ 49 (Dec. 25, 2014) (Isr.).

[192] Kretzmer & Ronen, *supra* note 56, at 211.

[193] HCJ 4481/91 Bargil v. Govt. of Israel, 47 PD 210 (1993) (Isr.).

render aid or assistance to international wrongful acts.[194] However, the exact content and scope of these obligations are unsettled, and it is beyond our scope here to analyze them further.[195] Unlawful resource extraction or use across supply chains might also entail responsibility under business and human rights paradigms, which are, again, beyond this book.[196]

6.3.4 Shared Resources

Article 55 Hague addresses natural resources in the occupied territory, but does not refer to interests of third parties in these resources, and, in particular, situations of *shared* resources such as transboundary waters. Concerning managing shared resources in occupied territories, three fundamental issues intersect: first, the requirements under article 43 Hague, to promote the interests of the local population; second, and relatedly, the extent to which the occupant is bound by treaties in force vis-à-vis neighboring riparian states; and, third, whether the occupant must take into account global community interests, as part of the global governance regime of transnational resources.

We considered the first and second aspects briefly in Section 6.1.5, addressing whether the occupant is bound by the treaties in force in the occupied territory. Applied in the context of shared resources, the conclusion must be that article 43 Hague requires the occupant to respect the treaties in force—or the relevant customary international law, for that matter—concerning the management of natural resources, even if the occupant is not considered a party to the treaties itself.

Global community interests also push for a recognition of the occupant's power to participate, on behalf of the occupied territories and for the duration of the occupation, in regional arrangements and institutions designed to attain the optimal and sustainable utilization of shared resources of all

[194] Eva Kassoti & Antoine Duval, *Setting the Scene: The Legality of Economic Activities in Occupied Territories*, *in* The Legality of Economic Activities in Occupied Territories 1 (Antoine Duval & Eva Kassoti eds., 2020).

[195] *See* Rutger Fransen & Cedric Ryngaert, *EU Trade Relations with Occupied Territories: Third Party Obligations Flowing from the Application of Occupation Law in Relation to Natural Resources Exploitation*, *in id.* 47; *compare with* Eugene Kontorovich, *Economic Dealings with Occupied Territories*, 53 Colum. J. Transnat'l L. 584 (2015).

[196] See Introduction.

riparian states.[197] Functionally, this might be the only way in which the interests of riparian states, and indirectly the interests of the local population in the occupied territory, can be protected during occupation.[198] Disregard for the interests of riparian states might lead to retaliation which, in the short or long term, would mainly harm the occupied population.

However, as always under occupation, conflicts of interest may arise. This is particularly the case when the occupant is itself a riparian of a shared resource with the occupied territory. This is the case in the West Bank, in which Israel is in control of water resources shared by itself and the West Bank (the Mountain Aquifer), as well as water resources shared by Israel, Jordan, and the West Bank (the Jordan River). In such situations, it seems unreasonable that the occupant would represent both the occupied territory and itself, when participating in transnational arrangements.[199]

Many other complex problems can arise. For example, where a state's territory is only partially occupied, a transnational resource might be jointly controlled by the occupant, and by the sovereign in the unoccupied part of the state. In such situations, conflicts concerning resources can arise between the occupant and the sovereign in the unoccupied part of the state, or between both and third parties. It is impossible to enumerate in advance the complex circumstances that might occur in such situations, and it seems that the best approach would be to resolve such conflicts according to the general principles of the international law of transboundary resource management.[200]

[197] Convention on the Law of the Non-Navigational Uses of International Watercourses art. 5(1), May 21, 1997, 2999 U.N.T.S. 77; *see also* Eyal Benvenisti, Sharing Transboundary Resources: International Law and Optimal Resource Use 101 (2002).

[198] *See* Benvenisti, *supra* note 103, at 84.

[199] *Id.* at 85.

[200] *Id.*

7
Basic Issues in Economic Administration of Occupied Territories

A key weakness of the law of occupation is its lack of explicit regulation of most aspects of economic administration.[1] This is striking, considering that it devotes much attention to the protection of property. One explanation for the scant regulation of economic issues is the laissez-faire approach that characterized economic thought when the Hague rules were developed.[2] Yet, it is precisely in this field where there is much concern that the occupied territory be exploited, and historical practice demonstrates the frequent expansive interpretation by occupants of their economic powers.[3]

In absence of detailed rules, economic administration of occupied territories is regulated by the general principles of the law of occupation, manifested in article 43 Hague. Accordingly, the occupant must only take measures for the benefit of the local economy, and not for its own economic interests, while respecting, as a point of departure, the status quo ante. However, although frequently couched in terms of technical expertise, the question whether a certain economic policy indeed benefits the local population is not a neutral one, but requires a fundamentally political decision. This calls for a cautious approach to the economic powers of occupants. Indeed, economic transformation is no less of an intervention than what is usually considered "political" transformation, such as regime change. Moreover, the choice of economic system is an integral part of the right to self-determination.[4] This, too, pushes toward a restrictive view of

[1] *See* Gerhard von Glahn, *Taxation Under Belligerent Application*, *in* INTERNATIONAL LAW AND THE ADMINISTRATION OF OCCUPIED TERRITORIES: TWO DECADES OF ISRAELI OCCUPATION OF THE WEST BANK AND GAZA STRIP 341, 341 (Emma Playfair ed., 1992).

[2] *See* Dominique G. Carreau, *Military Occupation Currency*, 19 SAN DIEGO L. REV. 233, 239 (1982).

[3] *See* von Glahn, *supra* note 1, at 354–73.

[4] *See, e.g.*, International Covenant on Civil and Political Rights art. 1 (1), Dec. 16, 1966, 999 U.N.T.S. 171.

occupants' powers to make far-reaching economic changes, even if they genuinely believe that they would benefit the territory. This should be kept in mind, although, as we shall see, the practice of occupants has been quite permissive.

Nowadays, economic policies by occupants are further constrained by norms and institutions beyond the law of occupation, whether de jure or in terms of international expectation. In the past, international economic law was thin, and an occupant could not expect much international oversight of its economic policies. Today, however, economic decisions are regulated by a dense web of global governance institutions. From the standpoint of the principles of the law of occupation, this oversight cuts both ways. While international involvement limits occupants' unilateral discretion and as such might reduce abuse, it might also push occupants to transform the territory. Institutions like the World Bank or the International Monetary Fund are far more likely to press for reform, liberalization, and privatization, than for preserving the economic system in the territory.[5]

This chapter discusses select issues concerning the economic administration of occupied territories. Since economic administration, in essence, encapsulates almost every aspect of government—from antitrust to pensions, from banking to privatization—we focus here on issues that have traditionally been at the center of debate.

7.1 Taxation and Military Contributions

7.1.1 Taxation

Although taxation is the only aspect of economic administration that the law of occupation addresses explicitly, its relevant provisions are quite ambiguous.[6] The HCJ went as far as to observe that in this context, "the parties which convened to draft the Conventions wished to avoid as far as possible any all-embracing positive determination of what is permitted and what is forbidden."[7] Unsurprisingly, the ambiguity of the black-letter law on taxation resulted in exceedingly permissible interpretation by states.

[5] *See* Kerry Rittich, *Occupied Iraq: Imperial Convergences?* 31 LEID. J. INT'L L. 479, 497–98 (2018).

[6] *See* von Glahn, *supra* note 1.

[7] HCJ 69/81 Abu Aita v. Commander of the Judea and Samaria Area, 37(2) PD 197 ¶ 24(b) (1983) (Isr.).

Articles 48 and 49 Hague provide the basic framework concerning taxation and "money contributions" in occupied territories. Article 48 provides that *if* the occupant collects the taxes due to the state under the status quo ante, it shall, "as far as possible," maintain the rules of assessment in force; and should likewise "defray the expenses of the administration of the occupied territory to the same extent as the legitimate Government was so bound." Article 49 adds that if besides the existing taxes under article 48, the occupant "levies other money contributions," these can only be imposed for military needs or for the administration of the territory. Importantly, article 48 only refers to taxes collected for the occupied state qua central authority. The occupant cannot collect taxation due to local government.[8]

Article 48 applies only *if* the occupant decides to collect the taxes in the territory. Theoretically, the occupant can decide not to intervene at all, and to allow the local authorities to manage taxation as they see fit.[9] If, however, the local authorities break down, the occupant might be obligated to collect taxes as part of its general duty to maintain the public order.

Furthermore, article 48 should be read against the conservationist principle. The power to tax is a key tenet of sovereignty, and tax policy is a central part of a given society's conception of distributive justice. Accordingly, occupants' powers to intervene in taxes cannot be unfettered.[10] The conservationist principle is embedded in article 48, in its requirement that the administration of taxation must be subject to the duty to maintain the situation *ante* "as far as is possible." Article 49 complements this requirement, by clarifying that if new taxes are levied, they can only be imposed for certain needs.

Relatedly, taxation is restricted with regard to the *use* of the collected money. According to article 48, the occupant must first use the money to pay for the administrative costs of the territory, in a manner similar to that which would have been required from the ousted government.[11] However,

[8] Gerhard von Glahn, The Occupation of Enemy Territory: A Commentary on the Law and Practice of Belligerent Occupation 152 (1957).

[9] *See Abu Aita*, 37(2) PD ¶ 22(b).

[10] The same conservationist notion should apply to the *cancellation* of taxes, since this, too, has societal ramifications. For instance, the CPA's cancellation of all property taxes in Iraq can be criticized as deviating from this principle. However, as mentioned before, in the case of Iraq the occupant acted on the basis of UNSC resolutions. *See* Governing Council Resolution 93 of 2003 [Cancellation of All Property Taxes] (Nov. 4, 2003), *reprinted in* 2 Stefan Talmon, The Occupation of Iraq: The Official Documents of the Coalition Provisional Authority and the Iraqi Governing Council 1168 (2013).

[11] With the possible exception of expenses that are directly detrimental to its war effort or security. *See* von Glahn, *supra* note 8, at 150, 155–56.

article 48 is silent regarding surplus tax revenue exceeding these expenses. Some have read this silence as allowing the occupant to use surplus for *any* purpose.[12] The logic behind this approach might be that law already permits the occupant to seize the state's cash, so it should likewise be allowed to take surplus tax revenues.[13] However, this view allows the occupant to continuously exploit the occupied territory's economic base. It is one thing to take possession of immediately available cash reserves, but it is another thing to continue, once in control, to exploit the population through taxation for the benefit of the occupant. A view more in line with the object and purpose of the law of occupation is that the surplus can only be used for the administration of the territory in line with the occupant's general trusteeship duties.[14]

The conservationist rationale of article 48 allows deviation in two main ways. First, it requires that taxes be collected "in accordance with the rules of assessment and incidence in force." If, however, the same rules in force allow for adjustments of tax rates in accordance with economic circumstances, the occupant would be permitted to adjust these rates accordingly.[15] Second, article 48 requires the occupant to respect the status quo ante in taxation only as far as possible. In the past, a controversial question has been whether this caveat means that the occupant was permitted to impose *new* taxes, in cases where it was impossible to maintain the tax policy *ante*. Feilchenfeld, for example, argued that while increasing existing taxes is not forbidden per se by article 48, it is unclear whether the article permits imposing entirely *new* taxes. He nonetheless suggested that the duty to maintain public order might justify imposing new taxes.[16]

The question of new taxes was raised in the HCJ's *Abu Aita* case. The military commanders of the West Bank and Gaza decided to introduce value added tax (VAT) in the territories, in rates similar to those within

[12] *See Abu Aita*, 37(2) PD ¶ 22(d).
[13] Hague Convention (IV) respecting the Laws and Customs of War on Land and its annex: Regulations concerning the Laws and Customs of War on Land art. 53, Oct. 18, 1907, 187 C.T.S. 227 [hereinafter Hague IV]. *See* Section 6.2.2.
[14] *Compare* VON GLAHN, *supra* note 8, at 150.
[15] *See* YORAM DINSTEIN, THE INTERNATIONAL LAW OF BELLIGERENT OCCUPATION 137 (2d ed. 2019); von Glahn, *supra* note 1, at 350. *Compare* Governing Council Resolution No. 42 of 2003 [Approval of the Level of Income Tax] (Sept. 16, 2003), *reprinted in* TALMON, *supra* note 10, at 1140.
[16] ERNST H. FEILCHENFELD, THE INTERNATIONAL ECONOMIC LAW OF BELLIGERENT OCCUPATION 49–51 (1942); *see also* von Glahn, *supra* note 1, at 351.

Israel.[17] This raised two main questions. The first concerned whether such integrationist measures are unlawful as forms of "economic annexation," and relatedly whether imposing VAT indeed benefited the local population.[18] The second question, relevant here, was whether occupants could introduce new taxes to begin with. The petitioners—small business owners from the West Bank and Gaza—argued, *inter alia*, that the occupant was unauthorized to do so, even if, *arguendo*, the new taxes would benefit the local population.[19] The state responded that article 48 must be adapted to prolonged occupation, and in this case, it should be read to facilitate the proper economic relations between Israel and the occupied territories. It argued that absent the imposition of VAT, trade barriers between Israel and the occupied territories would be erected, and in any case, the proceeds of the VAT were "earmarked" for the local population.[20] Interestingly, the state argued that even if article 48 would be construed as prohibiting new taxes, this would not apply to indirect taxes such as VAT. This is because in the 19th century, when the provision was formulated, taxation was only used to cover government expenditures. Nowadays, however, taxes are conceived as economic measures meant to stir the economy. For this reason, it claimed, article 48 did not consider the possibility of indirect taxes such as VAT, and these must therefore be allowed.[21]

The HCJ ruled that the "as far as is possible" caveat in article 48 Hague implies that there is no absolute prohibition on new taxation.[22] It added that the caveat should be interpreted in light of the spirit of article 43 Hague, which obliges the occupant to maintain public order.[23] As it held, "as far as possible" does not only refer to technical impossibility such as missing land registers or lists of debtors, but also to "substantive economic fiscal changes that have a decisive effect on the economic situation and that could render meaningless" the previous taxation policy. It ruled that in prolonged occupation, where many years have passed since the introduction of the existing rules of taxation, this can indeed be the case.[24] Reading articles 48

[17] HCJ 69/81 Abu Aita v. Commander of the Judea and Samaria Area, 37(2) PD 197 (1983) (Isr.); for a critique, see Hisham Jabr, *Financial Administration of the Israel-Occupied West Bank*, *in* Playfair, *supra* note 1, 377, 377–89.

[18] Section 4.1.2; *see* von Glahn, *supra* note 1, at 372–73.

[19] *Abu Aita*, 37(2) PD ¶¶ 2–3.

[20] *Id.* ¶ 4.

[21] *Id.* ¶ 4(b).

[22] *Id.* ¶¶ 26–45.

[23] *Id.* ¶¶ 22(c), 25(h); *compare* DINSTEIN, *supra* note 15, at 139.

[24] *Abu Aita*, 37(2) PD ¶ 22(c).

and 43 together, it held that introducing new taxes, can be lawful, for instance, when required to coordinate "between the economic systems [of the occupant and the occupied] so as to maintain orderly economic life in the territory."[25]

The application of the doctrine of prolonged occupation to taxation suffers from the similar problems discussed in detail in Chapter 4. In relation to taxation—like in other cases in which the occupant might invoke the prolongation of occupation as grounds for wider powers—it makes sense that if increased powers are recognized, so will be increased participation rights for the local population.[26] This is especially true in the context of taxation, which implies accountability to the taxed population.[27]

Ultimately, the debate whether article 48 itself permits new taxes loses much of its salience, since article 49 clearly recognizes the power to levy "other money contributions." Since both new taxes and money contributions reach into the pocket of the local population, the formal distinction between them is of secondary importance at best. Despite some controversies on the exact relationship between articles 48 and 49,[28] it is suggested that they be read together: article 48 sets forth the general principle that the status quo ante be maintained unless it becomes impossible, while article 49 clarifies that if new taxes or "contributions" are imposed they can only be used for certain purposes.[29]

A further question concerns situations in which the tax base is insufficient to allow the occupant to fulfill its obligations on the basis of the local resources alone. This might be a common situation, owing to the power gaps in modern wars, and due to the likely economic consequences of war. In such cases, must the occupant "reach into its own pocket"?[30] The language of the law does not answer this question explicitly. However, the occupant cannot be released from its obligations under article 43 simply because the local tax base is depleted.[31] In this context, the law of occupation can be supplemented with positive obligations under IHRL, including obligations to ensure social and economic rights.[32] On its face, this obligation

[25] *Id.* ¶ 50(d).
[26] Section 4.1.
[27] *See* Jabr, *supra* note 17, at 390.
[28] *Abu Aita*, 37(2) PD ¶ 23(a).
[29] *Compare* Dinstein, *supra* note 15, at 137.
[30] *See Abu Aita*, 37(2) PD, at 75.
[31] *Compare* von Glahn, *supra* note 1, at 351; Feilchenfeld, *supra* note 16, at 85.
[32] *See* Legal Consequences of the Construction of a Wall in the Occupied Palestinian Territory, Advisory Opinion, 2004 I.C.J. Rep. 136 (July 9).

is not limited by the economic capacity of the occupied territory itself, and might ultimately require the occupant to use its own resources.

7.1.2 Military Contributions

Beyond taxation in the conventional sense—which is intended for the civil administration of the territory—article 49 allows, on its face, imposing money contributions also for the needs of the army qua occupying force.[33] This practice was quite common during the 19th century and in WWI.[34]

The institution of "military contributions" seems anachronistic and difficult to reconcile with the modern understanding of the law of occupation. Unlike requisitions on the basis of article 52 Hague, money contributions for military needs, as per article 49, do not require compensation.[35] This seems arbitrary. If requisitions require compensation in accordance with the market value, why are money contributions—imposed for the exact same purposes—not treated as loans? Contributions for military needs are also difficult to justify normatively. It is one thing for the occupant to tax the population in order to fund the administration of their own needs, but it is quite different to force them to finance the occupant's *military* needs in the territory. This runs counter to the spirit of the law of occupation.[36] These anomalies explain why military contributions have been highly controversial since the early 20th century, and calls for their abolishment have often been made.[37] Notably, in the most legalized and prolonged occupation of modern times—the Israeli occupation—no use has been made of military contributions.[38] Considering this, it is quite possible that this institution has fallen into desuetude.[39] Even if this is not the case, occupants must

[33] Feilchenfeld stresses that the needs, in this context, refer to those of the occupying army and not to the interests of the occupant at large, including its general war efforts. Feilchenfeld, *supra* note 16, at 41.

[34] For a brief survey and criticism, see *id.* at 41–45.

[35] *Id.* at 41.

[36] This harkens back to the notion that "war pays for war." *See Abu Aita*, 37(2) PD ¶ 25(b). *Compare*, however, Convention (IV) relative to the Protection of Civilian Persons in Time of War art. 51(2), Aug. 12, 1949, 6 U.S.T. 3516, 75 U.N.T.S. 287, which deals with forced labor, and raises the same problem.

[37] *Compare* 2 Paul Fauchille, Traite de Droit International Public 1224 (1921); Feilchenfeld, *supra* note 16, at 44 n.4.

[38] *Abu Aita*, 37(2) PD ¶ 23(b); Dinstein, *supra* note 15, at 139.

[39] *Compare* von Glahn, *supra* note 1, at 374.

consider that imposing military contributions is likely to draw resistance, which also makes it unwise in policy terms.

7.2 Regulation of Trade and Liberalization

Traditionally, states impose customs and other restrictions on international trade in order to protect the local industry against a flood of imports. Since WWII, however, the desirability of trade liberalization and related market reforms such as deregulation and privatization has become an orthodoxy in international economic forums. Yet, nowadays, there is increasing disillusion with the uncritical adoption of such measures, as well as growing critique of their portrayal as neutral and apolitical.[40] Of course, assessing the outcomes of market liberalization is beyond the scope of this book. However, this disagreement emphasizes that the adoption of such measures should be a sovereign decision as part of the right to self-determination.[41] Accordingly, measures of economic transformation through liberalization should be beyond the powers of an occupant qua trustee. Nonetheless, here, too, the practice of occupants has been quite permissive.

We first address the issue of customs, both in terms of their increase, and in relation to their decrease or elimination (liberalization). In general, customs in occupied territories are regulated by article 48 Hague, and are subject to the principles that apply to taxation.[42] Nowadays, increasing or imposing additional customs—as is the case with other trade restrictions—might also be in tension with the occupied state's obligations under international trade agreements. Whether these obligations must be taken into account by the occupant is another sub-question of the effects of the occupied state's treaties on the occupant.[43] The duty to respect the status quo regarding customs might therefore include consideration of the treaties in force. Recall, however, that the occupant does not become directly bound by such treaties; rather, it is only bound to respect them as part of the status quo ante. Accordingly, and in line with article 43, the occupant may impose

[40] *See, e.g.*, Martti Koskenniemi, *Enchanted by the Tools? An Enlightenment Perspective*, 113 PROC. ASIL ANN. MTG 3 (2019).

[41] Such decisions are the focus of complex negotiations in international bodies such as the WTO. For an overview, see SIMON LESTER, BRYAN MERCURIO, & ARWEL DAVIES, WORLD TRADE LAW: TEXT, MATERIALS AND COMMENTARY ch. 1 (2018).

[42] *Compare* FEILCHENFELD, *supra* note 16, at 83; von Glahn, *supra* note 1, at 354.

[43] *See* Section 6.1.5.

trade restrictions in furtherance of the interests recognized by the law of occupation, notwithstanding the occupied state's international obligations.[44]

Yet, the key concern is not that the occupant would impose additional barriers to trade—although that may happen[45]—but that it would reduce or eliminate customs and other restrictions on trade or investment, in a self-interested manner detrimental to the local economy. Such liberalization measures might also transform the local economy, infringing on the economic self-determination of the population.

While it is possible to imagine situations where certain necessary goods are scarce in the territory, and temporary suspensions of trade restrictions can be undertaken to ensure their supply, wholesale and structural liberalization—as was done in Iraq—are a different thing. Soon after Iraq's occupation, the CPA abolished all tariffs and trade restrictions in the country, subject to limited exceptions.[46] Additionally, the CPA significantly liberalized foreign investment, and established foreign investment protection.[47] Unsurprisingly, these measures were criticized as prioritizing foreign interests, placing the Iraqi economy at a disadvantage, and fundamentally transforming the economic system.[48]

Nonetheless, it should be pointed out that the CPA was at pains to emphasize, in most of its liberalization orders, that the measures were coordinated with the Iraqi Governing Council.[49] Whether this coordination was effective is beyond our scope here;[50] however, it reveals the expectations that liberalization measures, if at all, should be taken with the participation of the local population. Furthermore, some of these orders empowered local authorities to regulate—albeit in a limited manner—their execution.[51] This also reflects the understanding that local authorities must have a role

[44] This conclusion is strengthened by international trade law itself, which recognizes that obligations might be suspended for security reasons. *See* General Agreement on Tariffs and Trade, art. XXI, Oct. 30. 1947, 61 Stat. A-11, 55 U.N.T.S. 194.

[45] *See* von Glahn, *supra* note 1, at 354.

[46] CPA Order No. 12, Trade Liberalization Policy, CPA/ORD/7 June 2003/12 (Feb. 26, 2004). Yet, the order was limited only until the end of 2003, and a "reconstruction levy" on imports was imposed soon after. CPA Order No. 38, Reconstruction Levy, CPA/ORD/19 September 2003/38 (Sept. 19, 2003).

[47] CPA Order No. 39, Foreign Investment, CPA/ORD/19 September 2003/39 (Dec. 20, 2003).

[48] Rittich, *supra* note 5, 494–95. *See also* Section 4.2.5.

[49] *See* Eyal Benvenisti, The International Law of Occupation 83, 262–63 (2d ed. 2012).

[50] *See* Gregory H. Fox, Humanitarian Occupation 266–67 (2008).

[51] *See* for instance, CPA Order No. 39, Sec. 7(3), Foreign Investment, CPA/ORD/19 September 2003/39, *amended by* CPA Order No. 46, CPA/ORD/20 December 2003/46 (Dec. 20, 2003).

in economic governance. Last, the CPA repeatedly emphasized that its economic measures have been coordinated with international financial institutions.[52] This demonstrates the significance—whether in constraining or legitimating terms—of international financial bodies in relation to the occupant's economic policies.

In fact, the coordination with national and international bodies for the purpose of economic reconstruction and development in Iraq was required by UNSC Resolution 1483.[53] As we have already pointed out, it is difficult to generalize conclusions concerning the law of occupation from the case of Iraq, since these UNSC resolutions have been relied on for transformative powers.[54] Clearly, equivalent measures of economic transformation would not be lawful in "regular" occupation.[55] What is perhaps generalizable, from the case of Iraq, is that coordination with local and international institutions was required *even* when such measures were seemingly authorized by the UNSC. Arguably, a "regular" occupant, enjoying no international mandate at all, cannot disregard them in its economic policies.

7.3 Integration

The previous section discussed measures of liberalization in general. No less significant is the possibility that the occupant would attempt to integrate between the occupied territory and its own, inter alia by eliminating customs between the two territories. Indeed, occupants might argue that such measures benefit the local economy. Sometimes, perhaps, due to the unavailability of certain basic products, the occupant might be justified in temporarily suspending certain customs between the territories to facilitate the import of these products.

However, if integration measures are wide, several concerns arise. First, integration might benefit the occupant's economy at the expense of the occupied territory. For example, if the occupant enjoys a trade advantage over the occupied territory, eliminating customs between the territories might benefit the occupant while harming the local industry. Second, even if

[52] BENVENISTI, *supra* note 49, at 262.
[53] S.C. Res. 1483, ¶ 8(e) (May 22, 2003).
[54] *See* Section 4.2.5.
[55] *See* James Thou Gathii, *Foreign and Other Economic Rights upon Conquest and Under Occupation: Iraq in Comparative and Historical Context*, 25 U. PENN. J. INT'L ECON. L. 491 (2004).

integration might, according to some measures, benefit the local economy, it can still affect the local market significantly, sometimes irreversibly. Again, such decisions go beyond the authority of the occupant qua trustee. Third, and relatedly, integration measures can promote de facto annexation. For this reason, Feilchenfeld, albeit accepting that the occupant can adjust customs in line with the requirements of article 43, doubted that it can abolish all customs between the occupied territory and its own state.[56]

Unfortunately, the practice of occupants concerning integration is frequently at odds with the logic of the law of occupation. There are many historical examples of occupants abolishing all customs between occupied territories and their own.[57] In fact, von Glahn claimed that this has been the case in *most* occupations.[58] Moreover, integration was usually asymmetrical. Occupants suspended customs and other barriers concerning goods that they wished to export to the territory, while maintaining or introducing trade restrictions in the opposite direction.[59] Clearly, if an occupant claims that integration is pursued for the benefit of the local economy, it cannot simultaneously act in a protectionist fashion concerning its *own* interests.

Economic integration has been a prominent feature of Israel's occupation of the West Bank and Gaza, at least until the Oslo Accords of the 1990s. In 1967, soon after the onset of the occupation, Israel established a "common market" with the occupied territories.[60] Among other integration measures, it abolished customs between Israel and the occupied territories, and established a de facto custom union by equalizing customs rates for goods entering both territories from abroad. However, integration was unequal: while Israeli export to the occupied territories was free, this was not always the case vice versa. Permits were required for the export of certain goods from the occupied territories, not only into Israel, but also to competing third-party markets.[61] As mentioned, VAT was introduced in the territories simultaneously with its introduction in Israel.[62] Unsurprisingly, in the *Abu Aita* case, the HCJ held that integration measures might be justified as part of the duty to promote the welfare in the territories, in light

[56] Feilchenfeld, *supra* note 16, at 83.

[57] *See id.* at 83–84.

[58] Von Glahn, *supra* note 8, at 154.

[59] Von Glahn, *supra* note 1, at 354.

[60] Benvenisti, supra note 49, at 224.

[61] *Id.* at 225; Hisham Awartani, *Israel's Economic Policies in the Occupied Territories: A Case for International Supervision*, *in* Playfair, *supra* note 1, 399, 411–16.

[62] *See* Benvenisti, *supra* note 49, at 224–27.

of article 43 Hague.[63] While early on, integration arguably contributed to growth, it did not contribute to the development of a local economic base, which was often curtailed when there was potential competition with Israeli interests.[64] For these reasons, Israel's policy, and the reasoning of the HCJ, were criticized as establishing a form of unequal economic annexation. Economic policies were adopted in Israel, in accordance with its own internal priorities, and were then followed by the imposition, through the military commander, of similar policies in the occupied territories.[65] Awartani lamented this situation as one in which Israel acted "as its own negotiating partner in the establishment of bilateral economic relations between its own state and the territories it occupies."[66]

If mass liberalization, as discussed in the previous section, is at odds with the principles of the law of occupation, economic integration should be equally, if not more, suspect.[67] First, this is because economic integration might serve as a measure of de facto annexation. Second, there is an inherent concern that integration would mainly benefit the occupant. This is especially true when integration is unequal. Third, like other forms of liberalization, integration transforms the local market, and in this sense reflects a decision that should be reserved to the sovereign.

7.4 Currency

The law of occupation does not address expressly the use of currency in occupied territories, nor, for that matter, monetary policy at large. As with most aspects of economic administration of occupied territories, the conclusion must be that the occupant must respect the status quo ante as a point of departure, subject to the powers recognized under article 43.[68] Within these confines, the power to regulate currency was usually recognized by the courts of the returning sovereign and by third parties.[69] The regulation of currency and its potential effects is a highly technical issue that we

[63] HCJ 69/81 Abu Aita v. Commander of the Judea and Samaria Area, 37(2) PD 197 (1983) (Isr.).

[64] Awartani, *supra* note 61, at 400–09; Jabr, *supra* note 17, at 392.

[65] Benvenisti, *supra* note 49, at 242–43.

[66] Awartani, *supra* note 61, at 400.

[67] *Compare* Benvenisti, *supra* note 49, at 244.

[68] Feilchenfeld, *supra* note 16, at 70; Dinstein, *supra* note 15, at 129; Carreau, *supra* note 2, at 242.

[69] *Id.* at 246–47. *See, e.g.*, Aboitiz & Co. v. Price, 99 F. Supp. 602 (D. Utah 1951).

cannot address here.[70] Rather, we only offer some observations about the main questions which have arisen in this context.

7.4.1 Regulation of Local Currency

Concerning the regulation of local currency, the default would be to maintain its circulation, as well as the monetary policy and operation of the central bank—while limited changes can only be justified within the terms of article 43.[71] This would mean, for example, that the central bank should be allowed to regulate the local currency, to the extent that one exists in the territory. However, where central banks cease operating, occupants might increase or decrease the amount of local currency in circulation, as part of their general duty to maintain public life. This has been the practice during occupations in the 20th century where not infrequently occupants encountered scarcity of local money.[72]

Ultimately, the occupant's duties regarding the local currency follow its general trusteeship obligations: currency must be managed for the benefit of the local economy, and not for the benefit of the occupant. In this context, Skubiszewski has suggested a list of duties vis-à-vis local currency. These consist, inter alia, of the duty to avoid harmful measures to the local currency; the prohibition on disrupting the monetary unity of the occupied area; the duty to reduce the number of local currencies in circulation; the duty to prevent deflation; the duty to protect the currency's value; the duty to fix the exchange rate for the benefit of the local economy; the duty to prevent inflation; and the duty to regulate exchange.[73] Nowadays, the occupant must also take into consideration, when regulating the local currency, the relevant global regulatory environment.

In line with the general principles of the law of occupation, security considerations can also affect the regulation of currency and central banks. For instance, the occupant is not required to accommodate the local central bank's banking activities for the ousted government, and it has indeed been the practice of occupants to cut off these relations. This is especially true

[70] *See* Krysztof Skubiszewski, *Currency in Occupied Territory and the Law of War*, 9 German Y.B. Int'l L. 161 (1961).
[71] *Id.* at 162–63
[72] *See id.* at 167.
[73] *Id.* at 182–91.

when the ousted government continues to conduct hostilities against the occupant from unoccupied parts of the state.[74]

7.4.2 Introduction of the Occupant's Own Currency

A more problematic issue concerns the active introduction of the occupant's own currency as legal tender in the occupied territory.[75] Like other integration measures discussed above, such actions are intuitively suspect, since they raise the concern that the occupant seeks to annex the territory. Indeed, the extension of currency is a prominent feature of annexationist policy. For example, when Russia annexed Crimea in 2014, it introduced the Russian ruble as the only legal currency in the territory.[76] Russia has also introduced the ruble in Ukrainian territories it occupied in 2022, even without formal annexation.[77]

It should be conceded that the law of occupation has been usually interpreted quite liberally in this context, when introduction of the occupant's currency could be justified under article 43.[78] However, when it is undertaken within a broader context which raises the suspicion of de facto annexation, it would be unlawful as part of the illegality of the annexationist policy at large.[79] In 1967, Israeli currency was introduced as sole legal tender in Gaza, while in the West Bank it was introduced in parallel with the Jordanian dinar, which continued to be legal. The exchange rate between the two was thereafter adjusted by the military commander.[80] While there might have been valid reasons, at the time, to introduce Israeli currency,

[74] *Id.* at 164–65.

[75] That a currency is legal tender in a certain territory means, in general, that a currency is (a) valid in the territory; (b) that it can be used by any debtor for payment of all debts; and (c) against which no creditor can legally refuse payment. *See, e.g.* CPA Order No. 43, New Iraqi Dinar Banknotes, CPA/ORD/14 October 2003/43, Section 1 (Oct. 14, 2003).

[76] *Russian Ruble Becomes Only Valid Currency in Crimea*, RT (June 2, 2014), https://www.rt.com/business/162992-crimea-adopts-ruble-currency/.

[77] Adam Taylor, *Shift to Ruble in Kherson Fuels Concerns About Russia's Aims in Occupied Region*, Wash. Post (May, 2022), https://www.washingtonpost.com/world/2022/05/01/kherson-russia-ruble-internet-referendum/.

[78] *See* Skubiszewski, *supra* note 70, at 168.

[79] *See id.* at 168–69.

[80] Benvenisti, *supra* note 49, at 225–26. *See* Order Concerning the Establishment of the Israeli Currency as Legal Tender (Judea & Samaria) (No. 76), 5727–1967.

these measures must be evaluated in light of the greater context of Israel's control, as discussed throughout this book.

In the Turkish-controlled areas in northern Syria, the value of the Syrian lira plummeted, leading Turkey to increasingly introduce its own currency into the territory.[81] While the local population was undeniably in need of a stable currency, this measure was criticized as intended to tighten Turkey's long-term control over the area.[82] Here, too, the introduction of Turkish currency must be assessed in accordance with the transformative Turkish policies in the area.[83] Turkey has connected areas in Syria to its electricity grid and to its cellular infrastructure, and has placed Syrian areas under the responsibility of adjoining Turkish provinces.[84] It has also established higher education institutions in the area, which are affiliated to universities in Turkey.[85] The introduction of Turkish currency cannot be analyzed separately from these measures.

Often, even when there is no formal decision to introduce the occupant's currency as legal tender, the occupant's currency will still make its way into the territory. Historically, this was because the occupant's soldiers, as well as requisitions, were usually paid in that currency. A dual system might emerge, in which the occupant eventually fixes the exchange rate to facilitate the use of its own currency.[86] Of course, this exchange rate must reflect the occupant's duties under article 43, and not as a means to impoverish the local population.[87]

[81] Nicholas Frakes, *Turkish Lira Becomes Unofficial Currency in Syria's Economy Sinks*, AL ARABIYA (June 15, 2020), https://english.alarabiya.net/features/2020/06/15/Turkish-lira-becomes-unofficial-currency-in-Syria-as-economy-sinks.

[82] *See* Isabel Coles & David Gauthier-Villars, *Turkey Uses Its Currency to Tighten Grip on Northern Syria*, WALL ST. J. (June 24, 2020), https://www.wsj.com/articles/turkey-uses-its-currency-to-tighten-grip-on-northern-syria-11593019438.

[83] *See* Eyal Benvenisti & Eliav Lieblich, *Assessing Turkey's "Resettlement" Plans in Syria Under the Law of Occupation*, JUST SECURITY (Oct. 23, 2019), https://www.justsecurity.org/66679/assessing-turkeys-resettlement-plans-in-syria-under-the-law-of-occupation/.

[84] Carlotta Gall, *In Turkey's Safe Zone in Syria, Security and Misery Go Hand in Hand*, N.Y. TIMES (Feb. 16, 2021), https://www.nytimes.com/2021/02/16/world/middleeast/syria-turkey-erdogan-afrin.html.

[85] *See, e.g.*, Saeed Abdulrazek, *Erdogan Orders Establishment of Campus for Turkish University in Northern Syria*, ASHARQ AL-AWSAT (Feb. 2, 2021), https://english.aawsat.com/home/article/2790256/erdogan-orders-establishment-campus-turkish-university-northern-syria.

[86] *See* VON GLAHN, *supra* note 8, at 203.

[87] Skubiszewski, *supra* note 70, at 182–91.

7.4.3 Introduction of New Currency

Some occupants have introduced "occupation currency" in occupied territories, which differs both from the occupant's own currency and the local one.[88] In situations where local currency is scarce—or, historically, when there was no metal coverage for the local currency in the territory[89]—there might be several reasons why an occupant would opt to introduce occupation currency rather than its own currency. One concerns the risk of inflation, and other possible adverse effects to the occupant's currency if extended to the occupied territories.[90] Another can be the fear that the occupant's money would fall into the hands of the enemy state.[91] Furthermore, when a territory is occupied by a coalition, introducing a single occupation currency—as was the case in the allied occupation of Italy and Germany in WWII—can be better than introducing a plurality of currencies.[92]

While issuing occupation currency lessens the concern of economic annexation, and therefore might seem a preferable policy, it raises the different concern of potential economic transformation. One policy, which seems less transformative and has been frequently employed by occupants, involves the introduction of new currency, which circulates *in parallel* with the local currency.[93] Be that as it may, it is clear that if an occupant decides to introduce occupation currency in any form, it incurs an additional duty to properly regulate it.[94]

The most problematic situation in terms of its transformative potential, arises when the occupant seeks not only to introduce new currency into parallel circulation, but to replace the local currency altogether. Some argued that this radical action might be lawful only when it proves *impossible* to maintain the old circulation, for example, due to hyperinflation or the prevalence of counterfeit bills in the territory. In general, whether it is impossible to maintain the local currency is a question of economics which we do not address here.[95]

88 *Id.* at 171.
89 *See* Feilchenfeld, *supra* note 16, at 71–76; Skubiszewski, *supra* note 70, at 176.
90 Skubiszewski, *supra* note 70, at 170, 173.
91 *Id.* at 175–77.
92 *Id.* at 174.
93 Carreau, *supra* note 2, at 243. For examples, see Feilchenfeld, *supra* note 16, at 71–76; von Glahn, *supra* note 8, at 204; Skubiszewski, *supra* note 70, at 173–76.
94 *See id.* at 174–76.
95 For examples, *see* Skubiszewski, *supra* note 70, at 174–80.

A pertinent case is that of Iraq. In 2003, the CPA mandated the Central Bank of Iraq to issue new Iraqi dinars.[96] As reasons for its actions, the CPA noted that that there were different series of Iraqi banknotes circulating in Iraq, and explained that new banknotes would "instill public confidence and facilitate the use of money." The CPA established the official conversion rates between the new dinars and the old currency, and organized the transition between the currencies.[97] It should be recalled, yet again, that it is difficult to derive any precedent from the CPA's actions, since as usual, the CPA invoked the authority granted to it by relevant UNSC resolutions.[98]

Whenever an occupant introduces new currency in occupied territory, a question arises concerning the responsibility to "back" occupation money remaining in the territory post-occupation, if the returning sovereign decides to withdraw it from circulation. The main disagreement revolves around the question whether the issuing occupant retains the duty to redeem this money, or whether it is the responsibility of the returning sovereign. A related question concerns the extent to which the legality of the occupant's decision to issue currency affects this responsibility. Both practice and scholarship are inconsistent on these questions, and usually, such issues were resolved in ad hoc agreements between the occupant and the returning sovereign.[99]

[96] CPA Order No. 43, New Iraqi Dinar Banknotes, CPA/ORD/14 October 2003/43, preamble (Oct. 14, 2003).

[97] *Id.* § 5.

[98] *Id.* preamble.

[99] For a detailed analysis of this question, see Skubiszewski, *supra* note 70, at 192–97; Carreau, *supra* note 2, at 260–61, 266–72.

Concluding Thoughts

The Present and Future of the Law of Occupation

This book demonstrated both the compelling normative basis of the law of occupation and its inherent limitations. At the basis of this legal framework is the need to ensure that occupants respect the rights of people under their control, including their right to self-determination. Like other areas of IHL, this comes with the pragmatic recognition that the occupant's security interests must be given some weight in order to induce it to fulfill its obligations. Furthermore, the limited powers of the occupant, coupled with the assumption of temporariness, are meant to prevent the transformation of military occupation into illegal forms of control, such as annexation or apartheid.

Yet, as this book demonstrated, an unease permeates all aspects of the law of occupation. First, the very treatment of the occupant as a trustee, given the inherent conflicts of interest, raises many challenges. Even if we set this aside, there are significant tensions between the various interests protected by the law of occupation itself. Namely, the conservationist principle, and the right to self-determination at its core, frequently clashes with the duty to maintain public order and life; and security considerations often conflict with the rights of the local population. Furthermore, the indeterminacy of many of the law of occupation's provisions—a product of competing interests during negotiations—have allowed states to advance, at times, narrow interpretations of the applicability of the law of occupation, and in other cases exceedingly permissive interpretations of their powers as occupants, coupled with restrictive construction of their obligations. Perhaps most significantly, while the law of occupation assumes temporariness, it has been interpreted by some actors as imposing no concrete obligation to end the occupation. This book therefore suggested that for the law of occupation to survive as a potent legal framework, it must be interpreted in a manner that enables it to "make a difference." While this seems obvious, many instances, discussed in this book, demonstrate that this has not always been the case.

Several other processes cause uncertainty regarding the enduring viability of the law of occupation as an autonomous body of law. We discussed these contemporary challenges in the Introduction. We briefly recount some of them here. The first problem has plagued the law of occupation since its inception: in the vast majority of cases, states have sought to disapply the law of occupation. This problem is compounded by third-parties' hesitation to qualify situations as occupation, for diplomatic and political reasons.

The second problem is more recent, and concerns the disaggregation of the concept of control. While the law of occupation assumed, traditionally, physical control on the ground, control can nowadays be exercised through various measures. It remains uncertain whether and how the law of occupation would be able to accommodate this transformation.

Third, while in the past, the law of occupation was the sole legal framework regulating the hostile control of foreign territory, there are nowadays many potential parallel frameworks, ranging from IHRL to international economic and environmental law. This makes the isolated treatment of the law of occupation impossible.

Fourth, in the past, the state was the primary actor in occupied territories. Today, however, the presence of transnational private entities in the territory requires much attention to be shifted from the acts of states qua occupants to issues of business and human rights. International law has been generally slow to do so, and the relations between business and human rights and the law of occupation are relatively underdeveloped.

Fifth, and relatedly, as most modern armed conflicts are non-international, control by non-state actors is no longer rare. Since the law of occupation has not been traditionally extended to such forms of control, the source of obligations toward the local population in such cases, as well as their content, is still very much unclear.

The latter problems haunt the law of occupation at present. We end this book, however, with some thoughts on the *future* of this law. Perhaps the most general among these is the realization that contemporary problems transcend national boundaries, which complicates the concept of trusteeship. While the law of occupation's classical dilemmas pit the interests of the occupant against those of the occupied, modern problems might require inserting global interests into the equation. Transnational environment problems, the climate crisis, and pandemics require sovereigns to consider wider interests than their immediate own. The law of occupation, too, would have to accommodate such interests, as global crises become more acute.

Moreover, the law of occupation traditionally seeks to regulate the occupant's discretion. However, modern governance increasingly relies on algorithmic decision-making, which challenges the mere idea of administrative discretion, and complicates notions such as transparency and accountability.[1] These developments would inevitably find their way into occupied territories. In the West Bank, for example, Israel has applied predictive algorithms that monitor behavior on social networks, as well as facial recognition technologies.[2] Beyond questions addressed by IHRL, such as interference with privacy, it is yet unclear how the framework of article 43 Hague can accommodate these developments. Additionally, militaries are pushing for the increased autonomy of weapons system.[3] If these developments become fully operational, autonomous systems might be deployed to control territories and populations. While the debate on autonomous weapons systems has mostly focused on issues relating to the conduct of hostilities, scant attention has been given to specific problems that might arise in the context of autonomous systems and control over territory.

Additional future challenges might arise from the extension of forms and spaces of state control. As discussed only briefly in this book, states nowadays claim interests and rights in areas beyond their territorial waters. With the possible development of deep seabed mining—and in the future, resource exploration in space[4]—it is quite possible that states would attempt to claim jurisdiction or rights, in whatever form, on areas far beyond their traditional reach.[5] Wherever a state claims any form of control over an area or an activity, there is at least the potential that the latter can be subject to hostile control by another. The law of occupation, however, is still far from developed in these contexts.

Although much remains open to debate in relation to these future challenges, we believe that the first principles of the law of

[1] *See, e.g.*, Eyal Benvenisti, *Upholding Democracy amid the Challenges of New Technology: What Role for the Law of Global Governance?*, 29 Eur. J. Int'l L. 9 (2018).

[2] *See, e.g.*, Rohan Talbot, *Automating Occupation: International Humanitarian and Human Rights Law Implications of the Deployment of Facial Recognition Technologies in the Occupied Palestinian Territory*, 102 Int'l Rev. Red Cross 823 (2021).

[3] *See* Eliav Lieblich & Eyal Benvenisti, *The Obligation to Exercise Discretion in Warfare: Why Autonomous Weapon Systems Are Unlawful*, *in* Autonomous Weapons Systems: Law, Ethics, Policy 244 (Nehal Bhuta, Susanne Beck, Robin Geiβ, Hin-Yan Liu & Claus Kreβ eds., 2016).

[4] *See* Artemis Accords, Principles for Cooperation in the Civil Exploration and Use of the Moon, Mars, Comets, and Asteroids for Peaceful Purposes, Oct. 13, 2020.

[5] *See, e.g.*, Surabhi Ranganathan, *Ocean Floor Grab: International Law and the Making of an Extractive Imaginary*, 30 Eur. J. Int'l L. 573 (2019).

occupation—understood in light of their inherent connections with the laws regarding sovereignty, self-determination, and human rights as they develop over time—can guide the way in which these and other novel questions are addressed. We hope that this book will serve as a helpful point of departure for the analysis of the law of occupation in the future, in light of these significant challenges and others that will surely arise.

Suggested Recent Monographs in English

Arai-Takahashi, Yutaka, The Law of Occupation: Continuity and Change of International Humanitarian Law, and Its Interaction with International Human Rights Law (2009)

Ben-Naftali, Orna, Sfard Michael, & Viterbo Hedi, The ABC of the OPT: A Legal Lexicon of the Israeli Control over the Occupied Palestinian Territory (2018)

Benvenisti, Eyal, The International Law of Occupation (2d ed. 2012)

Bisharat, George Emile, Palestinian Lawyers and Israeli Rule: Law and Disorder in the West Bank (1989)

Cuyckens, Hanne, Revisiting the Law of Occupation (2017)

Dinstein, Yoram, The international Law of Belligerent Occupation (2d ed. 2019)

Duval, Antoine & Kassoti Eva (eds.) The Legality of Economic Activities in Occupied Territories (2020)

Erakat, Noura, Justice for Some: Law and the Question of Palestine (2019)

Fox, Gregory H., Humanitarian Occupation (2008)

Gross, Aeyal, The Writing on the Wall: Rethinking the Law of Occupation (2017)

Hajjar, Lisa, Courting Conflict: The Israeli Military Court System in the West Bank and Gaza (2005)

Kalandarishvili-Mueller, Natia, Occupation and Control in International Humanitarian Law (2021)

Kretzmer, David & Ronen Yaël, The Occupation of Justice: The Supreme Court of Israel and the Occupied Territories (2d ed. 2021)

Longobardo, Marco, The Use of Armed Force in Occupied Territory (2018)

Shehadeh, Raja, From Occupation to Interim Accords: Israel and the Palestinian Territories (1997)

Wilde, Ralph, International Territorial Administration: How Trusteeship and the Civilizing Mission Never Went Away (2008)

Index

For the benefit of digital users, indexed terms that span two pages (e.g., 52–53) may, on occasion, appear on only one of those pages.